MUSIC
THE BUSINESS

MUSIC
THE BUSINESS

THE ESSENTIAL GUIDE TO THE LAW AND THE DEALS

FULLY REVISED AND UPDATED 2ND EDITION

ANN HARRISON

This edition first published in 2003 by
Virgin Books Ltd
Thames Wharf Studios
Rainville Road
London
W6 9HA

First Virgin paperback edition published in Great Britain in 2000 by Virgin Publishing Ltd

ISBN 1 85227 013 6

Original page design by Roger Kohn Designs
Typeset by Phoenix Photosetting, Chatham, Kent
Printed and bound in Great Britain by CPD, Wales

contents

acknowledgements

THANKS TO:

In addition to those already thanked in the first edition I'd like to thank Debbie Hooker, the librarian at Harbottle & Lewis, for once again coming up trumps with the research I needed.

To Antony Bebawi for his invaluable help with and knowledge of new-media issues. To Lawrence Abramson for his input on the Robbie Williams 'Campervan' case. To Richard Penfold for the information on the 'Liberty X' case, and Ben Bye for his behind-the-scenes legwork on the fact-checking.

To Amanda Gilbert for her continued support, sense of humour and hard work in producing this new edition efficiently and professionally, and her help in researching the sections on Media Courses and Further Reading.

To my parents, Eric and Sadie Harrison, for their love and unfailing support.

preface

I qualified as a solicitor in 1983 and began working for a firm that did general work but also had a good reputation as entertainment lawyers. At first I just did general commercial litigation but found that I was naturally attracted to the entertainment cases. Somehow they seemed more 'sexy'!

When I moved to another firm to get more experience of the entertainment business I made a big mistake. The firm I joined was good at entertainment work, but in fact wanted someone to clear 180 people off a large holiday camp in the North of England. I spent most of the next two years running 180 separate property cases with no connection to the entertainment business at all. Still, I got to know Scarborough pretty well.

Luckily for me I'd kept in touch with a former flatmate who had become a very successful music lawyer at Harbottle & Lewis. He spent some time trying to persuade me to do the same work that he did. I thought my future lay in sorting out disputes in court and wasn't convinced. Then the law firm I was working for closed and that decided it. Luckily, the job at Harbottle & Lewis was still open and I joined the music group in March 1988. But not before I had gone through about four interviews with different people at the firm, including one where I was asked if I wanted to be the next Madonna. I wish!

For the next six months I was convinced that this had been the second big mistake I had made. My litigation training and instincts made it almost impossible for me to appear friendly towards lawyers on the other side, signing letters 'Kindest personal regards' when often I could cheerfully have strangled them. I eventually got over that and have just celebrated ten years as a partner there. I became head of the music group in 2000.

I work mostly for artists and songwriters, managers and small record labels and publishers. I also give legal advice to music business executives and A&R people on their employment contracts. I like working for the creative end of the business. I'm not one for toeing the party line. I also like being able to sack a client if the relationship isn't working out for some reason. I couldn't do that if I worked for a company. I've been lucky over the last seventeen years to work with some of the leading players in the business. My clients come from every part of the music spectrum from drum and bass, dance and experimental music via classical and opera singers through rock and blues to chart-topping 'pop' acts.

If I could go back in time and change anything, would I? Yes, I would have fought harder, earlier to get into this great, exciting, often frustrating, but incomparable business.

In writing this book I hope I will be able to convey some of the excitement of the music business to you. I have followed the usual convention of using 'he' throughout. This is not intended as a slur on female artists or on the many excellent women working at all levels in the music business. Indeed, how could it be when they were so kind as to give me an Accolade award at the Women of the Year awards ceremony in October 2001, something I will always cherish. Recognition by your peers and clients is just the best.

Ann Harrison
31 October 2002

introduction

When I started work in the music business I had very little idea how it worked. Record and publishing companies were a mystery to me. It felt a little like trying to do a very hard jigsaw puzzle without the benefit of a picture on the lid of the box. I looked for books that might help me but there weren't many around. Those that were, were mostly out of date or applied to the USA and not to the UK music business. I had to learn from my colleagues as I went along. I was lucky in that they were very knowledgeable and very generous with their time.

Now there are many more sources of information available on the UK music business and there are several good full- and part-time media and law courses available to give you a head start. And yet I often wished for a good, easy-to-read guide to how the business works from a legal viewpoint – one that explains what a publisher does and what copyright is. Every trainee lawyer that comes to work with me asks if there's a guide to the music business they can read as a kind of road map through the industry. Managers and artists often ask me the same thing. This book aims to be that guide. Where I've used technical expressions I have tried to give a non-technical explanation alongside. Where industry jargon has been used there is an explanation in the glossary at the end of the book. For the legal eagles among you the detail is there in the footnotes. This book is not, however, intended to be a substitute for legal textbooks on copyright, other Intellectual Property rights or contract. There are many good examples of these sorts of books around, some of which are listed in the Further Reading section at the end of the book.

The music business, like most businesses, is a constantly changing and evolving one. In the first edition, published only two years ago, online distribution, webcasts and other uses of new-media technologies were new. They are much more familiar concepts now and online business has changed significantly. The chapter on New Media (Chapter 7) has been completely rewritten for this edition.

Wherever possible I have tried to illustrate points with practical examples. Because my experience is in acting for the creative end of the business – for the 'talent' rather than the big record or publishing companies – I tend to favour the artist's viewpoint. But I would not have got anywhere in the music business if I had not also learned all the arguments that could be used against me by the other side. So I have also tried to give both sides of an argument except where this would have made the text too confusing. Publication of the first edition led to a couple of mild grumbles that I had been too hard on some record companies. Where I think they may have a point I have noted this in the text.

We've all been fascinated by newspaper reports of this or that artist in court over disputes with their ex-managers, record companies or even other members of the band. Are these reports accurate? Do these cases have any long-term effect? Do they matter? In this book I'll highlight the facts of some of the more important cases, what was decided and the effects of these decisions on the music business.

I also have to add a health warning that the examples produced and the guidelines given are mine alone and others may not agree or may have had different experiences.

What I've tried to do is to let you into some of the things I have learned over the last seventeen years in the music business. There is, however, no substitute for legal advice on the particular facts of your case. Chapter 1 deals with choosing your advisers. Please read it. Good advisers will save you from what can be expensive mistakes. Most artists only have one chance of a successful career in this business – make sure you don't lose it through poor advice.

ABBREVIATIONS

In this book the following abbreviations have been used.

FSR	Fleet Street Reports
EMLR	Entertainment & Media Law Reports
CDPA	Copyright Designs and Patents Act 1988 (as amended)

1: **GETTING STARTED**

INTRODUCTION

How do you get into the music business as a performing artist or songwriter? How do you get your foot in the door and how and when do you start gathering your team of advisers around you?

This isn't a book on how to become a star or how to make your band a success, although it will try and help you avoid some of the mistakes you might make along the way. It is about understanding the music business, the deals and how you get yourself started.

CREATING A BUZZ

How do you get your work noticed? The idea is to create a 'buzz' by whatever means you can. We'll see later that lawyers and accountants can help you to get noticed but you also need to work out your own way to get your work heard.

You can play as many gigs as you can and hope to be recognised by a scout on the lookout for a record or music publishing company or you can make a demo of your performances or songs and send it to an A&R person and hope.

There's no guarantee of success. As someone said to me once, 'Just because you've got a phone doesn't mean anyone will call.'

You could try to improve your chances by using gimmicks. Bands have been known to hire open-top buses and drive past record companies playing as if their life depends on it. Others take their guitar along to record companies and hope to do an impromptu audition. This is very hit or miss, as these record company people have seen it all before.

You can also shamelessly exploit any and all contacts you have with anyone who has even the remotest connection with the music business. You can pester these hapless souls to 'get their mate to the next gig' or to listen to your demo. This can improve your chances of at least getting your work listened to, but that isn't any guarantee it will lead to a record or publishing deal.

A&R people are bombarded with sacks full of demos and lots of artists have contacts in the music business promising to do them a favour. You need to be more enterprising than ever to bring your music to the top of the pile, to get yourself heard above the 'noise'.

Scouts do find undiscovered talent playing in out-of the way pubs. If you happen to be based outside the M25 your chances of being spotted are much slimmer than if you're in London. However, there are other areas of the country that get the attention of scouts – Sheffield, Liverpool, Manchester, Birmingham, Bristol, Cardiff and Glasgow among them. Sometimes you get an ambitious scout who goes and checks out what is happening in a part of the country not on the traditional circuit. When this happens you can get a rash of signings from that area. Who knows, your area could be next.

A&R people are largely conservative although there are exceptions and none of them will admit it. They like to have their hunch about an artist confirmed by someone else whose opinion they respect. This could be someone in their own company but, somewhat surprisingly, they will often talk to A&R people from rival companies. You would think that if they found someone they thought was good they would keep it to themselves until the deal was done. Some do, but many seem to need to be convinced that they have got it right even though this might push up the cost of the deal if the rival company also gets in the running to sign the same artist. For the artist this is a dream come true. He can choose the company that works best for him, and his lawyer will negotiate between the companies to get a better deal. This is what we call using your bargaining power. The more bargaining power you have the better your overall deal is likely to be. In the last couple of years the trend has been for several successful artists to make their mark elsewhere before becoming big with a major record company. Moby had made at least two albums before the phenomenally successful *Play* album and David Gray had been plugging away for many years before making it big. It seems that the A&R people want actual evidence of an artist's ability to complete recording an album *and* promote it. Sales success in another country, e.g. Ireland, is also helpful. This can be a depressing thought for a band just starting out, but it could also be seen as an opportunity to create and develop your own style on a smaller independent label first. Of course you also need to be able to keep body and soul alive while you are doing it. The government has given a little bit of assistance with this by allowing musicians, in certain circumstances, to continue to draw benefit while trying to earn a living as a musician. This is called the New Deal for Musicians.

THE BAND NAME

The name a band chooses is a vital part of its identity, its brand. It's a very difficult thing to get right and it's quite common for bands to go through various name changes before they settle on one they're happy with. It should be memorable, because if you combine a good name with a clever logo then you are already halfway to having the basis of a good advertising campaign. However you decide to market yourself, a distinctive name makes it that much easier. If it's a name that you can do some wordplay with, so much the better. There was a tendency a few years ago for bands to have short, one-word names – Blur, Pulp, Oasis and Suede, to name but a few. But a name doesn't have to be short to be memorable. More recently bands have appeared with names like And You Shall Know Them By The Trail Of Their Dead.

Finding a good name is easier said than done. I'm sure you've all sat around at some time in the pub after a beer or three and tried to come up with good band names. Despite all my advice on branding, I suspect that most bands choose their name for much more down-to-earth reasons, like it sounds cool, or it is the only one they can think of that is not naff and that no one else has already nabbed. Raiding books, old films and song titles are other good sources, for example, All About Eve, His Latest Flame and Janus Stark (from a comic). History is also a fertile source (the Levellers, for instance).

You might decide on a name not knowing that anyone else has already claimed it. You may then invest a lot of time and maybe some money in starting to develop a reputation in that name. You are not going to be very happy if you then find out that someone else has the same name. So how do you check if someone else is already using a band name?

There are some easy and cheap means of doing this. Firstly, go to the nearest large record store and ask to borrow their catalogue listing all available records. Have a look if the name you want to use appears – the lists are usually alphabetical by artist name so that's not as horrible a task as it might seem.

If you've access to the Internet you can widen your search. Using a good search engine check to see if the name you've chosen appears. You could just do a UK search but if you plan to sell records overseas (and you do, don't you?) then you should do a worldwide search. You could apply to register a domain name and see if anyone has claimed any of the main top-line domain categories for that name. If it is available do register it quickly.

THE BAND REGISTER

You can also apply to register your band name with the Band Register (see Useful Addresses). The Band Register is run as a commercial operation and many firms of lawyers subscribe to it as a means of searching for band names on behalf of their clients. Its stated aim is to try to head off disputes over names by acting as a filtering process at the beginning and before a band gets too attached to the name they have chosen. The names that they list are taken from a number of sources. As well as taking the details from people who apply to them they also trawl through the gig listings in the newspapers and online and, to a lesser extent, adding to their database the names of artists who are doing gigs around the country. One thing you do have to think about if you apply or ring them up about a name search is that, if the search reveals there is another band with the same name and you then choose to ignore that and go ahead with the name anyway, the Band Register has evidence that you knew about it when you decided to go ahead. An Internet search on their website www.bandreg.com might be more anonymous or neutral.

Just because a band is listed on the Band Register database doesn't mean that they will automatically succeed in stopping you from using the same name. You have to also look at whether they have an existing name or reputation, whether they have registered a trademark or a domain name, and whether they had a reputation in the same area of the business as you. If you choose a name and another artist objects to you continuing to use it because it is the same as one they have been using for a while, they may sue you. This could be for a breach of their trademark (see Chapter 8) or, if they have not registered a trademark, they would have to argue that they had a reputation in the same area of music, in the same country as you and that you were creating confusion in the mind of the public and trading on their reputation. This is called 'passing off' (see Chapter 8).[1] If they *can* establish these things (and that is not always easy to do) and they can also show that they are losing or are likely to lose out as a result, then they can ask the court to order you to stop using the name and also to award them damages against you. They would have to establish a number of things including an existing reputation. Just because a band has done a gig or two under the same name as you doesn't necessarily mean that they have a reputation or that they can satisfy the other tests of 'passing off'. You may have the greater reputation or the greater bargaining power. If you've already got a record deal or are about to release a single or album under that name you may be

---

1 For a more academic overview of branding, see Chapter 21 of *Copinger and Skone-James on Copyright*, Sweet & Maxwell, 1998.

able to persuade them that they are in fact trading on *your* reputation and that they should stop using the name.

If you do find another band with the same name then you could do a deal with them to buy the right to use the name from them. You pay them a small amount (or a big amount if you really want the name) and they stop using it, allowing you to carry on. If you're going to do these sorts of deals you should also make sure that you get from them any domain name that they have registered in the band name and, if they have a trademark, an agreement to assign the registration to you.

A recent, well-publicised case was that involving the members of Liberty, the band formed from the runners-up in the television programme *Popstars*.[2]

THE LIBERTY X CASE

V2 Music, the record company, had an exclusive recording contract with the members of Liberty and were preparing to release and promote their first album. The claimants were a funk band formed in the late 1980s who also went by the name Liberty. This band had had a lot of publicity and played a number of live concerts in the period up to 1996 but never got a record contract. Their three independent releases made between 1992 and 1995 sold only a few thousand copies. The public interest in them had become virtually nonexistent by the mid-1990s, although they kept going in the business, where they were known and respected, and appeared as session musicians on other people's work.

The question was whether they had sufficient residual goodwill left in 2001 to be entitled to be protected against passing off.

The pop group Liberty argued that even if there was residual goodwill their activities could not be seen to interfere with the old Liberty as they were in different areas of music.

The court found that the amount of residual goodwill had to be more than trivial which was a question of fact. The judge found that while the case was 'very close to the borderline' there was a small residual goodwill that deserved protection. He granted an injunction against the new Liberty band's continued use of the name. The band has renamed itself Liberty X and continues to release records even though the winners of *Popstars,* the band Hear'Say, announced its demise in October 2002.

TRADEMARK SEARCH

You can run a trademark search to see if there is someone else with the same or a very similar name in the classes of goods or services that you would be interested in (for example, Class 9 for records). In the US the record company often makes it a condition of the record deal that they run a trademark search and charge you for it by adding on the cost to the unrecouped balance on your account. If the search reveals another band or artist with the same name, the record company will usually try to make you change your name.

SHOWCASING YOUR TALENT

Let's assume you've got a name, can legitimately use it and are getting some interest from the business. Record companies have had their fingers burned by signing artists for large sums of money who they haven't seen perform and then discovering that they can't

---

2 *Keith Floyd Sutherland v. V2 Music and others* Chancery Division (2002).

play or sing at all. So most record companies will insist on seeing you play live. If you are already playing the club circuit they may just turn up to a gig. If you aren't then they may pay for the hire of a venue. This is called a showcase. The venue will either be a club or a rehearsal studio. Sony Records' showcases often take place in their staff canteen. These showcases may be open to the public but more often they will be by invitation only.

You could hire a venue yourself and send invitations out to all the record companies. However, just because you've invited them doesn't mean they'll come. Don't be at all surprised if they say they're coming and then don't show up. It's a very fickle business. They probably got a better offer on the night. The more of a 'buzz' there is about you the more likely it is that they will turn up, as they won't want to miss out on what could be 'the next big thing'.

I once asked the MD of a major record company why he was paying for an artist to do a showcase which would be open to the public when he knew that the artist would then be seen by the A&R people from rival record companies. His answer was quite revealing. He said that he knew how far he was prepared to go on the deal and so was not worried that it would be hyped up. He felt that if this artist really wanted to be with his record company he wouldn't be influenced by the interest from other companies. Confidence indeed. In fact the artist did sign to his company and at the time of writing is still on that label, although the MD has moved on.

PRESENTING YOURSELF WELL

Here are some tips that may help you showcase your talents successfully. First, do your homework. Read the music press. Find out the current 'happening' venues, the places that regularly get written up in the music press. Pester that venue to give you a spot, even if it's the opening spot, and get all your mates to come along so that it looks like you've already got a loyal following. Before you get to that stage you may need to start out in the clubs outside the main circuit and work your way in.

You should also find out what nights the venue features your kind of music. If you play radio-friendly, commercial pop you don't want to get a gig on a heavy metal night.

Make sure the songs you play (your set) are a good cross-section of what you do. What goes down well with your mates in the local may not work for a more sophisticated (or uptight) urban audience (but you'll want to play one or two of the firm favourites to give you a confidence boost).

Be professional. Rehearse, rehearse, rehearse. Think about your image and style. Don't send mixed messages. Think about your relationship with the audience. If yours is the 'say nothing, the music will speak for itself' style, that's fine – but make sure you're sending that message clearly to your audience. We all like a 'personality'. If your band has got one make sure you use him or her to their best advantage.

Always tell your audience who you are at the beginning and end of your set. You'd think this was obvious but you'd be surprised how many gigs I've been to where it's been impossible to tell who the artist is unless you've seen them before. The line-up of the bands on the night can change and no gig ever starts at the time it's supposed to, so you can't even make an intelligent guess. Make life easier for us – tell us who you are.

Try and get your local press behind you. I know of one Nottingham band that did this very successfully. They made a fan of the arts reporter on the local newspaper and kept him up to date on what they were up to and when they were playing. This made sure they got good reviews. A scout read one of these and went to the next gig, which was on the outer-London circuit. The band took 'rent-a-crowd' with them and were spotted by an A&R man tipped off by the scout. A record deal followed. The local reporter was the first one they told – after their mum, of course.

SHORT CUTS

It's a long haul and it needs determination and dedication to plug away on the gig circuit like this. Are there any short cuts? Yes, there are some. There are 'battle of the bands'-type competitions, and if you get through to the final three or even win then that will give you valuable exposure and should ensure a number of follow-up gigs in the local area and some useful publicity. They don't often lead directly to deals although, if you win, you may get free studio time to make a demo (see below).

There are also 'open mike' evenings at clubs, when anyone can turn up and ask to play one or two numbers. In London these are held at places like West 14, the 12-Bar Club, the Kashmir Club, and the Borderline. Scouts regularly check out these places.

Music industry organisations – such as the Performing Rights Society Limited (PRS) or its US equivalents, The American Society of Composers and Publishers (ASCAP), or Broadcast Music, Inc. (BMI) – occasionally arrange nights at a Central London venue to showcase two or three acts who are either unsigned or have signed a record deal but not a publishing deal (or vice versa). ASCAP sends out a CD containing a track by each of the acts it's promoting. These are popular with A&R people because someone has already filtered out a lot of the rubbish for them. See Useful Addresses for contact details.

There is also an annual UK music industry convention called In The City. Attached to it is a series of showcases for unsigned acts at venues in the city where the conference is being held. It's quite expensive to register for the conference but it's often possible to get into the bar of the main conference hotel where the executives meet to relax. You could get lucky and meet one or two A&R people and get your demo to them. Remember, however, that they get given many CDs, often late at night, and possibly after several pints of beer and they will probably need to be reminded who you are in a follow-up call a few days later. If you're chosen for one of the unsigned showcases, it will guarantee that at least one A&R person will be at your gig. In past years Suede, Kula Shaker and Oasis have all played 'In The City Unsigned'.

THE DEMO RECORDING

One thing several of these short cuts have in common is that someone has to hear a recording of your work first. The demo recording is your calling card, your way of introducing a stranger to your work. It should be recorded to the best standard you can afford.

STUDIO DEALS

What if you haven't any money? How do you afford to make a recording? One way is to beg 'down-time' from your local recording studio. This is time when the studio is not being hired out commercially. It may be at really unsociable hours such as 2 a.m. to 8 a.m. But who needs sleep – you've got a record deal to get.

The studio may give you the time cheaply or even free, but they are more likely to let you have the time in return for promises of what they will get when you get your first deal. The studio owner may want some of the income (the royalty) you earn from the sale of your records. This is sometimes called an override royalty. This is fair if you get a deal using recordings made at the studio, but take care that the studio is not asking for too much. A 1% override royalty is usually enough. By that I mean that if you are offered a 12% royalty you have to give 1% to the studio owner, leaving you with 11%. Some studios try to get royalties on your second and third album too. They argue that you wouldn't have got your chance to record at all without their generosity. This is true, but there comes a time when your success has nothing to do with that original generosity. One album is plenty in most cases.

The studio may also want a guarantee that you use their facilities when you make your album. Or the studio owner may want to produce your first commercial album. You should be careful about agreeing to these sorts of conditions. Record companies don't like package deals on studio and producer. They like to have some say on these things themselves.

The demo should feature a good cross-section of your work. Most people think that it should contain no more than three or four different pieces, with your best one first, your second-best one last and contrasting style pieces in the middle, but be careful of sending a confusing message by mixing too many different styles on one CD. The opening number should have immediate impact in case the listener fast-forwards it before you've got into your stride. Many A&R people listen to demo tapes in their car. If you don't grab their attention they'll hit the eject button and move on to the next in the pile. The case and the tape/CD/DAT should both contain details of who you are, the names of the pieces, who wrote them and, most importantly, a contact number, otherwise when, inevitably, the case gets separated from the CD or tape itself, there is no way of telling who the band are and how to get hold of them.

If the A&R person likes your tape he'll undoubtedly want to hear more. He may want to pay for some studio time for you to record some more material or to try out different versions of what you've already recorded on your demo. He may offer you a demo deal.

DEMO DEAL

The deal will usually guarantee you a certain amount of time in a professional or in-house recording studio. Many record and publishing companies have their own studio facilities, which they may offer to make available. Perhaps you shouldn't look a gift horse in the mouth, but if the studio doesn't have the equipment you need to show yourself off to best advantage you should say so, and either ask for that equipment to be hired in or ask to go into a commercial studio. Cheeky, yes, but you can do it politely – it's your chance, so don't blow it.

The record or publishing company will expect to own the copyright in what you record (see Chapter 3). The company will want to own the right to control what happens to the recording. A record company will not usually expect to own rights in the song but a music publisher might. Try and take advice before you agree to give away rights in the song. At the very least they shouldn't own the song unless they offer you a proper publishing deal (see Chapter 4). The company offering you the deal will also own the physical recording or 'master'. This is fine as long as they don't stop you recording the same song for someone else if they don't offer you a deal. They should also agree that they won't do anything with the master without first getting your permission. This is important. When you finally sign your record deal you will be asked to confirm that no one else has the right to release recordings of your performances. The record company will not find it funny if a rival company releases the very track that they had planned as your first single. The company who paid for the demo will usually agree that you can play it to other companies if they decide not to offer you a deal.

The record or publishing company will normally want some exclusivity in return for the studio time they are giving you. They may want you to agree not to make demos for anyone else or not to negotiate with another company for a period of time.

They may be slightly more flexible and want the right of first negotiation or refusal. This means that they will want either to have the first chance to try to negotiate a deal with you or they will want to have the right to say yes or no first before you sign to another company. This is a difficult call. You will no doubt be excited and perhaps desperate not to risk losing the deal but, before agreeing to exclusivity or these negotiating options, you need to be sure that the exclusive time period is not too long. If they tie you up for months you may miss your moment. If they have first negotiating or rejection rights then they should tell you as soon as possible where you stand. If they're not interested then you need to move on as quickly as possible.

Bear in mind, though, that the record company has to go through a number of stages before they can make a decision. They have to listen to the recording, probably then discuss it at a weekly A&R meeting and then maybe also with their immediate bosses or even overseas colleagues. All this takes time and they may not want to risk losing you to a rival company. So you need to get a balance between the needs of the two sides.

Don't be surprised or depressed if, after you make the demo, the company decides not to offer you a deal. I know several artists who got demo time from two or three record companies and ended up with an excellent set of demos that they took to another company who then signed them up. What you don't want to happen is that people feel that you've been around for a while and are sounding a bit stale. This is a difficult balance to strike.

On a more positive note, the first company may love what you've recorded. The demos may confirm the A&R man's faith in your abilities and he may be ready to do a deal with you. You've passed go and, once you've read the rest of this chapter on getting yourself some good advisers, you should go straight to Chapter 3 (What Is A Good Record Deal?)

GETTING HELP AND PUTTING TOGETHER YOUR TEAM

All of this may seem a bit daunting. Don't worry about negotiating or signing a studio or demo deal. There are people that you can turn to for help. You should be looking to put your team of advisers in place as soon as you start to get a bit of a 'buzz' about you so that you are ready to move quickly.

THE LAWYER
A good lawyer with experience of the business can be of enormous help to you. So where do you find one and what can they do for you?

Finding a lawyer
You can ask the Law Society for their suggestions (see the Useful Addresses section for details). They have entertainment firms on their referral lists but make no judgement on the quality of the advice.

Some law firms have their own websites, which will tell you a bit about the firm and its areas of expertise. It will usually contain an e-mail address, so you could try sending them a message asking for further information.

Some websites contain details of the last big deals the firm did and, where their clients allow them to, list the names of some of their clients. It is not necessarily a bad thing if there aren't many clients mentioned. Professional rules mean we have to keep client information confidential and not even say that someone *is* a client without the client's permission or unless it is public knowledge. If a client is kind enough to give me a credit on the album sleeve, I take it that he's happy for people to know I'm his lawyer, but if in doubt I have to ask.

Directories
Not all law firms have websites, so you could also look in the two main books listing UK legal firms – *Chambers* and *Legal 500* (See Useful Addresses). The guides can be found in most of the larger public libraries. Both have a similar approach, breaking down the lists into areas of the country and particular specialisations. Most UK music lawyers are based in London, but there are one or two in places like Manchester and Glasgow. *Chambers* writes short pieces on those it thinks are the leading players in a particular field. *Legal 500* operates on a league principle. When it interviews lawyers it notes which names are mentioned most frequently by others in the business and grades the firms accordingly.

The *Music Week Directory* also lists UK law firms, but an entry in the directory is not any guarantee that they are any good.[3]

Managers and accountants
If you already have a manager or an accountant they may be able to recommend a lawyer to you. You should check if your manager has the same lawyer. Most managers realise that for some things (for example, negotiating the management contract) you have to have a separate lawyer from your manager. There is a conflict in the interests of the two of you that means you must be separately advised. Where there is no conflict of interest there is nothing wrong in you and your manager having the same lawyer.

Other bands
Other bands or contacts in the business may be able to recommend someone to you. This may be their own lawyer or someone they have heard others say is good. We

---

3 *Music Week Directory* is published annually by Miller Freeman Entertainment. If you subscribe to *Music Week*, you are entitled to receive a free copy of the directory and a free entry in it. For subscription details contact *Music Week* (see Useful Addresses).

lawyers love personal recommendations as a source of new work. It means we must be doing something right.

Other sources of information

Other sources could be the Musicians' Union, the International Association of Entertainment Lawyers and the Music Managers Forum. See the section on Useful Addresses at the back of the book.

How do you go about choosing and employing a lawyer?

Sometimes lawyers have moments when they are in the public eye because of a particularly high-profile piece of work they have done and everyone wants to have them as their lawyer. You must, however, try to find out whether the lawyer is experienced and not a one-hit wonder. How do you do that? Ideally you should have two or three names on your list, possibly gathered from a variety of sources. You should call them, tell them you are looking for a lawyer and ask to meet with them. Be wary of lawyers who promise the earth. We don't have all the answers. Before you meet up with the lawyers have some questions ready for them. Ask how long they've been doing this and who their main clients are. As we saw, they may be a bit coy about this because of their duty to keep clients and their business confidential.

You should also ask the lawyers the all-important question of what they charge, when they expect to send you a bill and when they expect it to be paid. Will they accept payment in instalments and, if so, do they charge interest on the balance like you would on a credit card bill that you were paying off monthly? Can you *pay* by credit card? Beware of a lawyer who is reluctant to discuss his costs. If he tells you what he charges by the hour you may need to sit down. But quoting hourly rates doesn't really help you to compare two firms, as one lawyer may work faster than the other. A better way to do it is to ask them to give you a ballpark figure for what it usually costs for them to do a record or publishing deal. If you ask each lawyer the same question you'll have a better basis for a comparison. Don't necessarily go for the lowest price. It may be that the deal gets done faster but it's a short-term view. Where the lawyer really comes into his own is when something goes wrong in six months' or a year's time. Then the thoroughness with which he has done his job in protecting your interests really gets put to the test.

Your lawyer is a fundamental part of your team. Take your time in choosing one and don't be afraid to say if you're not happy with a piece of work, including voting with your feet and changing lawyers if it doesn't work out. The same goes for your accountant and any other advisers you have. We're only as good as the last job we did for you.

Potential problems

There are firms of lawyers that work mostly for record and publishing companies and others that work for what we call the 'talent' (the creative end of the business). It is important to know this. If the record label interested in you uses the same firm for their own legal advice there will be a conflict of interest which will make it difficult for that lawyer to work for you if you're ever in a dispute with the record company. Some say it's possible to build Chinese Walls (artificial barriers where, in theory, one lawyer within a firm knows nothing about what another is doing, so can't be influenced in any negotiation). When things are going well this can work, provided everyone knows it is happening. When things aren't going so well will you feel confident that your lawyer is looking after your interests?

Another potential problem area concerns fees. The Law Society now requires your lawyer send you a letter setting out the basis on which he is going to work for you, including details of what he expects to charge. The letter should also tell you who in the lawyer's firm you should complain to if you can't get the problem sorted out by speaking to your own lawyer. If the worst comes to the worst you can ask for a Remuneration Certificate (provided you ask for it within a month of getting the bill). You can also ask the court to tax (i.e. check) the bill. As a last resort you can appoint another firm of lawyers to sue the first. The Law Society can recommend firms to you that do that sort of work. But this is all very negative. In the majority of cases there isn't a problem that can't be sorted out with one phone call.

Beauty Parades

When you go to meet lawyers it's only fair that you tell them that you're seeing lawyers from other firms. Lawyers call these meetings 'Beauty Parades' when we set out to impress you. There's nothing worse than spending an hour giving advice to someone you think has already chosen you as their lawyer only to be told as they walk out of the door, 'Thanks for that, I'll get back to you when I have seen the other firms on my list.'

If you're asked what other firms you've seen you don't have to say, but if you do it helps that lawyer, who then knows who he is in competition with and can adjust his 'sales pitch' accordingly.

When you've decided who you want to work with, you should tell the others who've given up an hour or more of their valuable time that they are out of luck. You never know, you may want to change lawyers at some point and there's no harm in keeping things civil.

What does your lawyer do for you?

A trite answer may be to say whatever you instruct him to do (provided it is legal). We do work 'on instructions' from you, but that's really not a true picture of all that we can do for you. We're there to advise you, to help you decide what's the best deal for you. We give you the benefit of our experience of similar situations. In larger firms, where there's more than one music lawyer, you're also getting the benefit of all their experience as well, as we share information on who's doing what deals and for how much.

If you want, we can help you to target companies that our experience tells us should be interested in your type of music. This can help you to be more focused. This doesn't mean to say that we act as A&R people, although I have come across one or two lawyers who do think they are. The type of music you're into shouldn't influence your lawyer, who should be able to represent you whatever style of music you make, provided it's not so far out of his area of expertise that he doesn't have the necessary experience or commercial knowledge of whether the deal is good, bad or indifferent.

There's also a growing band of lawyers who, following the American trend, are acting as quasi-managers, only taking on clients who they think they can get a deal for. Managers seem a little uncomfortable about this, as it blurs the edges between their respective roles. It also means that the lawyer is making a judgement call, and those who really need advice may be losing out.

Our role can be as wide or as narrow as you want it to be. If you are already clued-up on the type of deal you want, or have a manager who is, then you won't need that sort of advice. If you're quite happy about negotiating a deal direct with the record or publishing company, then you bring your lawyer in later when the commercial terms are agreed and you need to get the legal contract in place. On the other hand, if you're new to the business and aren't confident enough to negotiate commercial terms, you'll want to involve your lawyer at a much earlier stage.

I work differently with different types of clients. If it's a new artist that either doesn't have a manager or has a manager who isn't very experienced I run with things right from the beginning when a record company says it wants to do a deal. I contact the record company, get their deal proposal and, after talking to the client, I go back to the record company with any counter-proposals, continuing this process until the deal is in its final form. I then get the draft contract, check it, make any necessary changes, and negotiate those with the company until the contract is ready for me to recommend to the client for signature.

With other clients there may be an experienced manager on board who knows exactly what his bargaining power is and what sort of deal he would ideally like to end up with. My role at the beginning is more that of an adviser or sounding board. The manager will usually make sure I get a copy of the proposal and any counter-proposals, but won't want to involve me directly in the negotiations. He may telephone from time to time to ask if I think company X can do better than what they are offering. I'll tell him what I think based on other deals my colleagues or I have done with that company. We keep the details and the names of the clients confidential, but we can say whether we know they can do better on a particular point or not. Once this type of client is happy with the commercial terms I'm then brought in to do the negotiation of the contract itself.

You should establish with your lawyer what kind of relationship you want to have. This may well change from deal to deal as you grow in experience.

I like to take an interest in my clients' work. I'm delighted to be sent a copy of the new album or single. It helps to cement the relationship between us. I also like to go and see my clients play live. I have to admit, though, that when I'm in the middle of a very long week at work and a client rings up and says, ' Hi, I'm on stage tonight at the Laughing Cow at 10.30 p.m.' (which means 11 p.m. at the earliest) then my wish to support the client is tested to the full.

What you don't want to happen is for your advisers to embarrass you. And yes, it does happen. I can still remember a gig a few years ago when four members of a top entertainment accountancy firm were standing proudly in the front row wearing the band's T-shirt over their work suits.

When should you get a lawyer?

There are a number of different views on this. Some say that there's no need to get a lawyer until you've a contract in front of you. Funnily enough, I think you should get a lawyer earlier than this. I think that the whole process of getting a deal is so much of a lottery that anything you can do to reduce the odds must be worth doing. Most of us are happy to give initial advice and guidance for free, or only charge you when your first deal is in place. Just be careful and check this before going ahead.

With the new breed of lawyer who claims to be able to get you a deal, you need to be clear what they are expecting to charge you. Is it their normal rate or is there a premium for this service?

Your lawyer can also help you to find a good accountant.

ACCOUNTANTS

This leads me neatly on to discuss how you find a good accountant and what they can do for you.

The Institutes

The Institutes of Chartered Accountants in England & Wales, Scotland or Northern Ireland and the Association of Chartered and Certified Accountants can recommend firms to you (see Useful Addresses). It's important that the accountant is qualified, preferably a Chartered or Certified accountant. Anyone can set up in business giving financial advice, so you should check that they're properly regulated. You shouldn't allow them to keep your money in an account to which they can have access without your knowledge. If they are to have signing rights on cheques make sure two signatures are needed at least, with one from your side as well as the accountant.

Directories

There isn't any general guide similar to the *Legal 500* or *Chambers*. The accountancy profession is broken down into the big international firms like Ernst & Young and Deloitte & Touche, medium-sized national firms with international networks like BDO Stoy Hayward, and smaller local firms. Firms come and go out of the directories.

In 2001 the Tenon Group Plc acquired the goodwill and assets of the law partnership Statham Gill Davies (SGD). As a consequence, SGD lost its stand-alone office and identity and was rebranded as Tenon Statham Gill Davies. While the name partners of SGD are still at TSGD, they and their fellow partners and employees are not allowed to call themselves solicitors (and so have had to be removed from the relevant directories). Instead they describe themselves as lawyers or business advisers. The Tenon website[4] confirms that Tenon is, like Numerica,[5] an aggregator, bringing together accountancy practices and other related service providers, such as lawyers, financial services and corporate recovery firms. Despite this change, TSGD continue to be a force in the music business.

For a time after this happened a number of other boutique firms wondered if this might be a way forward for them. It hasn't happened, however.

The *Music Week Directory* has a section on accountants. The directory is not a recommendation that they're any good, but it is a good starting point. See the Useful Addresses section for contact details.

AMIA

You could always try the Association of Music Industry Accountants (see Useful Addresses). They will be happy to recommend accountants from within their own membership and, as their name suggests, they are all associated with the music business.

---

4 www.tenongroup.com
5 Numerica Business Services Limited, part of the Numerica Group Plc.

Music Managers Forum

The MMF can give you recommendations for accountants as well as for lawyers. They have firms of accountants who are corporate members (see Useful Addresses) as well as individual accountants who provide business or quasi-management services.

Lawyers

Your lawyer should have had dealings with a number of accountants and should be able to recommend two or three to you that they know have experience in the music business.

Bank managers

Your bank manager may have one or two names of accountants he can suggest, but it must be someone who is familiar with the music business. Certain banks, such as Coutts and some branches of Barclays, NatWest and HSBC, concentrate on the entertainment industry and they would certainly be able to suggest some names to you. It's also important that you find a sympathetic bank manager who will understand that your income doesn't come in neat monthly wage cheques. Your accountant can put you in touch with those he's found to be helpful.

Other sources of information

Your A&R or other record or publishing company contacts or friends in the music business may be able to suggest some names. It's always good to get a recommendation from someone who rates a particular accountant highly.

How to choose an accountant

As I suggested when choosing your lawyer, you should see more than one accountant. You should ask them the type of work they can do for you. Some are strong on tour accounting or in auditing (inspecting) the books and records of companies. They may also do general bookkeeping and tax advice – but they may not, so ask.

If you expect to do a lot of touring, it's worth having an accountant who's experienced in putting together tour accounts and is familiar with tour budgets and all the necessary arrangements to deal with VAT on overseas tours and taxes on overseas income (see Chapter 10).

It's less important that your accountant's offices are in the same city as the record and publishing companies. They don't have to be in London. The main thing is that they are familiar with the music business and how it works. They must know the sources of income and how and when it's paid. They need to know how to read and understand a royalty statement. These things are often, literally, written in code. You need to know what country A is and what the code for CD sales is. Your local family accountant can, of course, do the basic accounting work as well as the next man, but this isn't enough once you start getting deals. Just as you need a lawyer with specialised music business knowledge, so you need the same expertise from your accountant if he's to be able to look after your interests properly. The basic accountancy and tax rules do, of course, apply to artists and songwriters, but there are a number of specialised rules and regulations aimed at them. Your accountant must be up to date on these rules.

Some accountants don't claim to be experts in tax planning or advice and, if that is an area that you need to have covered, you would be best advised to go to an accountant that can provide that and then get a specialist accountant in to do the tour accounting or auditing.

As your accountant will have intimate knowledge of your finances and may have some control over your bank account, it is vitally important that you trust them, that they have a good reputation and that there are suitable checks and balances in place to protect you and your money.

Business managers

There is another breed of accountant that could provide the sort of services you are looking for, and that is a business manager. This is a term that has come across from the US, where they're quite common. In the US they generally act as the business and financial adviser alongside a personal manager who looks after the day-to-day and creative aspects of the artist's career (see Chapter 2). In the UK the term means something slightly different. They provide day-to-day business advice and bookkeeping services. They'll do your VAT and tax returns for you. They can provide business plans and advice and some also do tour accounts. Most don't provide international tax planning or audits. Their argument is that this makes them more cost effective as you are not paying for a full tax planning and audit service when you don't need it. This means they can charge less than the bigger firms of accountants do. When specialist tax or international advice is required, they have relationships with more than one of the bigger accountancy firms and other financial advisers and can refer you to the right company for you, to get the advice you need when you need it.

How do they charge?

Accountants usually charge fees rather than commission. They may quote you a rate per annum for advising you. Some of the bigger accountancy firms run special schemes where the first year's work for you is done at a special, discounted rate. You don't have to stay with them after the first year. If you're tempted by these schemes you should ask what exactly is covered by the discount rate. It's likely that you won't get the same service as the full-price one. You should also ask what the non-discounted rate would be after the first year so that you can decide whether you think you'd be able to stay with them afterwards or will have to start the search for a new accountant, which could be disruptive.

You should ask them what their experience is and who will be doing the work. Often you find that the person who sees you and does the hard sell is the partner or even the marketing person. Someone quite different and possibly much less experienced may be doing the work. This sort of thing is more likely to happen in the bigger firms, particularly those that are offering a discount rate. You can be reasonably sure that it will not be a partner that will be doing the cut-price work.

What does an accountant do?

Accountants can do a number of things for you. They do the accounts books for you, and advise and help you to complete your tax return. They register you for VAT, if necessary, and can do your quarterly VAT returns. Depending on your accountant, they may also do your tour accounts and help prepare a tour budget. Your accountant will advise you on whether you should be a sole trader, in partnership or a limited company (see Chapter 11). He can prepare partnership or company accounts. Some accountants can also act as the auditor of your company books; many can also act as the company secretary and can arrange for the company's registered office to be at their offices. Incidentally, this is also a service that a lawyer can usually provide, so you might want to compare costs and see which offers the best value before automatically plumping for one or the other.

Your accountant can act as your financial adviser, telling you where is the best place to invest your money. Because this area is very closely regulated, not all accountants are authorised to provide financial services advice. You should ask if your accountant is. If he isn't you will need a separate financial adviser.

Your accountant can be your tax adviser and help plan with you things such as whether you could consider putting your income in an offshore tax haven or, indeed, if you could, or should, become a tax exile.

Can your accountant help you get a record deal?

Yes, he can. You can use accountants in the same way as lawyers. Use their contacts and pick their brains for information on companies and A&R people. Accountants also send out demo tapes on behalf of artists and songwriters.

If your accountant does find you a deal then he shouldn't charge you a commission for doing so. He should just charge for any accountancy advice that he gives you on that deal. If your accountant offers to get you a deal, ask him on what basis he is doing it before you give him the go-ahead.

The accountant should be able to work as part of the team with you, your manager and your lawyer. It's important that you keep your accountant in the loop about the deal so that he can advise how it can be structured as tax-effectively as possible before you sign anything.

All accountants should give you a letter of engagement, setting out the basis on which they will work for you and how they will charge. They should give you the name of someone in their firm that you can complain to if you've a problem with your accountant. If the complaint is about fees you can ask for a breakdown of the bill. The professional body that your accountant belongs to is the first port of call for complaints about your accountant. If they don't deal with the complaint to your satisfaction you can take it to court. This is looking at the negative side and most relationships proceed smoothly.

An accountant can have conflicts of interest just as your lawyer can. If your accountants act for one of the major record or publishing companies, and you then want to do a deal with that company, the conflict may or may not arise at that stage. However, if later on you aren't sure whether the company is accounting to you properly and you want to send someone in to look at (audit) the books, then your accountant will have a conflict of interest and you will probably have to take that work elsewhere. There are, in fact, specialist firms of accountants who only do audits. Sometimes it's best to use their specialised knowledge even if there isn't a conflict of interest with your own accountant.

So now you've got your lawyer and your accountant lined up. You have two members of your team – getting a manager could be the critical third stage. I'll deal with this in the next chapter.

CONCLUSIONS

- If you hope to get noticed through doing live work, do your homework first. Investigate your venues and rehearse thoroughly. Tailor your material to your audience and tell us who you are.

- Consider short cuts like industry-organised showcases, open mike evenings or music conventions.

- Make sure your demo is the best quality that you can afford and that it has a good cross-section of your work. Put your name and contact number on the tape or CD as well as the packaging.

- If you do a deal with a studio for studio time, make sure it's for no more than 1% and don't agree they can be the producer of your first album unless there are excellent reasons to do so.

- If you do a demo deal, keep the exclusive period as short as possible and make sure that no one can do anything with the recordings without your agreement.

- When picking a lawyer or accountant, arrange to see two or three different firms and ask them for estimates of their charges for a particular piece of work. Find out their expertise and who their clients are.

- When you appoint a lawyer or accountant, get written confirmation from them of their charges.

- Your accountant and lawyer are vital members of your team – take your time to choose the right one.

2: MANAGEMENT DEALS

INTRODUCTION

In this chapter I'm going to look at how to find a good manager, what to expect from a manager, and what you have to think about when entering into a management contract. I'm going to look at it from the artist's point of view, but when we get to the part on contracts I'm also going to put the manager's side of the argument. The section on what to expect from a manager should also be useful to managers. It'll give them an idea of what it is reasonable to expect from them.

It gives me a real buzz to team up the right manager with the right artist; it's like watching a well-oiled machine going into action. It's also great to work with a good artist/manager team, as everyone's pulling in the same direction.

HOW TO FIND A MANAGER

DIRECTORIES

One of the main music business directories in the UK is the *Music Week Directory*. It lists managers and the acts they manage. The Music Managers Forum (see below) also issues a directory of its managers and who they manage, which can be an excellent starting point for finding a manager who looks after artists who are similar to you or who share a particular musical genre. *Gavin* is a directory for listings of US managers.[1] The *Musician's Atlas* lists managers in the independent sector of the US music business. For details of how to get hold of these directories see Useful Addresses.

The drawback with all directories is that they don't give you any clues as to whether the managers listed are any good. The information you get from them needs to be backed up from other sources.

MUSIC MANAGERS FORUM

One such source is the Music Managers Forum (MMF).[2] The MMF doesn't act as a dating agency for setting managers up with artists. It does, however, publish a directory of its members and is helpful in putting you in contact with individual managers.

Membership of the MMF is not a recommendation that a manager is any good but, if a manager is a member, it shows that he is interested in talking to other managers and in keeping up to date with what is going on in the outside world that can affect the music business and their or your livelihood. The MMF also runs very good training courses for wannabe managers (see the appendix on Working in the Music Business for more information).

---

1 *Gavin* is published annually by Miller Freeman. It is one of the leading directories of information on who's who in the US music industry and can be a useful source of information if you're looking for managers with American connections or offices in the US.

2 The MMF was formed in the mid-1990s by a group of like-minded managers who felt that they could achieve more both for their artists and for themselves if they grouped together. They act as a lobbying group on behalf of their members in relation to national and international issues facing the music industry. The MMF is also establishing links with managers in Europe. For contact details see Useful Addresses.

It can be lonely out there so, if you are a manager yourself looking for like-minded individuals, the MMF runs a group for new managers, whose aim is to educate and inform less experienced managers, but not in any kind of 'preachy' way.

RECOMMENDATIONS
You may by now have quite a lot of information about various managers, but you still may not know if they're any good or even if they're looking for new artists to manage. What you need are personal recommendations (references, if you like) from people who have worked with a particular manager or know him by reputation. Where do you get these? You can ask around among other bands to see if they have any good or bad experiences of particular managers. Bad reports can be as useful to you as good ones. At the end of the day you'll have to make up your own mind whether to trust a particular manager, but if people who know him keep saying bad things about him, you can't say you weren't warned.

LAWYERS AND ACCOUNTANTS
If you've already found yourself a lawyer or accountant then they should be able to tell you what sort of reputation a particular manager has. They are also good sources of information and can put you in contact with managers that you may not have discovered on your own. They may know that a particular manager is looking for more acts to manage or, conversely, is too busy to devote the necessary time to a new artist.

As with all major decisions you shouldn't rush into anything. In particular, if a lawyer or accountant has recommended someone, you should try and find out what the relationship is between him or her and that manager. If, for example, they get most of their work from that manager, how independent are they and is there any conflict of interest? They can't advise you independently if the rest of the time they are advising the manager. But just because a lawyer recommends a manager that they regularly work with doesn't mean that there is necessarily a conflict of interest. You just have to be clear who is looking after your interests.

SURGERIES
The Performing Right Society Limited (PRS) holds occasional 'surgeries' (see Chapters 4 and 15). These are meetings where music business professionals such as lawyers, managers and A&R people discuss particular topics and answer your questions. They are sociable events, held in a pub or club, and are a good place to meet other songwriters and music business people. Details of their meetings are given in the PRS Newsletter or direct from the PRS. ASCAP (one of the equivalent societies in the US) also holds informal evening sessions when managers get together. See Useful Addresses.

A&R CONTACTS
Record or publishing company scouts or A&R people can be an excellent source of information on managers and whether a particular manager is looking for new artists to manage. They can put you in contact with managers. In fact, they may insist on you getting a manager before they are prepared to discuss a possible deal with you, because they're happier dealing with a middleman (and preferably someone with a track record).

MANAGERS

There is always the possibility that a manager will approach you direct. They may have heard about you from an A&R man, a lawyer or accountant, or they may have seen you play live. It's not unheard of for a manager to come up to you after a gig to say that he wants to manage you. A word of warning. Just because a manager approaches you doesn't mean they're any good, nor does it mean that you've to leap at the chance of being managed by anyone regardless of who they are. You still have to do your homework and make as sure as you can that this is the right manager for you.

You should always ask for a trial period to make sure that the relationship is working. It takes time to build up the necessary trust between you. The manager should agree to that, but he will be looking for commitment from you before he spends any significant amounts of his own money on you. He'll certainly be looking for you to confirm that you want him to manage you before he approaches record and publishing companies on your behalf. If he's prepared to commit time and spend money on you then it's reasonable to expect some commitment from you in return. Sometimes they ask you to sign a short agreement to cover their expenses and any deals they may get for you during the short trial period. As with any legal agreement, if in doubt – get it checked out by a lawyer.

Having discussed how to find managers we should now look at one or two of the principles behind the artist/manager relationship. Many of these principles have been developed and applied to management contracts through a series of cases involving some of the leading players of the time.

THE PRINCIPLES

The first thing you have to understand is that it's a relationship based on trust. If the trust is lost then there's little hope for the relationship. The contract won't hold you together if the trust isn't there. All that a management contract will then do is tell you what your rights are and what happens if you part company.

This loss of trust has led to many disputes between managers and artists over the years. Some end up in court, many more settle before they get that far – even at the doors of the court. Most people don't want to air their dirty linen in public. It's not a pretty sight when you're sitting in court and the reporters are all lined up on the benches behind you ready to take down every sordid detail. One time I was in court and found myself sitting next to a journalist from one of the tabloid newspapers. He was obviously bored with the lack of juicy scandal and kept popping in and out of court. In one of the gaps in the proceedings I asked him if he'd been going out for a cigarette. 'Nah, love,' came the reply, 'I'm checking with my bookie who won the last two races at Sandown Park.' He then asked me if I fancied a bet on the outcome of the trial and could I tell him what he'd missed while he was outside on the phone. Ah, British journalism at its finest.

Anyway, the cases described below *did* get to court. Two of them were written up in the Law Reports, which means they can be quoted and relied on in later cases. The third one was unreported, but within days every decent music lawyer had a copy of the judgement because its effects were so far-reaching. The judgements in these cases helped to establish what lies behind the relationship in legal terms, what duties the manager has towards an artist, and what is acceptable in a management contract.

THE CASES

Gilbert O'Sullivan

One of the leading cases on management fall outs and the breakdown of trust involved Gilbert O'Sullivan (yes, he of the flat cap and mournful expression).[3]

Gilbert O'Sullivan signed a management contract with Management Agency and Music Limited (MAM) in 1970. He was young and unknown at the time and had no business experience (this theme comes up time and time again in music disputes). MAM and the man behind it, Gordon Mills, already had an international reputation. Mills managed the superstars Tom Jones and Engelbert Humperdinck. Through MAM Mills also had interests in a number of other music companies.

O'Sullivan trusted his manager completely and, at Mills's suggestion, he also signed recording and publishing contracts with those related music companies.

O'Sullivan didn't have any independent legal advice on these contracts. He wasn't told that it would be a good idea for him to get such advice. It seems that he trusted Gordon Mills to such an extent that it didn't cross his mind to get a second opinion. If his manager told him to do something, then he did it.

The agreements tied O'Sullivan to Mills and to his companies completely, and the terms were far worse than if O'Sullivan had done the deals with independent companies and if he had taken independent advice.

O'Sullivan's debut single on MAM was the very successful 'Nothing Rhymed'. Early UK successes were followed by a Top 10 hit in the US with 'Alone Again (Naturally)'. In 1972 he had two No. 1 singles in the UK with 'Clair' and 'Get Down'. His second album reached No. 1 in the UK and he had a number of further hits, but by the mid-70s his career seems to have been on a downward path.

By 1976 O'Sullivan's relationship with Mills had broken down; he'd lost his trust in him. This might have been because, for all these hits, he didn't seem to be making much money. He sued Mills, arguing that the various contracts should be treated as if they'd never happened (that they were void), because Mills had used his position of trust with O'Sullivan to wrongly influence him to sign them. He also argued that the terms of the contracts were so unreasonable that they unfairly restricted his ability to earn a living. These concepts of undue influence and unreasonable restraint of trade come up often in music contract disputes.

The court decided that Mills did owe a duty to O'Sullivan. This is called a fiduciary duty – a duty to act in good faith. Mills had a duty to put O'Sullivan's interests first. The court also decided that the contracts were void and could not be enforced. If O'Sullivan chose to ignore them, Mills couldn't do anything about it. The court tried to put O'Sullivan back in the position he would have been in had the contracts not been signed. It ordered all copyrights that had been transferred (assigned) by O'Sullivan to be returned to him as well as all master recordings of his performances.

This was a dramatic decision and it caused uproar in the music business. Record and publishing companies were afraid that, if this decision were allowed to stand, there would be a rush of other artists making the same claims and trying to get their rights back. They knew that many of the contracts around at the time were no better than those that

---

3 *O'Sullivan v. Management Agency and Music Limited* [1985] QBD 428.

O'Sullivan had signed. They were really worried that all the deals they had done for the records or songs would be void and unenforceable. It's no exaggeration to say that the whole basis of the music business, and the financial security of many companies, was at risk.

The Appeal

Unsurprisingly, Mills and his associated companies wanted to have this dangerous precedent overturned. They appealed against the decision that the companies owed any duty to O'Sullivan. They argued that the record and publishing companies had not used any influence over O'Sullivan. They also argued that the contracts should be declared voidable and not void from the outset. If the Court of Appeal agreed with them, the contracts would be valid but could be set aside later if they were found to have been signed through undue influence or to be in unreasonable restraint of trade. Because the companies had already acted as if the contracts were valid, they argued it would be impossible to return everyone to the position they would have been in had the contracts not existed. They said that the copyrights and master recordings shouldn't be returned to O'Sullivan, but that he should be compensated by payment of damages.

In a very important decision for the music business, the Court of Appeal decided that the associated companies *did* owe a fiduciary duty to O'Sullivan, because Mills was effectively in control of those companies and was acting in the course of his employment by these companies when he used his undue influence over O'Sullivan. The court also confirmed that it *was* possible to set these contracts aside, even if the parties couldn't be put in exactly the same position they would have been in had the contracts not been signed. The court thought that this could be done if it was possible to reach a 'practically just' result for O'Sullivan.

So far so good for O'Sullivan, you might think. His lawyers must have thought they were home and dry, but there was a sting in the tail. The Court of Appeal decided that a 'practically just' solution would be for the copyright in the songs and master recordings already in existence to remain with the publishing and record companies, subject to suitable compensation for O'Sullivan. They also said that the contracts were voidable rather than void, that they were an unreasonable restraint of his trade and that O'Sullivan was freed from them but only for the future. What he'd written and recorded before stayed with the record and publishing companies.

The music business breathed a collective sigh of relief. The refusal of the Court of Appeal to order the return of the copyrights has made it very difficult, if not impossible, to successfully argue for a return of copyrights in cases of undue influence or unreasonable restraint of trade.

Joan Armatrading

At about the same time, another important case was reaching the courts. It involved Joan Armatrading.[4]

Joan Armatrading is a guitar-playing singer-songwriter who is still recording today. The case was about an agreement that Armatrading signed when she was young and relatively inexperienced and before she became famous. There's that theme again.

---

4 Armatrading v. Stone and Another (1985), unreported.

Stone was a partner in the Copeland Sherry Agency, which had signed a management agreement with Armatrading in March 1973. This was shortly after she released her debut album *Whatever's For Us,* which was produced by Gus Dudgeon, who also worked with Elton John and who was recently tragically killed with his wife in a car accident. Copeland is Miles Copeland, who managed The Police and Sting for some time. Stone advised Armatrading on business matters. She took charge of most creative issues herself. It seems she was confident enough to select the studios and producers she wanted to work with without needing advice from her managers, but didn't have a clue when it came to the business end of things.

In 1975 Armatrading released her second album *Back To The Night.* It didn't reach the charts. She then began work on an album that turned out to be the first to bring her properly to the public's attention.

In February 1976, as the term of the original management contract was about to run out, she signed a new contract under which Stone was to manage her on his own. He may have been worried she would go off to another manager when the original contract ran out and just as her career was starting to take off. Although he denied that in his evidence, the album that she released in 1976, *Joan Armatrading,* went into the Top 20 in the UK and one of the singles released off it became her most famous and successful song. It was called 'Love And Affection' and it reached the Top 10.

Things continued to go well for her at first and in 1980 she released her most successful album to date, *Me Myself, I,* which also contained the hit single 'All The Way From America'. Shortly after that she seems to have become disillusioned with Stone and commenced proceedings for the management contract to be declared void on the grounds that Stone had used undue influence to get her to sign the contract and that the terms were unreasonable and a restraint of her trade.

It became clear from the evidence given in the case that the lawyer who drew up the contract had been introduced to Armatrading by Stone and had done some work for her. Coincidentally, I worked with that same firm of lawyers for a couple of years. The contract was done before my time there, but the court case was going on when I was there and I know it caused a lot of strain on everyone concerned. When preparing the management contract, it seems the lawyer acted on the instructions of Stone and not Armatrading. In particular, Stone asked for two specific things to be added to the draft contract. The lawyer billed Stone for the work and it's clear from the description on the bill that he thought he was acting as Stone's lawyer.

At a meeting on 4 February 1976 at the lawyers' offices, Armatrading received a copy of the draft contract to take away with her. She returned the next day to sign it. She didn't ask for any changes to be made to it.

Stone claimed that the lawyer acted as lawyer for both of them. When he gave evidence the lawyer said that he thought he was just acting as lawyer to Stone. A very confusing state of affairs. Stone and Armatrading were both present at the meeting with the lawyer on 4 February when the contract was discussed. That must have been very awkward. If a manager turns up at a meeting I'm due to have with an artist to discuss a management contract, I insist on him staying outside while I take the meeting. I can't be open with the artist about what I think about the contract or the manager if the manager is in the same room. The same would apply the other way around.

The contract was strongly biased in Stone's favour. It was for five years and during that time Armatrading was exclusively tied to Stone as her manager. The contract didn't say that Stone had to do very much at all for her. He could manage other artists. He was to be paid a management commission of 20% (which, as we will see, is quite common) but 25% on any new recording or publishing deals she signed (which is not). He got 20% commission on touring whether or not the tour made a profit. The court thought this was particularly harsh, as was the fact that Stone's right to commission was open-ended. For example, if Armatrading signed a new record deal in year three of the five-year management term, Stone would be entitled to 25% commission. He might stop being her manager two years later, but he'd still go on earning at 25%. If Armatrading got herself a new manager and he negotiated some improvements to the recording contract in return for, say, a two-year extension on the record deal, then Stone and not the new manager would get commission at 25% on the extended term. Not much of an incentive for the new manager (or expensive for Armatrading if she had to pay out two lots of commission to the original and the new manager).

When he gave evidence, Stone agreed that he knew that he had a duty to act in Armatrading's best interests and that she had trust and confidence in him. This fiduciary duty already existed when the 1976 management contract was being discussed. Stone knew that his interests under this contract were not the same as Armatrading's and yet he still seemed to think that the same lawyer could act for both of them.

Stone admitted that it was very likely that Armatrading didn't realise she should have separate legal advice. Even though he accepted his fiduciary duties existed, he didn't seem to accept the idea of a conflict of interest and couldn't seem to see that if something in the management contract was in his interests it would not necessarily be in Armatrading's best interests. This doesn't mean that a manager can't look out for his own interests, just that it's up to him to make sure that the artist has separate advice and is able to come to an informed decision.

The court found Stone's evidence was very contradictory. It decided that Armatrading relied heavily on Stone in business matters. She trusted him and he'd told her that he would look after her. The court thought it was clear that he had influence over her. She didn't look at the detail of the contract. She relied on Stone, who told her that it was a standard and fair contract, even though he had asked for two specific changes to be made to the draft.

The court decided that the contract should be set aside by reason of undue influence by Stone. The terms of the contract were said to be unreasonable ('unduly onerous and unconscionable' in the words of the judgement). The contract was voidable and not void from the outset. On this point they came to the same conclusion as in the O'Sullivan case.

The fact that Armatrading didn't have separate legal advice was seen as very important. On its own this wouldn't have been enough to set aside the contract. For example, if the contract had been a perfectly reasonable one, so that any lawyer who advised on it would say it was all right to sign it, then the absence of that advice wouldn't have been fatal. The absence of separate legal advice coupled with the particularly harsh terms of the contract was enough to convince the court to set it aside. The court found that, although she had some experience of the music business, because she concentrated on the creative side it was important that she be given a proper understanding of the business side of the contract. She hadn't understood the implications of the open-ended commission clause and hadn't been able to form an independent view after full, free and informed thought. She had signed the contract relying on her manager's claim that it was fine. He had failed in his fiduciary duty to her. She was freed from the contract and went on to record several more successful albums.

Although this case wasn't reported in the Law Reports, it had a very significant and practical effect on management contracts. We lawyers still use it as a yardstick to measure the reasonableness of management contract terms. It's also quoted as an authority for saying that artist and manager should have separate lawyers when discussing the management contract and whenever their interests are not the same.

After this case it became usual to add a clause to management contracts saying that the artist has been advised to take independent legal advice. I don't think this goes far enough. Just advising someone they should get advice and then not making sure that they do is not good enough. I think that the manager should insist on the artist having separate legal advice from a lawyer who understands the music business, and should make sure he understands what he's being asked to sign.

The Armatrading case also cast doubt on whether a five-year contract term was reasonable. After the case, some managers decided to go for a shorter term or otherwise tried to make their contracts more reasonable. No manager wants to risk having an artist walk away from a management contract at the height of his or her success. However, as we shall see below, the trend these days is back to longer minimum management terms.

The judge was also quite critical of the 25% commission rate on new record and publishing deals (25% rates are now rare, but do still occasionally occur). He was even more concerned about the fact that Stone took commission on touring money even if the tour made a loss. Music business lawyers reacted to these criticisms by introducing new protections for artists in this area.

Elton John

Another case on management contracts that was reported in the tabloids as well as the Law Reports involved Elton John.[5]

Elton John signed a series of publishing, management and recording contracts starting in 1967, when he was still under age and unknown. Although these themes come up quite often in these cases, each case played its own part in developing how the business operates and how contracts have to be adapted to deal with criticisms made by the judges.

Elton John and his lyricist Bernie Taupin were originally taken on as in-house writers for James's new publishing company, DJM. It's said they were on wages of £10 per week. It took quite a while for them to be commercially successful. The first successful album was produced by Gus Dudgeon and was called *Elton John*. The 1972 album contained the now-classic work 'Your Song'. Seven consecutive No. 1 albums followed in the next seven years.

Although Elton was making a lot of very successful records, he didn't seem to be seeing much of the proceeds. For example, the publishing set-up consisted of a number of inter-related companies, each taking its own slice of the income, so that a very small amount was left for Elton. What he did get he had to pay management commission on.

He sued to try and recover his copyrights and damages for back royalties. He relied on

---

5   *John v. James* (1991) FSR 397.

the tried and true arguments that he had signed the contracts under undue influence and that they were an unreasonable restraint of his trade.

He hadn't taken separate legal advice before signing any of the contracts. He'd placed trust and confidence in James. The contracts weren't as beneficial for him as they could have been had they been with independent companies. The publishers could take rights in his songs and not have to do anything with them. They could be shut away in a drawer and never seen again and Elton couldn't do anything about it. He was also signed up exclusively, so he couldn't take his songs to another music publisher.

The court decided that in these circumstances it was to be assumed that there was undue influence at work and that it was up to the manager to show that he didn't use his influence in the wrong way. The court found that James had failed in his fiduciary duties to Elton. It felt that James couldn't be acting in the best interest of Elton if James's publishing and recording companies were also entering into contracts with him. How could James be advising Elton as his manager while he also had an interest in making as much money as possible for his record and publishing companies out of those contracts?

Once again, the decision in this case had a knock-on effect on the music business. It was fully reported in the Law Reports, so had authority, and it confirmed the existence of the fiduciary duty owed not only by the manager, but also any companies under his control. It also brought home the importance of separate legal advice.

The other important thing it changed was what happens where your manager also has a record or publishing contract that he wants you to sign up to. If your manager also has an interest in a record or publishing company, the management contract will now usually ask the artists to confirm that he won't consider it a failure of the manager's fiduciary duty to him if he signs up to the record or publishing company on the manager's advice. I don't think this would be enough to get the manager off the hook if he did, in fact, break his duty to the artist – especially if the artist hadn't had separate legal advice. There's also usually a clause that says the manager can't take a double hit on the income from the record or publishing deals. For example, if the artist releases a record on the manager's record label, the manager should get his money from the record label's profits on the record sales. He shouldn't also take a management commission on the artist's record royalties.

The Pell Case

Not all disputes involving managers are claims by the artist against the manager or vice versa. Sometimes the manager has to look after the artist's interests in other ways, such as keeping their personal life confidential. One such case involved Elton John again and his long-term manager, John Reid, as well as a colourful character called Mr Pell.[6]

It is alleged that Mr Pell comes by confidential or interesting information on people in the public eye by, among other things, rummaging in their dustbins.

Mr Pell supplied material to the *Daily Mirror* about Elton John's spending habits, including information that was from sources expected to be confidential, such as a letter from a firm of accountants. John Reid Enterprises Limited (JRE) was Elton John's management company at the time and it seemed that the 'leak' of the information could be traced back to someone within JRE. JRE wanted to know who it was, so that they could be dealt with and the clients' belief in their ability to keep things confidential could be restored.

---

6 *John Reid Enterprises Limited v. Pell* (1999) EMLR 675.

JRE brought an application to the court for an order that Mr Pell deliver up all information and papers he had so that they could find the source. Mr Pell applied for no such order to be made on the basis that he was an investigative journalist with many sources of information that it was important for him not to disclose.

The court decided that it was of the essence of the trust relationship on which JRE's business was based that it could assure its clients of confidentiality. The court generally takes it as being less important that a source is protected where information has been obtained unlawfully. The court refused Mr Pell's application and ordered that the source be disclosed.

This touches on a fast-developing area of law, that of the rights of privacy under the Human Rights Act and the often contradictory rights of freedom of speech and of the press. This is dealt with in more detail in Chapter 8.

WHAT TO LOOK FOR IN A MANAGER

This all depends on what you expect your manager to do for you. You may only need a manager to advise you on business matters. You may want that but are also looking for creative advice, comment and guidance. Some artists already have a clear idea of what they are doing creatively and have a good business sense and grasp of contracts. They don't want an all-round manager and may only be looking for a good organiser. We saw in the Armatrading case (above) that Stone only looked after Armatrading's business interests. She looked after the creative side herself.

You may be looking for a Svengali, someone who will come up with the cast-iron plan for world domination in three years. Such managers do exist, for example, people like Tom Watkins, who has successfully managed acts like The Pet Shop Boys and Bros to considerable success. Then there are managers like Simon Fuller, whose marketing background meant that he could see the worldwide possibilities of an act like The Spice Girls and S Club 7. When you expect a manager to devise an all-encompassing gameplan and then to implement it, you can't expect to get away with no effort on your part. You and your manager will have to put enormous amounts of time and energy into making the plan work and both of you must completely buy into the whole idea behind it. There is, of course, also the type of artist who's been formed to a particular purpose, such as TV-based acts like S Club Juniors, or those who have won reality TV competitions such as *Pop Rivals*. Provided the artist fits in with this gameplan then all is well. It's only when the artist, or one or more members of the group, start to rebel or baulk at the situation that problems occur. We have recently seen the demise of the original *Popstars* group, Hear'Say, who said things hadn't been the same since one of the original members, Kim, had left to pursue a solo career.

IS IT ESSENTIAL TO HAVE AN EXPERIENCED MANAGER?

Someone who hasn't managed anyone before can make a good manager if they have the flair for it. They may have been a musician themselves, a tour manager, a producer or may have worked in-house at a record or publishing company. They will have seen how the music business works and can bring valuable experience to the job of manager. However, the skills that make a good producer are not necessarily those that make a good manager, so be careful. On the other hand, a manager may be experienced and still not right for you because his experience is in a different arena (for instance, as a tour manager) rather than skilled in managing an artist's career. So take your time before making up your mind.

QUALITIES TO LOOK FOR IN A MANAGER

The manager has to be a diplomat, motivator, salesman and strategic planner – and has to have the patience of a saint.

Record and publishing companies like to have managers around to act as middlemen so they don't have to have unpleasant conversations with you. They'd like you to choose someone who's already successfully steered an artist through getting a deal, getting a record made and who's already done the whole touring and promotion side of things. This doesn't mean to say that they won't work with an inexperienced manager – just that they would prefer one who was not. They would also like you to be managed by someone they already know, someone they know they can work with. This doesn't necessarily mean that that manager will be in their pocket. It could mean that they have a healthy respect for him for being tough but fair, someone that gets the job done. If you *are* being pushed by your record company towards a particular manager, take the time to stop and ask why and to do some research of your own before meekly accepting their choice.

WHAT DOES A MANAGER DO FOR YOU?

PERSONAL MANAGERS

A personal manager looks after your day-to-day needs. This usually includes some advice on the creative side of things. The personal manager also acts as go-between with the record and publishing companies and the outside world. A personal manager is usually someone who organises your life and tries to make everything run smoothly. They put into action plans others have come up with. They don't necessarily get involved in day-to-day business decisions or strategic plans.

BUSINESS MANAGERS

A business manager doesn't usually involve himself in the day-to-day business of running your life. He leaves it to the personal manager to make sure that you have your personal needs attended to, that your fridge is full when you get back off tour and that you get to where you are meant to be at about the right time. It's the job of the business manager to work out where you should be in terms of business planning and to help you put the plan into action. He will liaise with the record and publishing company, but usually more at the level of negotiating deals, changes to the contracts, setting video and recording budgets and getting tour support when it's needed. For more information see Chapters 3 (on record contracts) and 10 (on tour support).

It's much more common in the US to have a separate business and personal manager. There the business manager is often an accountant or financial adviser. The idea of these roles being filled by different people hasn't yet become popular in the UK. What tends to happen here is that one person will do both jobs, sometimes with the assistance of a personal assistant (see below).

If you do have separate business and personal managers, you need to be sure that you're not paying too much by having two people on board instead of one.

Don't assume that because you have a business manager you can do away with the need for an accountant. You will need one to oversee your tax and possibly VAT returns and someone to prepare company or partnership accounts (see Chapter 11 for more information on whether to be a partnership or a limited company). Bear this in mind when you agree what to pay your business manager. If you're paying your business manager 20% of your income, your personal manager another 10% and then paying an accountant, that's not a great bargain.

The manager is there to advise you, to guide you through your career in the music business. A successful career as a performer or composer can lead into other areas such as films, television, writing or modelling. One of the many things you have to consider in choosing your manager is whether the manager can also look after these other areas of your life.

The manager should spend a reasonable amount of time on your affairs and your career. He should help you to get a record and/or publishing deal, live appearances, sponsorship and merchandising deals.

The manager should advise you whether or not you should take up a particular offer. It may not fit in with the gameplan that you and the manager have worked out. Putting together that gameplan is a very important job for your manager. You and he need to be on the same wavelength on it.

PERSONAL ASSISTANTS

As you become more successful, so the manager may employ someone to act as your personal assistant (PA). If the PA is working full-time for you, the manager will expect you to pay their wages. If they work some of the time for you and the rest on general work for the manager or for other acts that he manages, then the cost is likely to be shared between you. If the PA works most of the time for the manager and only occasionally runs errands for you, then you would expect the manager to bear all the cost.

FIDUCIARY DUTIES AND PROBLEMS WITH BANDS

As we saw in the section on the cases (above), the manager has to always act in your best interests. He has a fiduciary duty to you, which means that he has to always act with the utmost good faith towards you.

This duty can cause problems when dealing with a band. Something that may be good for the band as a whole may not be good for one of the band members. There's a very narrow line that the manager has to tread. Sometimes you may feel that the manager has stepped the wrong side of that line.

This issue was one of several behind a dispute in the late 1990s between Nigel Martin-Smith and Robbie Williams.[7]

The Robbie Williams management case

I have to declare an interest here, as this was a case I inherited when I became Robbie's lawyer a few years ago. Martin-Smith was the manager of Take That from the early days to the height of their success. Take That was made up of five members, including Robbie. He became fed up at the direction his life was taking and was thinking about leaving the band.

---

7 *Martin-Smith v Williams* (1997), unreported.

His version of events is that he was prepared to see his commitments to a major tour through to the end before leaving the band. He says that, on advice from Martin-Smith, the band sacked him. The other members and Martin-Smith say he walked out.

When Martin-Smith later sued Robbie for unpaid commission (Robbie had refused to pay him), one of the arguments that Robbie used was that Martin-Smith had failed in his fiduciary duty to Robbie and was not acting in his best interests in advising the band to sack him.

Martin-Smith acknowledged that it was very difficult in such circumstances to advise a band when he also had a duty to each of them as individuals. He admitted that he had had discussions with the other band members about Robbie and how disillusioned he was, but he said he also tried to advise Robbie on what was best for him. He said that he had acted in the best interests of the band as a whole, while trying to balance this against the interests of the individual members. He denied that he'd advised the band to sack Robbie.

The judge accepted his evidence that he had acted in good faith and was not in breach of his fiduciary duty to Robbie. The judge acknowledged the difficulties that a manager faces in such circumstances, but decided that in this case Martin-Smith had stayed the right side of the line.

If you're in any doubts as to the good faith of your manager, you should seek independent advice, if only to be aware of your legal position.

WHAT IS IN A MANAGEMENT CONTRACT?

Once you've found yourself a manager you think you can trust and who will do a good job for you, you need to think about what should go into the contract between you.

This will be different depending on whether you are an artist or a manager. In what follows I'm going to take the artist's viewpoint, but in my time as a music lawyer I've acted for both artists and managers and so I'll try to present both sides of the argument.

INDEPENDENT LEGAL ADVICE

As we've already seen, when negotiating a management contract the artist must have separate legal advice. The manager may decide not to take legal advice at all. He may be experienced enough to feel comfortable with the deal he's prepared to do and doesn't need advice. If he's experienced with management contracts this isn't really a problem. If the artist decides that he doesn't want legal advice, then this is a problem for the manager. The manager should insist on you getting separate advice from someone who is familiar with the music business and with management contracts.

What if you haven't got the money to pay for a lawyer? The Musicians Union (MU) has a limited free legal advice service for its members, but you can't expect it to be as detailed as if you were paying proper rates for it and it may take some time for you to get the advice (contact details are in Useful Addresses). The Music Managers Forum has also come up with some management contracts they recommend to their members, but bear in mind these are drafted from the manager's perspective.

Some managers will loan you the money to take independent legal advice, because it's in the manager's interests to make sure you're properly advised. If the manager does loan you money to get a lawyer, he will usually put a limit on how much he'll contribute.

You'll either have to get the lawyer to agree to do the work for that much or you'll have to put some in as well. The manager will get his contribution back out of your first earnings. Your lawyer may agree to accept payment by credit card or in instalments – ask him.

TERRITORY

The first thing you have to decide is what countries the contract will cover. We call this the territory of the deal.

The manager will probably want to manage you for the world. This isn't just so that he can get as much commission as possible, although that is a factor. He may want to keep overall control of the gameplan, which he won't be able to do very easily if he only manages what you do in one part of the world.

You may be fine about this because you're confident that he can look after your interests around the world. But you must bear in mind that the way the music business operates, in the US in particular, is very different from the UK. Does the manager have an office in the States? Does he have an associate there? Or will he be spending half his time on planes crossing the Atlantic? If he is, who's going to end up paying for that? Sometimes it'll be the record company, sometimes it'll be part of a tour budget, but sometimes it'll be you.

If you don't think that the manager can successfully look after your interests worldwide, you could insist that he only manage you for part of the world, for example, the world outside North America.

Even if you aren't sure he's up to being a worldwide manager you could initially give him the benefit of the doubt. You could make it a worldwide deal to start with and, if he's not up to it, you could insist that he appoint a co-manager, probably for the US but possibly for other parts of the world, like Japan, to look after your interests there. This is a very personal thing and both you and your manager should agree the identity of this person.

The co-manager is usually paid out of the commission you pay to the manager. Apart from the co-manager's expenses, you shouldn't end up paying out more in total commission just because there's a co-manager on board.

There are several ways that the manager and co-manager can split the commission between them. They could just take the total worldwide commission and split it down the middle. They could each just take commission on the income earned by you in their particular areas of the world. For example, the co-manager could take commission on the income you earn in North America and your original manager on the rest of the world income. The manager could decide not to share his commission but to put the co-manager on a retainer or pay him a fee. It's a complex subject and the manager should take legal advice on it.

ACTIVITIES COVERED

The next thing to think about is whether the contract will cover everything you do in the entertainment business or just your activities in the music business. You might start out as a songwriter or performer and later move into acting or writing books. The manager may be perfectly capable of managing you for all those activities, or he may be an expert at the music business and know nothing about the business of writing books or acting. If you're not convinced he can look after your interests across the whole of the entertainment industry you should limit it to the music business only. The manager may be unhappy about this. He may think that it will be his management skills that will help turn you into a success in the music business which will in turn open doors to acting or writing books. He may feel that he should share in your income from those other activities. On the other hand, you may be concerned that he's not up to representing your interests and may want a specialised acting or literary agent involved.

Many managers will agree to compromise and say they have no objection to you bringing in specialised acting or literary agents if you are acting in roles or writing books that have nothing to do with you being a successful musician or songwriter first. If the acting role or book is directly connected to the fact that you are an artist, they will want to share that income and manage those projects. For example, if you are asked to write a behind-the-scenes look at your time out on the road with the band, the manager will expect to take commission on your income from that book. If, however, you are asked to write a book on climbing in the Himalayas that clearly has nothing to do with your fame as a successful musician or songwriter, the manager may agree not to take commission on that income.

By the time you get a manager you may already have established yourself in another part of the entertainment business. For example, you may already be a successful TV actor or model. The manager may agree not to manage those areas of activity. He may also agree not to manage or take commission on work that comes from a particular contact or source of work, such as a recording studio, that was in place before he came along. If, however, you ask him to manage projects that come from that source, for example, by chasing them for payment for you, then it's only reasonable that the manager should be allowed to take commission on that work.

EXCLUSIVITY

Once you've decided what activities he's going to manage and in what parts of the world, the manager will expect to be your only manager for those activities and those areas. He will want to be your exclusive manager. You will not be able to manage yourself or to ask someone else to manage a particular project unless he agrees. This is not only reasonable – it's practical. You can't go around accepting work without referring it to your manager – it might clash with something he is putting together for you.

KEY-MAN PROVISIONS OR, HOW DO YOU MAKE SURE THAT YOUR MANAGER IS THERE FOR YOU WHEN YOU NEED HIM?

What happens if your manager manages other acts or is part of a management company that manages a number of people? How can you make sure he'll be there for you when you need advice? How do you make sure you aren't fobbed off on to someone else because your manager is busy with the others he manages? Well, first of all you make sure that your management contract says that he has to spend a reasonable amount of time on a regular basis on managing you.

You could possibly go further and insist on what we call a 'key-man' clause being put into the contract. I believe this term comes from insurance policies that are taken out on the life of key individuals in an organisation, which pay out if the key-man dies or is unable to work. You name the manager as a key-man and say that if he's not available to you as and when you need him, you can bring the contract to an end.

Your manager may be very flattered at being named as a key-man, but he may feel that it's a bit harsh to allow you to end the contract so abruptly. He may want to say that you can only terminate the contract if he has regularly not been available to you or has been unavailable to you for over, say, six weeks at a time. You have to be sensible about this. If you're buried in a residential studio in the depths of the country, writing or rehearsing material for your next album, it may not be reasonable to expect your manager to be there all the time. If you're in the middle of a major renegotiation of your record contract, however, you can reasonably expect him to be around.

These key-man clauses are also sometimes put into record or publishing contracts, but the companies hate them because they give the artist and the key-man a huge amount of power. If they sack the key-man you can end the contract. Unconfirmed rumour has it that the band Oasis had a key-man clause in their record contract with Creation Records. When Sony first looked to buy the remaining shares in Creation that they didn't already own, they are said to have had to rethink things because Oasis could have walked out of their contracts at the height of their success if the key-man at Creation Records, Alan McGee, was no longer in control at the label. So it seems they had to do a deal with either Oasis at Creation or Alan McGee or with both.

HOW LONG SHOULD THE CONTRACT RUN?

The contract could be open-ended and carry on until one side or the other decides it's over.

It could be for a fixed period of, say, one or two years and then, if everything is going well, could continue until one party wanted to end the relationship.

More usually it's for a fixed period of three to five years and at the end of that time the contract is renegotiated or it just ends.

Until the early 1980s, terms of five years or longer were common, but the Armatrading case cast some doubt on that. More recent UK cases, including one involving Shaun Ryder of the Happy Mondays, have made it clear that a term of five years or longer is not acceptable here.[8] Personally, I'm not happy advising an artist to accept a five-year term. I feel three years is long enough. If it's working then they can renegotiate at the end of the three years.

I can be persuaded to agree to a three-year term with the manager having an option to extend it for one or two years. The right to exercise that option should be linked to the manager achieving something for the artist – what I call hurdles.

Hurdles

A hurdle could be that the artist has to have a record or publishing deal or have earned a minimum amount of money in the first three years, although it's difficult to say what the right minimum level of income is.

It's also possible to put hurdles in at an earlier stage of the contract. You could have a get-out if the manager hasn't got you a decent record or publishing deal in the first twelve to eighteen months. Or if he got you a deal in that time and it's come to an end and he hasn't got you another one within, say, six to nine months.

---

8   This is not the case in the US, where terms of five years or longer are still common.

Album cycles

This is a US concept. Sometimes the length of the contract is linked to an album cycle. An album cycle starts with the writing of the songs to be recorded on an album, and runs through the recording of the album and all the promotion that then goes on after its release. The cycle ends with the last piece of promotional work for that album.

There are one or two lawyers in the UK who now favour this way of measuring the management term. My problem with it is that it's very difficult to say how long it will last. You don't know at the beginning how long it will take to write, record and promote an album. I'm uncomfortable with agreeing to two- or three-album-cycle deals, which could easily run for five years or longer. If you're offered this type of deal, I advise you to put a time backstop on it, for example, two album cycles or three years, whichever comes first.

THE MANAGER'S ROLE

I've already explained a little of what you can expect the manager to do for you. What you can't do, though, is list every single thing that you expect a manager to do. Murphy's Law says that it will be the very thing that isn't listed that causes the problem. There are still some contracts around that try to list things the manager is expected to do: for example, the manager will advise on clothes, image, voice training etc. I think these have an old-fashioned feel about them. I end up imagining what the reaction would be if Oasis's manager tried to advise Liam Gallagher on his stage image or told him to get singing lessons. On the other hand, if you were in SClub, Five or Boyzone your image may be so important that it's right to expect the manager to advise on it. My management contracts just say that the manager will do all he reasonably can to further the artist's career and to do all the things expected of a manager in the entertainment or music business.

WHAT IS THE MANAGER PAID?

Some would say too much, but if you ever saw a manager working round the clock, seven days a week to make an artist successful, with not even a thank-you from him, you'd say it wasn't enough.

The average rate of commission for a manager is 20%. If you're very successful the 20% could be negotiated down to 10–15%. Some record-producer managers only charge 15% because, arguably, there is less management of projects or a career than there is with performing artists. Although a 25% rate was criticised in the Armatrading case, there are some circumstances in which it could be justified. The manager may have invested a lot of his own money in making an artist successful and may want to get that back in commission as soon as possible. He may agree to reduce his commission down to 20% when the artist becomes successful and he's got his investment back.

Percentage of what?

A percentage of your gross income is the simple answer. For example, if you were paid £100,000 on signing a record deal, the manager on a commission of 20% would take £20,000.

What if you have to use some of that money to record your album or pay a producer? What happens if you are advanced money by your record company (which they get back or recoup from your royalties) to make a video or to underwrite losses on a tour? Is it fair that the manager takes 20% off the top? The answer is no, it's not. There are a number of exceptions. It's *not* usual for the manager to take commission on monies advanced to you as recording costs, video costs, payments to record producers or mixers, sums used to underwrite tour losses and sometimes monies advanced to you to buy equipment.

Example: The record company sets a budget of £200,000 for you to make an album, £50,000 to make a video and £100,000 for you to live on for the next year. The manager often won't take commission on the £200,000 or the £50,000, but will take commission on the £100,000, i.e. £20,000.

Depending on the manager and the contract, he may say that if you decide to use £20,000 of your £100,000 to buy some equipment, then that's your choice and he's still going to take commission on the full £100,000. Or he might treat the £20,000 spent on equipment as an exception and take his commission on the balance of £80,000.

Commission on earnings from live work can be a problem. The manager usually has to work very hard putting together and running a successful tour. He may feel that he should take his 20% off the top from the income that comes in from that tour. What if the expenses of putting on the tour are so high that the tour makes little or no profit? For example, you take £50,000 in ticket sales and the expenses are £40,000. If the manager took his 20% off the £50,000 (i.e. £10,000) there'd be £40,000 left, which would be wiped out by the expenses. As an artist performing every night of the tour you may start to resent the manager making £10,000 when you're getting nothing. As we saw in the Armatrading case, the judge was very critical that Stone took 20% of gross income on touring regardless of whether the tour made a profit.

What tends to happen is that the manager takes his commission on net income after some or all of the expenses are taken off. There are various formulas to use to arrive at a fair compromise. Your lawyer will advise.

Post-term commission
This means how long after the end of the management contract the manager continues to get paid commission. It has two sides to it. Firstly, should the manager take commission on albums made or songs written after the end of the management term? Secondly, for how long should he earn commission on albums made or songs written while he was the manager.

What is commissionable?
Dealing with the first. Until the early 1980s it was quite usual to see management contracts that allowed a manager to go on earning on things the artist did long after he'd stopped being the manager. If he negotiated a five-album record deal while he was the manager and he stopped being the manager after two albums, he'd still take commission on the remaining three albums because that contract was done while he was the manager. Some contracts also allowed him to continue to take commission after he stopped being manager if someone else negotiated an extension of or substitution for that original contract. Again, because he had done the original work. This led to some very unfair situations. The new manager had no incentive to improve upon deals because it was the former manager who got the commission. Artists found it difficult to get new managers and were forced to stay with the original manager or the artist

ended up paying out two lots of commission. This situation was strongly criticised in the Armatrading case and led directly to a change in the way UK managers operated. They began to accept that they'd only get commission on work done, recordings made and songs written while they were the manager.[9]

How long should the manager continue to receive commission?

As to the second part, after it was established that managers should only take commission on what was recorded or written while they were the manager, the question then came up of how long they should go on earning commission on those recordings and songs.

Many managers take the view that they should go on earning commission as long as the artist goes on earning income from a particular song or recording. I can see the logic in this but again it can lead to some unfairness. A manager might have only been around for one album's worth of recordings. It may be a second manager that makes the artist successful. Fans of successful artists want to own all the artists' back catalogue of records and so buy the first album, or a track from the first album may go on a Greatest Hits album. The first manager has done nothing to help ongoing sales of that first album. Should he get full commission on it? Some managers insist that they should, but these days most accept that after a period of time their influence cannot be affecting continuing sales of early records, so they agree to a reduction in their commission rate. Most also agree that it should stop altogether after a given period. For example, the first manager could agree that his commission on the first album drops to 10% after five years after the end of the management term and stops altogether after ten years. This means the artist can give the second manager an incentive by giving him 10% of the income on the first album after five years and 20% after ten years. Or the artist could keep the saving himself and give nothing to the second manager.

These periods of time are negotiable. There are all sorts of variations, including some music lawyers who insist that the commission stop after two or three years. In my view this is far too short for a manager to be properly compensated for the work he has done. It may, however, be acceptable if the artist is established and successful and has greater bargaining power than the manager.

WHAT HAPPENS IF THERE'S NO WRITTEN CONTRACT?

Some managers prefer to work without any written contract. They say they'd rather work on a good-faith basis, trusting you to do the right thing by them. It's also possible for a manager to work for you for a trial period and then not carry on. No written deal is done but you still have to deal with what he gets paid for the work he did. You and the manager may have discussed the basis on which you'll work together but never got around to writing it down. It is, of course, perfectly possible for there to be a verbal contract in place. The difficulty with verbal contracts is that it's very difficult to prove what exactly was agreed.

If it's not possible to show that there was any sort of agreement, the manager has to rely on what would be a fair price for the work he has done (a *quantum meruit* claim).

---

9 In the US it is still common for managers to expect commission on the first if not the second album made after they have stopped being the manager.

If you and the manager can't agree this and there is a court case, the judge will take expert evidence of what's usual in the music business and will make an order of what he thinks the manager should be paid. The court will order payment for the work already done, but it's rare for them to order payments going forward. For example, if the manager got a record deal for you then the court might order that he's paid a percentage of the money payable on signing that deal; but rarely does it order that the manager is paid a share of ongoing royalties. So the manager wouldn't usually get post-term commission. For these reasons it's usually more important for the manager to have a written contract to protect his commission on future royalty income than it is for the artist. However, both sides may want the certainty of knowing where they stand and want to reach some form of agreement.

ACCOUNTING – WHO COLLECTS THE MONEY?

It's very important to know who's looking after the money. The manager may be unhappy at the thought of you looking after the money because you're an artist. Artists are notoriously bad at hanging on to money (they say). 'They can't even keep the money back to pay the VAT or the taxman; how can I trust them to keep enough back to pay me?'

On the other hand, you may feel you've got a fantastic head for figures and are very responsible with your money. So why aren't you an accountant then? You may not want your manager controlling your money, but do you really want to have the bother of looking after it yourself?

A compromise would be for you to appoint an accountant (see Chapter 1). The money is paid into a bank account in your name that the accountant looks after. The manager sends in an invoice for his commission and expenses. The accountant checks the sums are right and writes out a cheque for you to sign. If you've asked him to he'll deal with your VAT and he'll almost certainly tell you to keep some money back for tax. What he does with the rest of the money depends on what you've told him to do. He could pay it into another account for you or leave some in the bank account to meet expenses.

There's currently a trend for managers and artists to either jointly agree on an accountant or even to jointly appoint one. I don't have a big problem with the first but I'm concerned about the joint appointment. If you and your manager fall out, your band money is deadlocked as the accountant has to act on the joint instructions of you both, and you're not likely to be agreeing on these matters if there's been a wholesale falling out.

EXPENSES

On top of his commission, the manager is entitled to be repaid his expenses for working for you. That doesn't mean everything he spends. The costs of running his business, his office, staff, computers etc. are all paid for by him. These are called office overheads. If he pays for a taxi to pick you up from the recording studio or for a courier to deliver your demo recording to an interested A&R man, then you can expect him to reclaim that money from you.

He should keep receipts and bills and have them available for you or your accountant to check. He should also agree that he won't run up expensive items in expenses without checking with you first. I wouldn't expect him to buy a plane ticket to New York without checking that you're all right with him spending your money in that way. On the other hand, it's not practical for him to have to come running to you for every small item of expenses, in which case you might agree a float account. This is a special account with a fixed sum of money, say £500, in it. The manager is authorised to draw money out of that account for expenses and the account is then topped back up to £500 on a regular basis; a bit like a float in a till of a pub or shop.

TAX

You are responsible for your own tax and National Insurance and for paying your VAT. Don't expect the manager to do it for you. As we saw in Chapter 1, your accountant is a very important part of your team. Your accountant will keep your books, do your VAT returns and prepare your tax return for you. This doesn't mean you can sit back and do nothing. You have to tell your accountant what has come in and give him receipts for anything he might be able to reclaim or recharge. He'll tell you the sort of things he's looking for. Your accountant will also advise you of what you can expect to have to pay in tax and ways in which you can, legitimately, pay as little tax as possible. But remember, there are, they say, only two certainties in this world – death and taxes.

SIGNING AGREEMENTS

It's practical to allow the manager to sign one-off short-term contracts in your name. For example, when you do an appearance on *Top Of The Pops,* the BBC needs you to sign a short release or consent form before you can appear and get paid. If you're busy rehearsing, it's all right for the manager to sign that form for you.

What isn't acceptable is for the manager to sign a long-term contract, or indeed anything more than a one-off. It's dangerous for you – you won't know what's in it or what's been agreed. It's also dangerous for the manager. You may not object at the time, but when you find something in the contract that's not to your liking you can be sure you'll blame the manager for not telling you.

You should take responsibility for your career and for what is being done in your name.

CONCLUSIONS

- Different lawyers must advise the artist and the manager on the management contract.

- Treat with caution any contract capable of running for longer than five years.

- 20% is the average management commission for artist managers.

- Commission is on gross income. If exceptions are to be made, these must be spelled out in the contract.

- Commission on 'live' work should be after deduction of some or all of the expenses.

- The management deal doesn't need to be for the whole world.

- Make sure it is clear who is handling the money.

- Only the artist should be able to sign potentially long-term contracts.

3: WHAT IS A GOOD RECORD DEAL?

INTRODUCTION

Everybody's idea of what is a good deal is different. For some it's a question of how much money is on the table. For others it's how much commitment there is from the record company. Some artists are more interested in how much control they have over what sort of record they make. We call this creative control.

I'm going to look at these different ideas of what is a good deal. I'm going to do it from the artists' point of view because that's what I know best. But, because I've negotiated so many record deals over the years, I've heard all the arguments from the record companies, so I'll try and put their side too.

There's more than one type of record deal. I'm going to look at three basic types of deal – the licence, the development deal and the exclusive recording contract.

To understand record deals properly you also need to know some law, so I'm going to look at the basic performer's rights, at copyright and at what rights a record company needs in order to exploit your recordings.

Incidentally, in the music business we use the word exploit quite a lot. Some people react badly to the use of this word. They associate it with exploitation in the bad sense – misuse of the weak and that sort of thing. When we use it in the context of music business contracts we generally mean 'to use', 'to sell' or 'to make money from' recordings or songs. It's a positive use of the word not a negative one.

You won't be surprised to learn that there have been a few celebrated cases over the years to do with recording contracts. I'm going to look at three in this chapter to see what the problem was, what the court decided and what the music business learned from them, and also at a new model for recording deals popularised by Robbie Williams in 2002.

THE HYPE

We have all read in the press about new, unknown acts being signed supposedly to million-pound deals. Can you believe what you read? Well, I guess in one or two cases it could be true, but it's pretty unlikely if it's a completely unknown artist.[1]

What is much more likely is that the deal has been hyped up in the press to make it seem bigger than it is. If you add up all the money that the record company could spend on making an album you could get to a million pounds. That would include the recording costs, the cost of making one or two videos, marketing and touring costs. The artist might only see a fraction of that money himself.

When the record company is making up its mind about what to offer you, it will look at a number of things. First, and most importantly, how much it wants to sign you to the

---

1 The Americans are more likely to go for telephone-number-size deals. But then the rewards are much greater for the record company. In the US a successful album will sell many millions of copies. Here, a platinum-selling record is only 300,000 copies.

company. If they desperately want you, they'll pay over the odds to get the deal done. If you've got more than one company fighting over you then you've much greater bargaining power. Your manager and lawyer can play one company off against the other and get you a better deal.

If the record company is doing it scientifically they'll use various formulas to work out what's a reasonable deal to offer you. There are computer models that they can use. They look at the type of act you are, at how much they think it's going to cost to record the album and to make videos. They also look at other commitments, possibly to touring. They put these estimates into the model and it tells them how many records you'd have to sell before they break even. If they think that's an unrealistic number they may scale down the offer to you. This is the theory anyway. I suspect that while they do this number crunching they then go with their hunches anyway as to how well they think you're going to do.

We saw in Chapter 1 some of the ways in which you can get a 'buzz' going for you. The 'hotter' you are, the more the record company is likely to pay or the better overall deal you'll be offered. The better your lawyer is, the less likely it is that the record company will get away with paying below the odds – a very good reason to get a good lawyer on your side.

Your manager should sit down with you and discuss what's important to you. Are you only interested in big-money advances, or would you prefer to go for a smaller advance in return for creative control or more commitment from the record company? Once he knows what you want, your manager can make his 'pitch' to the record company along those lines.

It should be a balanced contract, where the record company can reasonably protect its investment, but also one where you get some commitment from the company and the chance to earn a decent living from the deal.

THE PRINCIPLES

Before I look in more detail at these questions of money, commitment and creative control, I need to run through with you one of the guiding principles in deciding what is a good record deal.

RESTRAINT OF TRADE

We have already seen in the cases of *O'Sullivan* v. *MAM*, *Armatrading* v. *Stone* and *John* v. *James* that the courts can be highly critical of clauses in contracts that are unfair on the artist.

In deciding whether a contract is fair, the court looks at a number of things. It looks at the bargaining power of the artist and the company. It will also look at whether the artist had independent specialist advice before he signed the contract, and at how experienced the artist was in the music business at the time the contract was signed. It does this against the background of what was the norm for these contracts at the time.

Another guiding principle behind the court's decisions is that of restraint of trade.[2] For years it has been well known that this doctrine applied to ordinary contracts of

---

2 For a more detailed description of restraint of trade, see *Chitty on Contracts*, Sweet and Maxwell.

employment or contracts for someone to provide their exclusive services. The leading case on the subject is one to do with garages.[3] What we didn't know until a 1974 case was whether the doctrine could also apply to recording and publishing contracts.

The basic principle behind the doctrine is that, where someone has to provide services or be exclusively employed and the contract contains restrictions on what someone can and cannot do, that contract is automatically a restriction on the ability to earn a living, or trade. Because it's an exclusive arrangement, the person concerned can't earn money in any other way than through that contract.

In the UK it was decided long ago that these contracts were contrary to public policy. A person should be free to earn his living wherever he can. That said, the courts recognised that there would be circumstances where it was commercially necessary to have restrictions in contracts. They decided that such restrictions would be allowed if they were reasonably necessary to protect the legitimate business interests of the person imposing the restrictions. If the restrictions were unreasonable they couldn't be enforced – the contract would be unenforceable.

Because it was so important to the music business, the case of *Macaulay* v. *Schroeder*[4] went all the way to the House of Lords before it was finally clear that the doctrine did apply to recording and publishing agreements.

Macaulay v. Schroeder

Macaulay was a young and unknown songwriter who entered into a music publishing agreement with Schroeder Music Publishing Ltd. It was an exclusive agreement for his services for five years. The contract was in a standard form used by the music publisher. Macaulay's copyrights in the songs he wrote were assigned for the life of copyright throughout the world. The contract specifically prevented him from working as a songwriter for any other music publishers during this five-year period. There's nothing wrong in signing someone up to an exclusive deal, but because it restricts that person's ability to go and work for anyone else, we have to look at whether as a whole such a contract is fair, at whether the restrictions still allow him to earn a reasonable living. The House of Lords looked at the specific terms of the agreement to see if, taken as a whole, they were reasonable. It found, in fact, that they were unduly restrictive and an unreasonable restraint of trade. Macaulay didn't have a reasonable chance to earn a decent living from his trade of songwriting.

In contrast, the George Michael case described below is an example of an exclusive contract that was found to contain reasonable restrictions.[5]

CREATIVE CONTROL VERSUS LARGE ADVANCES

Earlier in this chapter I spoke of getting the right balance in the contract terms. Behind that statement lies this principle of restrictions in an exclusive services contract having to be fair and not unreasonably restrict a person's ability to earn a living. So let's look at some of these terms.

---

3 *Esso Petroleum Ltd v. Harper's Garage (Stourport) Limited* [1968] AC 269.
4 *Macaulay v. Schroeder Music Publishing Co. Limited* [1974] 1 WLR 1308, HL.
5 The particular provisions that were found to be unreasonable are discussed in more detail in Chapter 4 on publishing contracts.

DO YOU GO FOR THE MONEY OR TRY TO PROTECT THE INTEGRITY OF YOUR ART?

Of course it's important for you to be able to eat, to have somewhere to live and transport to get you to and from gigs, rehearsals and the recording studio, but it may not just be a question of money. For many artists, creative control of their work is at least as important. The right to make a record with minimal interference from the record company is crucial to some artists.

If creative control is the most important thing for you, then getting that control would mean you had a 'good' deal, even if there was less money on the table as a result. Some record companies are more flexible than others on questions of creative control. If this is an important issue for you, you need to look at this at the point when various record companies are still courting you. You should ask each of them what their attitude is to this issue. What is their track record? If you can, you should talk to other artists signed to the record company to find out their experiences. You should also ask if the record company is prepared to guarantee creative control in the record contract.

Your wish to have creative control must be balanced against putting so many restrictions on what the record company can do that they can't sell your records properly. They may in such circumstances choose to use another artist's recordings – one who isn't so particular about creative control. For example, a proposal comes in from an advertising company to put one of two tracks into a major new jeans campaign. Band A has full creative control in its contract and is known to be completely against the idea of its work being used in ads. Band B, on the other hand, has an eye to the integrity of its work but realises that a campaign like this, if done properly, can really break it into the big-time. Band B reacts positively and the record company puts their track forward not Band A's.

You may be very interested in getting as much commitment as possible from a record company. If so, you'll concentrate on getting a commitment from them to release a minimum number of singles off each album, to make one or more videos, to commit to a specific figure in marketing 'spend' or to underwrite tour losses up to a fixed amount. The record company may be reluctant to go this far. They'd be in trouble if there weren't enough tracks on the album suitable for release as singles. It's expensive to make videos and they may not want to commit to making one that only gets played once on Saturday morning children's television. They don't like putting specific figures on marketing 'spend'. They say they'll spend what it takes. They might commit to the principle of underwriting tour losses but may not want to put a figure on it. They'd prefer it if it were discussed at the time. If these things are an important part of your gameplan, you'll want to push for some or all of them to be included in the contract. No matter what big statements and promises they make when they want you, if it's not specifically in the contract you won't have a chance of enforcing their promises if they go back on what they said or if the person who said it is no longer with the company.

Whatever your particular needs (and it may be a mixture of all of these things), if you get a reasonable number of them in your record contract you'll have what is a good deal for you.

This whole issue of creative control versus money has caused a lot of problems over the years. It's one of the reasons why Prince became Symbol became The Artist Formerly

Known As Prince and now just The Artist. He may have believed that by changing his name he could use a loophole to get out of his record contract. He was probably also hoping that it would show his record company, Warner Bros., the strength of his feeling over the type of records he wanted to make.

Many more such disputes take place on a daily basis between record company and artist or manager, but most don't get to court. One that did was the acrimonious case between George Michael and his record company, Sony Records.

The George Michael Case

To understand the case[6] and the decision you need to know a bit about the background.

As we all know, George Michael was part of the very successful pop duo Wham! along with Andrew Ridgeley. The first exclusive record deal that George and Andrew signed was with the record company Innervision, owned by Mark Dean, in 1982. As is often the case, they were young, unknown and inexperienced. The record deal was for up to ten albums, which was a lot even in those days. They were exclusively tied to the company until they'd delivered all the albums that Innervision wanted from them. Applying the doctrine of restraint of trade, the restrictions in the contract were immediately contrary to public policy and were unenforceable unless they were reasonable.

Innervision was a small record company. It had a deal with Sony whereby Sony provided funding and facilities for the manufacture, sale and marketing of Innervision's records. The Innervision contract with George and Andrew, therefore, also included Sony's standard business terms. If the Innervision contract was criticised as being unenforceable and an unreasonable restraint of trade, this could also have been an indirect criticism of Sony's terms of business.

At first things went well, and their second release, 'Young Guns', was a UK Top 10 hit in 1982. This was followed by 'Bad Boys', 'Club Tropicana' and the chart-topping album *Fantastic*. By 1983, however, the relationship between Wham! and Innervision had broken down. They sued the company to get out of the contract, arguing that it was an unreasonable restraint of trade. The case was settled before it got to court. It was part of the settlement that George and Andrew signed an exclusive recording contract direct with Sony label Epic Records. Again, that contract contained Sony's business terms, but an experienced music business lawyer negotiated it on George and Andrew's behalf.

Once again things went well at first. Their first single on Epic – 'Wake Me Up Before You Go Go' – went to No. 1 in the UK and was followed by four further No. 1s in quick succession.

In 1986, George and Andrew parted company. George embarked on a solo career with Sony. And it was a very successful one, although not until 1988 with the release of 'I Want Your Sex', which was a deliberate move to break with the playboy Wham! image. His first solo album, *Faith*, was a huge success, selling over 10 million copies. On the back of that success, George renegotiated his contract with Sony again with the help of that experienced music business lawyer.

In return for a substantial sum of money, George agreed to record three solo albums in the first contract period and gave Sony options for up to five more albums. *Faith*

---

6 *Panayioutou v. Sony Music Entertainment (UK) Limited* [1994] EMLR 220.

counted as the first of the three albums and he went on to record and release a second hugely successful album, *Listen Without Prejudice (Vol. 2)*, which also sold millions. His star was also rising in the US, where he had a No. 1 with 'Praying For Time' off that album.

Not surprisingly, Sony wanted George to continue in the same style with his third solo album. By this time, George wanted to move away from the out-and-out commercial pop style of records. He wanted to be regarded as a serious artist.

Because the contract ran until he had delivered up to six more albums, or for a maximum period of fifteen years, George couldn't record for anyone else. Sony also had the final say on whether an album by him met the necessary artistic and commercial criteria. They could go on rejecting more serious material from him, so a deadlock existed.

George sued, arguing that the record contract was an unreasonable restriction on his ability to earn a living, and as such was an unenforceable contract.

He refused to record for Sony and instead did a number of projects with other artists that were within the terms of his contract, just. For example, he did guest spots on other people's albums. He also concentrated on live work.

The case finally came to court in 1994. The decision to throw out George's case was made on somewhat surprising grounds. The judge ruled that, in order to decide if the 1988 renegotiation of the contract was an unreasonable restraint of trade, he would also have to consider the earlier 1984 contract. He decided that he could not reopen a review of the 1984 contract because it had been entered into as a result of a settlement of a dispute. It's contrary to public policy to reopen something that was agreed by the parties as being a final settlement of a dispute.

It wasn't difficult to imagine that George would appeal. Perhaps the judge realised this because, even though he had decided that he could not look at the 1988 contract, he went on to say what his conclusions would have been if he had done so.

The contract was an exclusive worldwide deal. It was for potentially a very long time and Sony had the absolute right to reject recordings and a limited obligation in the contract to do much with any recordings that it did accept. Obviously, Sony argued that the contract represented only the contractual obligations that it had and that, in fact, it would have done far more to help sell as many records as possible. In deciding whether the contract was unfair and unenforceable as being an unreasonable restraint of trade, the judge looked at the relative bargaining power of the two sides. By 1988 George Michael was a very successful and powerful artist and well able to stand up to Sony. He had had the benefit of advice from his long-standing lawyer, who was very experienced in music business contracts. Finally, the judge looked at what George would get out of the contract. Financially, he stood to get a great deal.

Balancing out all these factors, the judge decided that the benefits George got out of the contract meant that the restrictions in it *were* reasonable to protect Sony's investment and its legitimate business interests.

Sony, of course, was delighted, but it was nevertheless seen by most of the 'talent' in the business as a blow for creative freedom.

While the case was going on it was much easier to get improvements in record contracts, particularly those parts of the contracts that George was specifically attacking. For example, on CD sales, Sony was only paying 75–80% of the royalty at the time. While the case was going on Sony was much more inclined to agree a 100% royalty rate. As soon as Sony won the case it was business as usual.

George, as expected, appealed. The thought of prolonged, expensive litigation with an artist who clearly wasn't going to record for Sony, and who could see his own recording career stalling with all the delays, led to a settlement before the appeal was heard. George was released from the contract and signed to Virgin/Dreamworks in return for a payment back to Sony. As part of the settlement, he later recorded some new tracks or new versions of old tracks for a Greatest Hits album that was released on Sony.

TYPES OF DEAL

Once you've decided what's important to you in a contract, you need to know what types of deal may be on offer. You'll also need to know what basic rights a performing artist has, what copyright is and what rights the record company needs in order to release records.

Although there are many variations, there are three basic types of record deal – the licence, the development deal and the exclusive long-term recording contract.

LICENCE DEALS

Let's look first at the difference between a licence and the other two. To do this I need to explain some legal principles before we go any further.

LEGAL PRINCIPLES

'Licensor' is the technical term for a person or company who owns rights, which it is licensing to someone else. I am going to substitute the word 'owner' in this section, as it fits more easily into the text.

Licensee is the term for the person or company to whom the rights are licensed.

A **licence** is an agreement to allow someone to do certain things with the rights that an owner has to a particular product – a recording, a song and so on. A licence can be for as long as the life of copyright (see below) but is usually for a shorter period. The owner continues to own the rights but gives someone else permission to use some or all of those rights.

An **assignment** is an outright transfer of ownership of rights by an owner to someone else. It's usually for the life of copyright, although sometimes the rights are returned (reassigned) to the owner sooner than that. The assignment can be of some or all rights and can have conditions attached.

An **assignor** is the owner of the rights being assigned. The assignor no longer owns the rights once they have been assigned.

An **assignee** is the person or company to whom the rights are assigned.

Life of copyright is now the same throughout the EU. For literary and musical works (e.g. songs), it's 70 years from the end of the year in which the author dies. For sound recordings and performer's rights it's 50 years from the end of the year in which the recording was released or the performance was made.[7]

The rights I'm talking about are the intellectual property rights of copyright and performer's rights.

---

7 Sections 12 and 13A CDPA.

The **author** is the first owner of the copyright.[8] The CDPA 1988 says that in the case of sound recordings it's the producer. This could be confusing, and for a time record producers were going around claiming they were the copyright owners. It was soon clarified that the position was the same as before the 1988 Act. The copyright owner of a sound recording is the person 'who made the arrangements for the recording to be made'. This is generally taken to mean the person who paid for the recording to be made.

Copyright is the right that an author has to prevent anyone else doing certain things with his work without his permission. The basic rights of copyright are the right to copy the work; the right to issue copies of the work to the public; the right to rent or lend out copies of the work to the public; the right to perform, show or play the work in public; the right to broadcast the work or include it in a cable programme; the right to make an adaptation of the work and the right to do any of the above acts in relation to that adaptation.[9] Before anyone can do any of these things with a copyright work, they have to get the permission of the copyright owner. There was some doubt until 2001 as to whether the copyright laws of the EU extended as far as the exercise or prevention of the exercise of these rights online, by digital, online or Internet-based means. It was clarified in April 2001 by the passing of a European Directive[10] that copyright did indeed extend to such new media but, as we will see in Chapter 7 on New Media, there was extensive lobbying as to what constituted a copy. The Directive has to be implemented in the UK within 18 months, i.e. by December 2002. The Government has issued a consultation paper and intends to bring forward changes in the law in the summer of 2002, but it looks as though implementation may be slightly delayed. However, as the Directive is already in force it is binding on the UK Government.[11]

Performing rights are the rights performers have to prevent someone else from doing certain things with their performances, or with recordings of their performances, without their permission. The basic performing rights are in some respects similar to the rights of copyright. They are the right to prevent someone making a recording of a live performance; the right to prevent the making of a broadcast or its inclusion live in a cable service programme. It is also a performer's right to prevent someone from making a recording of his performance directly from a broadcast or cable programme.[12] The performer's permission has to be obtained to do any of the above.[13] Recordings of performances for personal use are allowed. The performer also has the right to refuse to let someone make a copy of a recording; to issue a copy of a recording to the public; to rent or lend copies of the recording to the public; to play a recorded performance in public; or to include it in a broadcast or cable programme service. The EU Directive referred to above also extends the performer's rights to online methods of broadcast.

LICENCE VERSUS ASSIGNMENT

When he grants a licence, the owner keeps the underlying copyright. He only gives the licensee permission to do certain things with the copyright for a period of time (the licence term).

---

8 Sections 16(2) CDPA.
9 Sections 17–27 CDPA.
10 Directive 2001/29/EC.
11 For more information see www.patent.gov.uk/copy/notices
12 Sections 181–184 CDPA.
13 Section 185 CDPA.

It is clear from the Gilbert O'Sullivan case that, even where the court finds that a contract is unenforceable, it won't usually say that it's void but voidable and won't usually order the return of copyrights or other rights that have been assigned. If it's a licence then the underlying rights haven't been assigned; there is nothing that needs to be returned to the original owner because it never left him. If O'Sullivan had licensed his rights rather than assigned them he wouldn't have had such a problem. The licence would have come to an end because MAM were in breach of its terms and he would still have had his copyright in his songs and masters. So from the point of view of an artist, a licence should always be preferable to an assignment, all other things being equal.

There are two problems with this. The first is that the record company will probably be the one who made the arrangements for the recording to be made (i.e. paid for it) and so will be the first owner of copyright. The artist may have his performing rights, but will probably not own the copyright in the sound recording. The second is that record companies don't want to do licence deals if they can take an assignment of rights instead. They have investments to protect. It can take half a million pounds or more for a major record company to launch a new act. They will want to own the copyright outright. They can't risk losing their rights if a licence ends.

The more successful an artist is, the more chance he has of being the owner of the copyright in the sound recording and in a position to licence it to the record company.

The other scenario where you may find a licence rather than an assignment is when one record company (perhaps a small label or an individual) has paid for a recording to be made and then licenses the copyright to another (perhaps bigger) record company, either non-exclusively or exclusively.

In time, and particularly as a result of changes in how records are made (see Chapter 5) and with new methods of distribution such as the Internet (see Chapter 7), artists and smaller record companies won't need as much or any direct financial investment from a bigger record company. They may be able to fund themselves cheaply and efficiently, and this could see a shift in the balance of power in favour of artists doing more licence deals. At the present time, however, they generally remain the province of the super-successful or 'hyped' artist and intercompany arrangements. Even those artists who have a significant Internet presence and fanbase acknowledge that they need the infrastructure and funds of the record companies to market their records.

EXCLUSIVE AND NON-EXCLUSIVE DEALS

When a record company is putting out a compilation (The Best Dance Records In The World Ever Vol. 3 or similar) then you might licence rights in a recording that you own to that record company for that compilation only, and probably on a non-exclusive basis. You might want to put the recording out yourself or licence it to another company for a different compilation. You couldn't do that if you'd given the first record company an exclusive licence.

On the other hand, you may be an artist or a small label that has recorded a track or an album yourself so that you own the copyright in it. You may not have the financial resources to do anything with that recording. Perhaps you can't afford to press up copies of it to sell or you can't promote it properly. You might go to another record company for those resources. If they agree, the licence is likely to be an exclusive one to protect their investment.

THE LICENCE TERM

How long should the licence last? If it's non-exclusive it probably doesn't matter too much. An exclusive licence could be as long as the life of copyright or as short as a year. Three- to five-year licence terms are common. The licensee wants to have long enough to get a reasonable return on his investment, but if it is a short licence term the owner will get the rights back sooner and may be able to re-license them to someone else (perhaps with a new mix) or release them himself. Most licence deals I'm doing at the moment are for five years, but there have been one-off superdeals recently where an artist has been so hyped that one-year licence terms have been agreed to by the prospective licensees.

TERRITORY

It could be a worldwide licence or it could be limited to particular countries. If, for example, you've already licensed the rights exclusively to a company in the US, you can only then grant other licences in the same recordings for the rest of the world outside the US.

Although exclusive recording contracts can be for limited countries, this is more common in licence deals. A distinction always used to be made between the UK and other European counties, but one of the consequences of closer European integration has meant that Europe-wide deals, including the UK, are now more common than UK-only deals.

There are people who specialise in trying to get you licence deals for particular countries. They usually take a commission (called a finder's fee) from you of 2–5% of what you get in advances or royalties. Sometimes they also take a finder's fee off the licensee for bringing the recording to them and so are rewarded by both sides. Nice work if you can get it, but be aware that if they do have such arrangements with record companies they may only take your recordings to that record company rather than to where it's best for it to be.

The main problem with individual-country deals is that you have to keep on top of a number of different licensees. You have to co-ordinate record releases and marketing campaigns and there isn't just one company to chase for payment of royalties. The main advantage is that you have a chance to licence the recording to the company that most wants it in each country, subject always to what I have just said about finders. Another possible advantage is that you may end up with more in total advances from individual-country deals than you'd get from one multi-territory deal, and may also receive more than you need in contributions to make videos or do remixes.

OPTIONS

When you're doing a non-exclusive licence of a single track for a compilation, you don't usually give the licensee any options to any further recordings you may make. It's usually a one-off.

If it's an exclusive licence for something other than just on a compilation, the licensee may be keen to get follow-up products. The licensee may be encouraged to invest more in promoting the first track if he knows he's going to get the follow-up.

When doing your exclusive licence deal, you can agree up-front the basis on which you are going to give them any follow-up product, or you can leave it to be agreed at the time they exercise the option. This can be to the owner's advantage if the first track has been successful, as his bargaining power will be higher. It's not a very certain state of affairs though and often leads to problems, so I don't generally recommend it.

Another possibility would be to give the licensee an option, which gives the licensee the chance to be the first to try and do a deal with you for the follow-up. For example, you might deliver a demo of the follow-up and give the licensee the exclusive rights for two to four weeks to try and negotiate a deal with you. If he doesn't succeed in that time you can take it into the market place. This is called a first negotiating right.

You could give the licensee a matching right. This is the right to match any offer for the follow-up that you get from someone else. You have to tell the licensee the details of the offer, and if the licensee matches or betters it within a given period of time you've to do the deal with him.

DEVELOPMENT DEALS

These take two forms.

THE TRADITIONAL FORM
In its traditional form this is precisely what it says. You may still have to develop your skills and musical direction as an artist. The record company may not want to put too much pressure on you in the early stages while this is happening. The deal is usually a low-key one. In the early stages, the personal advances offered to you will be low to reflect the fact that you're not yet ready to make and promote an album. Recording costs will probably be paid on a track-by-track basis until, say, five recordings have been finished and the direction in which you are developing is becoming clear. At this point the record company usually has to decide whether or not to commit to a longer-term record deal with you.

Rights
Traditional development deals are usually exclusive worldwide deals. The record company will usually expect you to assign any copyright you may have in the recordings made under the deal.

You will probably have performed on the recording and so will have performer's rights. If the deal develops into a full-blown exclusive recording contract, you may be happy to give your consent as a performer to your rights being exploited by the record company. If it doesn't, and the record company doesn't go ahead with the deal, then you won't want them to be able to release the recordings. You could stop them from doing this in a number of ways. You could, for example, withhold your consent as a performer for the recordings to be used commercially. You could also require the record company to reassign the copyright in the sound recording to you if they don't do a full deal with you.[14] The record company may be happy to do this with no strings attached, but they might say you can have the copyright if you repay to them the recording costs.

ALTERNATIVE FORM OF A DEVELOPMENT DEAL
In its alternative form, a development deal could be a cheap exclusive recording contract dressed up as something else.

---

14 Reassignment doesn't have to be in writing but it is wise to have it recorded. The original assignment must be in writing – section 90(3) CDPA.

The record company may not be quite convinced that you've got star quality, but believe that there's enough there to make it worth doing an exclusive deal with you. The company will want to be able to get out of it at an early stage and their investment in recording costs and payments to you will be low. They won't usually commit to a big spend on recording or video costs or in supporting you on tour.

They'll usually want an assignment of all your sound-recording copyright and unconditional permission to use your performances. If the deal doesn't progress they are unlikely to automatically reassign copyright to you. They'll probably want their recording costs back, or a share of any royalty that you make from exploiting the recordings (an override royalty).

WHY SHOULD YOU DO ONE OF THESE DEALS?

Well, you may not have much choice. This may be the only offer on the table. You may decide to take it and see if you can manage to make it a success. If it is you can hope to renegotiate the terms.

If you're not desperate for a deal you might decide to hold out for a proper exclusive recording contract – perhaps by doing a publishing deal first to keep you going (see Chapter 4). Or you might decide to find the money to make some recordings yourself and licence them to another company or release them yourself (see Chapter 6). This is becoming easier and cheaper to do with advances in technology. In the late 1990s, when Internet fever was at a peak, the availability of digital recordings over the Internet was seen as the greatest challenge to the traditional record company means of distribution. In fact, while we have seen a consolidation of warehousing facilities and distribution companies to reduce overheads, digital distribution is still in its infancy. The vast majority of all records are still distributed in a physical (usually CD) form, through the usual 'bricks and mortar' retail outlets. Until such time as a secure means of earning money through Internet digital distribution is established, it's likely to remain either a specialised minority sport or a free-for-all for students with cheap Internet access and MP3 players (see Chapter 7 on New Media for more on this).

EXCLUSIVE RECORDING CONTRACT

This is the third type of record deal and the one that most new artists want to get. This type of deal gives you the greatest potential investment and commitment from a record company. In return, of course, the record company will expect to be able to protect its investment. You won't be able to walk away from it when you choose.

It will be up to your advisers to make sure that the contract is a fair one. It should also be in the record company's interest. If the contract is so unfair that it's an unreasonable restraint of trade it will be unenforceable and you can walk away from it. Most major record companies have now moderated their contracts to deal with this issue and, while individual cases will still arise of unenforceable contracts, you should never enter into a contract thinking you can tear it up if it no longer suits you.

Although it's likely that the sound-recording copyright will be owned by the record company, the contract will usually make sure by making you assign any copyright you may have to the record company. The record contract will also make sure that the record company will be able to exploit your performances by getting all necessary performers' consents from you. Your lawyer ought to make sure that you have plenty of creative control over what the record company can do with the recordings and with your performances.

One thing you might not want them to do is to put your recording with an advert for a product that you don't approve of. I was once involved in a case where Sting was furious that a recording of his track 'Don't Stand So Close To Me' was used in an advert for deodorant. Tom Waits also took exception to a use of one of his songs in a Levi ad. Not everyone wants, or perhaps needs, to make money at any cost.

TERM OF THE CONTRACT

The contract will usually run for an initial period of one year (possibly six months if it's a deal for singles rather than albums). The record company will usually have a number of options to extend the contract term. In each contract period they'll expect you to record a minimum number of tracks. It could be single tracks or enough tracks to make up an album. If you really want to make money, you'll want your record company to commit to recording albums as early as possible in the contract. In the first contract period the record company may want a couple of singles first, but they should also then commit to the number of tracks required to make up an album (usually at least ten tracks in total).

Each contract period is usually extended until three to four months after you deliver the last of the recordings the record company wants. The more slowly you record and deliver recordings, or the longer it takes to release them, the longer each contract period will be.

WHY IS IT ONLY THE RECORD COMPANY THAT HAS OPTIONS?

The record company will have invested a lot of money in making your records. It will probably also have made videos and may have supported you while you've been out touring. These costs are recoupable (i.e. the record company gets some or all of them back from your earnings or royalties from sales of your records) but, if you don't sell enough records, or you were to walk out of the contract before you'd given the record company the chance to recoup their investment, then all these unrecouped costs would be down to the record company.

Then there are the promotional and marketing costs, which for a major release can run into hundreds of thousands of pounds, as well as the manufacturing and distribution costs. Most of these costs are non-recoupable from your royalties. If you could just up and walk away from the contract whenever you felt like, it the record company wouldn't be able to protect its investment, its business interests. Which is why the options are in their favour not yours. If you could walk away at any time they wouldn't invest anything like as much money in you or in developing other artists.

Various labels do deals that do give the artist the option to walk away after he has completed all the promotional work needed on a particular record. The problem is that there's a great deal of suspicion about these types of deal and investors are unwilling to invest large sums of money.

WHY CAN'T YOU GET YOUR COPYRIGHT BACK?

I can understand why a record company justifies its ownership of copyright in the recording by the fact that it's invested a lot of money. What's less easy to understand is why the company won't transfer that copyright to the artist once they've recouped that investment. George Michael argued this point in his case with Sony, but the way the case went meant that there is no definitive decision on the point. Given the reluctance of the courts in cases like O'Sullivan's to upset the economic order, it seems that the courts would be very unlikely to order a return of copyrights.

Record companies claim that the vast majority of artists don't recoup their investment. This is a depressing thought, but let's press on. They also say that they have to spend a lot of money in researching and developing new talent. If they had to return the copyrights of successful artists they say they wouldn't be able to invest as much in new artists in the future and that the culture of the nation would suffer as a result. Well, I can think of a few bands that made barely a dent in the cultural richness of my life, can't you?

Some record companies, mostly those owned by former artists or managers, have offered to return copyright to an artist that has recouped his costs after a period of time, usually at least fifteen years, but there are often lots of conditions attached. I'm not aware of any UK companies who are offering such deals at the moment. Obviously, such deals are possible in individual negotiations with artists with enough bargaining power.

If you're a very successful artist, you may also get some or all of your copyrights back when you renegotiate your record deal. You may make it a condition of you re-signing to a record company when your deal comes to an end.

HOW MANY OPTIONS SHOULD THE RECORD COMPANY HAVE FOR FUTURE ALBUMS?

Most major record companies in the UK want options on four or five further albums.[15] Independent record companies may accept less. That said, 2002 has seen one or two highly unusual deals where record companies have been so keen to sign up particular artists that they have done non-exclusive, one-album deals, with no options and reputedly very large sums of money; for example, the £1million supposedly paid by Ministry of Sound for Fischer Spooner. In some cases the deals are seen as purely short-term deals to improve the record company's share of the record sales in a particular quarter or before a company's financial year end. A good or improved slice of market share can significantly improve the company's share price and the A&R or label head's end-of-year bonus.

The number of options, and therefore the overall length of the contract, is a key issue when considering if a contract is an unreasonable restraint of trade.

This issue was at the heart of a major court case between Holly Johnson of Frankie Goes To Hollywood and his record company ZTT.[16] (He also had a similar dispute with the sister publishing company, Perfect Songs, which I will deal with in Chapter 4 on publishing deals.)

ZTT v. Holly Johnson

Holly Johnson and the other members of Frankie Goes To Hollywood were unknown when they attracted the interest of the directors of ZTT, Jill Sinclair and her husband, the highly successful record producer, Trevor Horn. The band was broke and very keen to work with Mr Horn. They were told that ZTT would only do the record deal if they also

---

15 In the United States options for six or seven further albums are commonplace.
16 *Zang TumbTum Records Limited and Perfect Songs Limited v. Holly Johnson* [1993] EMLR 61.

signed an exclusive publishing deal with Perfect Songs. Now you might detect a whiff of undue influence here but, in fact, this point was not seriously argued in this case. The band signed up to both deals. Although they were inexperienced and had very little bargaining power, they were represented by a lawyer who was experienced in music business contracts.

Frankie Goes To Hollywood had two very successful singles with 'Relax' and 'Two Tribes', both of which attracted a great deal of controversy because of the subject matter in the case of the first and the video for the second. At one stage the tracks were Nos. 1 and 2 in the UK singles charts. The band's first album *Welcome To The Pleasure Dome* sold well and produced two more hit singles. They failed to make a success in the US and by 1986 the pressure was on them for the second album to be a success.

The band had a lot of trouble with the recording of this album, to be called *Liverpool*. Trevor Horn controlled the recording costs, he was the record producer and the recordings were being made in his studios. The costs were escalating alarmingly and the band was horrified by how much they would have to recoup. After a lot of problems the band split up but ZTT (and Perfect Songs) wanted to hang on to Holly Johnson. Johnson didn't want to continue with them and sued on the grounds that both the recording and publishing contracts were an unreasonable restraint of trade.

The term of the record contract was for an initial period of six months and was extendable by two option periods and up to five contract periods, all in favour of the record company. Each contract period was to be for a minimum of one year and extendable until 120 days after they fulfilled their minimum obligations to the record company (known as the Minimum Commitment). There was also no maximum extension of the contract period. It was open-ended and depended entirely on when the band fulfilled its Minimum Commitment.

The Minimum Commitment was one single in each of the initial period, first and second option periods and one album in each of the third through to seventh option contract periods. This is a very odd way of structuring a contract, but basically it meant that if the record company exercised every option the band had to record three singles and five albums.

The record company was free to bring the contract to an end at any time. The record company also had the right to reject recordings delivered to it by the band. As the term continued until after delivery of recordings that were satisfactory to the record company, this meant that the record company controlled how long the contract lasted. There are echoes of this in the George Michael case.

The court decided that the contract was one-sided and unfair and was an unreasonable restraint of trade and unenforceable. It thought that the potential term of the contract was far too long, as it could easily last eight or nine years. In that time the court felt that the band wouldn't have had the opportunity to earn a decent living from their work. The record company wasn't obliged to do very much with the recordings. There was no commitment to release them. The court freed Mr Johnson from the contracts and awarded him substantial compensation.

As a result of this case, record contracts now usually contain a clause committing the record company to releasing records in at least the home country. For example, if you did a UK record deal, you would expect to be able to insist on your records being released in the UK. If records are not released the contract usually gives the artist the right to end the contract and sometimes to get the recordings back, possibly in return for an override royalty. The term of UK record contracts also became shorter and maximum backstops are now usually placed on the time each contract period can run. All this happened as a reaction to this one highly influential court decision.

TWO-ALBUM FIRM DEALS

If you've enough bargaining power, it's possible to get a record company to commit in advance to a second album. These types of deal are called two-album firm deals. Record companies are more likely to agree to these when they're in competition with another record company. Most record companies don't want to give this commitment. They want to see how the first album does before committing to a second. These types of deal go in and out of favour. Some artists and managers favour them because they provide commitment and certainty, which allows them to do some forward planning. Others feel they only work if things are going well. If things aren't going well, the record company will probably try and get out of it after the first album. If your only alternative is to sue the company for failing to honour their side of the bargain, you'll probably agree to accept the offer they make to end the contract, so the commitment may not mean much in the end. While I have done one or two of these two-album firm deals in the last twelve months they aren't currently popular, possibly reflecting the fact that at the moment there is a fear of economic recession, fewer record deals are on offer and many managers are keen just to get a record deal for their artist without worrying about a commitment to a second album up-front.

TERRITORY AND SPLIT-TERRITORY DEALS

Long-term exclusive record deals will usually be offered on a worldwide basis. This may be perfectly acceptable to you, particularly if the record company has a strong presence in most major markets of the world. However, because the US is a very different marketplace from that of the UK, an artist sometimes asks for what is known as a split-territory deal.

This means that you do one deal with a record company for the world excluding the US and another deal with a different record company for the US. To make these type of deals work the artist and his manager have to juggle the demands of two record companies. If you get it right it means that you have two companies protecting your interests in the two main English-speaking music markets in the world. Record companies don't like doing these types of deals, because they say they need a worldwide market in which to recover their investment. They also say that their own companies are strong worldwide and should be given the chance.

Split-territory deals are usually offered to artists with considerable bargaining power, to those with an already established track record and occasionally to new artists managed by a manager with a track record for finding and developing new artists. Sometimes these deals are done because the record company has a strong reputation in one part of the world but not in another. A US branch of a UK record company may not have a track record in 'breaking' non-US artists in the US.

If you're thinking of doing a deal with a smaller record company, you may find that they don't have branch offices or companies in other parts of the world. They may have a network of licensees in different countries. Those licensees might take all the records they produce. These are called catalogue licence deals. Alternatively, the UK company may look for different licensees for each artist. For example, the UK record company could do a deal with Atlantic Records in the US for all its acts or it could do a deal with Atlantic for its mainstream acts and with a smaller label for its indie acts. Whatever the situation, you need to know who the licensees are going to be. They need to be well-established, trustworthy companies that will do a reasonable job of selling your records in the country concerned. If a licence deal isn't in place in a particular country when you do your record deal, you should have the right to approve that part of the licence deal that affects you at the time the licence deal is done.

Smaller companies use overseas licence deals to help to fund their operation in the UK. For example, a company in Germany could pay an advance against the royalty it expects to pay on sales of records in Germany. It may also pay a contribution to the cost of making a video in return for the right to use the video in Germany. If the artist does a promotional or concert tour in Germany, the German licensee will usually provide some financial back-up. If you've a small low-key deal in the UK with a label that can't afford to pay you very much up-front, you could ask that some of the advances paid by overseas licensees of your recordings should be paid through to you. For example, if the German licensee paid an advance against royalties of €100,000 you might get 25% (i.e. €25,000). This will help to make up for the low advances in the UK. This is something that should be negotiated at the time the original UK record deal is done.

OTHER ASPECTS OF RECORDING CONTRACTS

Now that I've looked at the three main types of deal and some of the things that distinguish them, I want to look at some aspects of contracts that are common to all three types.

DELIVERY REQUIREMENTS – MINIMUM COMMITMENT

Each type of record contract has a minimum that is required from the artist. Licence deals can be for single tracks or albums. Development deals may start out as being for four or five tracks and then develop into a commitment to record albums. Exclusive album deals can either be for a single track or an album initially, usually with options to acquire further product. One of your obligations will be to deliver the required minimum number of recordings.

Your obligation may be simply to deliver the master tapes of these recordings to the record company. More often, however, the commitment is not fulfilled until the record company has agreed that the recordings meet the required standards. As we saw in the George Michael and Holly Johnson cases, if these standards are not met the company can reject the recordings and make you re-record them until they are satisfied. It's important that these standards are realistic and that they're set out in the contract. They could be technical requirements or commercial ones or a combination of both. What you should try and avoid is a subjective standard. This is someone else's view of whether you meet the required standard or whether the recording is commercially satisfactory. What a record company executive thinks is commercially acceptable may not be anything like your own views on the subject. It's best if you can try and set an objective standard, a standard against which the quality of your recording can be measured. For example, measuring it against a recording of yours that the record company has previously accepted as being satisfactory.

It's also usual to try and put a time limit on when the record company has to give you an answer as to whether a recording is satisfactory. It must be a realistic time period, as the company may have to go through various stages and processes before it can give you an answer. Your A&R man will have to listen to it and probably play it to his colleagues at the weekly A&R meeting. He may talk to record producers to get their view of the recording. He'll probably talk to your manager for his views. He may have a hunch that the record could be improved if one or more tracks are remixed by someone other than the record producer or original mixer. Depending on the contract, he may have to get your permission before he does that. The contract with the record producer may mean that he has to give him the first chance to remix the track in question. This process takes time.

If it makes artistic sense, then you're going to agree to one or two remixes; but they can cost more than £10,000 a time including additional recording costs, for a good remixer. Some or all of this may be recoupable from your royalties, so you don't want to do too many remixes or it'll get very expensive for you. Until these have been done and accepted you may not have fulfilled your Minimum Commitment.

Once the record company's happy with the standard of your recordings it may say that the recordings have been accepted and that you've fulfilled your Minimum Commitment, but most companies want more information from you before they do that.

Acceptance of fulfilment of Minimum Commitment usually means that the record company has to start planning the release and maybe has to pay you a further instalment of your advance. The record contract may set a last date by which the record must be released. The record company won't want that time to start running until they're in a position to start the processes for a release. This means that they usually require you to hand over a number of other things before delivery is said to have taken place and before they accept the recordings. This could be artwork for the packaging of the records, details of who performed on the masters, and confirmation that those performers have given their performer's consents. If there are samples of anyone else's recordings or songs in your masters, the record company will want to know that you have permission from the copyright owners of those recordings or songs to use the samples (see Chapter 13). If permission to use the samples hasn't been agreed then the record company can't put your recordings out without being in breach of copyright.

Because it's vital to know when a recording has been accepted, I often ask the record company to agree that the recordings are said (deemed) to be accepted if the record company has not said that they aren't within four to six weeks of you delivering the masters, artwork etc. to them. Depending on how long they think it will take for them to go through the acceptance process, they may agree to this or they may not.

ADVANCES

For many artists this is one of the most important issues. Remember that these monies will have to be recouped out of the royalties you earn from sales or other uses of your recordings. Unlike a loan, however, advances aren't usually repayable if the record company doesn't sell enough of your records. That's the record company's risk. If, however, you take their money and then don't deliver any recordings, they may try and come after you to get the advance back. If you've spent it and haven't got any money, they may not bother to sue you because it would cost them more in legal fees than they would get back. I wouldn't like to rely on them not suing though.

If you take their money it's only reasonable that you deliver some recordings to them. Obviously this is sometimes out of your control if the band splits up or the singer gets ill. But I have seen artists who cynically wait to split the band up until after they receive the first instalment of their record advance. One band I know waited until they'd delivered the finished album to the record company and had taken the advance they were due on delivery. They then split up before the record was released. The US record company that they were signed to was furious. They'd spent all the recording costs and paid all the personal advances due to the band, only to have an album with no artist to promote it. They were so angry they sued the band for return of the advances and breach of contract. We had to settle it by agreeing to give them an override royalty on the next album any member of the band released.

What is a good advance?

A good advance is one that meets your needs. You may only care about getting as much money as possible and aren't concerned if you never sell enough records to recoup. There are a lot of cynical managers with that view in the business – take the money and run. In that case you'll just be looking for the most money you can get up-front. It's a short-term view because the greater the record company's investment in advances, the more pressure there is going to be on you to perform and the more likely it is that the record company will want to dictate to you. If you go for a more reasonable advance payable in reasonable instalments, the record company is going to put you under less pressure to deliver. You should also recoup the advances sooner out of your royalties. Because so few artists recoup advances and costs, this will put you in a strong bargaining position with the record company. I have, however, recently heard a very successful and influential music manager take completely the opposite position. His view is that an artist who has proved that he can sell records if the record company does its job properly can get more commitment out of a record company by being unrecouped, as this will encourage the company to work harder. This could well be the case with certain labels or individuals, but I'm not yet convinced that this applies to everyone.

Whatever the position on recoupment, a good advance is going to be one that allows you to live and have a roof over your head for at least a year (preferably eighteen months) while the recordings are being made and then promoted. It's a good idea for you or your manager to do an outline budget of what you may need.

Outline Budget for a Record Deal

Personal Advances: Wages to cover your basic living requirements, such as food, rent/mortgage and personal expenses, multiplied by the number of members of the band and on a monthly basis over, say, 18 months. The record company may bargain you down to 12 months, but 18 is more realistic.

Example: A 4-piece band needing £1,500 a month each would need a total of £6,000 × 18 = £108,000

Equipment: You may need to invest in certain equipment, for example, microphone stands, a better PA or guitars, an upgraded drum kit, etc. This throws up arguments about who owns this equipment. The record company usually retains notional ownership and in theory could require the band to return it once the deal ends, but this is rarely enforced.

Example: Say £5,000

Transport: You may need to buy or upgrade a transit van to get to gigs or to and from the studio.

Example: Say £5,000

Rehearsal Time: You may suggest a sum of money to cover the cost of hiring a hall or rooms to rehearse. You might argue that a long-term rental is cheaper than hiring commercial rehearsal rooms. One band I know took a lease on a room over the local chip shop to rehearse in.

Example: Say £1,000 a month for 12 months = £12,000

Debts: It would be unusual if you had reached this stage without running up an overdraft or other debts. If you're looking for justification for a particular level of advance, then an amount to repay debts would be a valid item to include in the budget.

Example: Say £2,500 per artist × 4 = £10,000

Professional fees: Don't forget you're going to have to pay a lawyer and an accountant.

Example: Say £10,000

Management fees: If you have a manager you'll also have to allow for him taking a 20% commission of the gross amount, so you should uplift your total figure to allow for this.

The Hype Factor: This is unquantifiable. My suggestion would be for you to look at your basic budget first.

Budget

Personal Advances	£108,000
Equipment	£5,000
Transport	£5,000
Rehearsal Time	£12,000
Debts	£10,000
Professional Fees	£10,000
	£150,000
Management Commission @ 20%	£30,000
	£180,000

Add the 'hype' factor, which is whatever your instincts or your advisers say the deal can be pushed to.
Say: £225,000–250,000 plus recording costs

Be prepared to be flexible.

If your manager is only interested in getting as much of the advance as possible as early as possible you should be suspicious. Is he only concerned about his commission? Is he only in it for the short term? Doesn't he expect to be around when the record is finished or when it's time for the option to be exercised? Whose interests is he looking after – yours or his? It may be a perfectly legitimate approach, but don't accept it without question. If he's pushing for a very short deal with most of the money up-front, is it an agreed approach of 'take the money and run' or doesn't he have faith that you can cut it beyond one album? What happens if you do a very short, very expensive deal and then find that the album bombs or only sells an average amount and won't recoup anywhere like the level of advances you've been paid? Do you say, 'Not my problem,' and walk away? If you do, how sure are you that you would get another deal?

You may accept a lower advance in return for other things such as greater creative control. It's possible to get both, but usually only when you have a lot of bargaining power. If you go for a lower advance you should also be able to argue for a higher royalty.

Min-max formula
The level of advances payable could be calculated according to a formula (called a min-max formula). Under this formula a minimum advance is payable to you and a limit is also set on the maximum the company will pay. The actual amount is calculated as a percentage of the royalties you've earned. The formula usually applies from the second contract period or album onwards.

At the beginning of the second contract period, the record company looks at how much you've earned from sales of the recordings you made in the first contract period. It then takes a percentage of that and, if the amount then arrived at is more than the minimum and less than the maximum, then that is the advance payable for that period. For example, in the twelve months following the release of your first album you may have earned £100,000 in royalties. The formula for calculating your advance for the second contract period is linked to 66% of those earnings. 66% of £100,000 is £66,000. The minimum advance payable in the next contract period is, say, £50,000. You are above that. The maximum advance payable is, say, £100,000, but you've not got to that point so the advance you get is £66,000.

This formula can work and many record companies favour them because they give them a degree of certainty for budgeting purposes and a payment linked to success. If you're offered a deal with this type of formula for calculating advances, you need to make sure that the minimums are enough to meet your minimum living requirements. In the example I gave above, could you live on £50,000 for a year or longer in the second contract period?

The maximums are usually double the minimum, but may be more in later contract periods. Is the maximum a reasonable advance if you're doing very well? To be honest, I don't worry about the maximums as much as the minimums. If you're hitting the maximums it's because you're doing well and the record company is more likely to want to keep you happy by renegotiating these figures upwards.

There are a number of variations on how you calculate what has been earned in the previous contract period. The actual percentage can change, as can the period over which it's calculated. It can also make a big difference whether income earned but not yet credited to your account is taken into account (so-called pipeline income). It's wise to take legal advice on these kinds of deals.

Payment terms

Advances are normally paid in instalments, usually one on signing the deal, another when you start recording the Minimum Commitment for that contract period, and the final instalment either on delivery of the completed recordings to the record company or on commercial release of the recordings. As the release could be some months after delivery, you'll want the final instalment to be paid on delivery. The record company may want to protect itself by only paying the last instalment when the record is released, when there is a reasonable prospect of record sales reducing its financial exposure.

However, a lot can happen between delivery of the finished masters and their release. A client of mine once delivered finished masters to the record company and they were accepted. A few months later, and before the last date on which the record company had to release the recordings, the company closed down and the copyright in the client's recordings was transferred to another record company. That record company then hesitated for a few months more about whether or not they were going to release the album. In the end the artist's manager asked me to send the record company a formal notice under the terms of the record contract requiring the record company to release the album and pay the final instalment due under the deal. When the record company got the notice it rang me up and said that it had decided that it didn't want to release the album. It offered to give my client the copyright in the album back in return for an override royalty until such time as it had recovered the recording costs that had been spent on the album. The client and his manager decided to take this offer, but more than seven months had passed since the recordings were delivered and the artist didn't get the advance due on release of the album.

Costs-inclusive advances

The advances I have been describing so far are called personal advances. They go towards the artist's personal needs. The costs of making the recording are separate recoupable amounts (see Chapter 5). The record company may offer you an advance, which includes the costs of making the recordings. These costs-inclusive deals are called recording-fund deals. Both you and the record company have to be quite careful that the amounts advanced under a recording-fund deal are at the right level. You have to be sure that you can make the album you want to make with the available funds and still have something over to live on. Often, costs-inclusive deals work out at less money than one for a personal advance plus recording costs, unless the artist can record very cheaply. The record company has to know it's not being too generous but also that you won't run out of money before the recording is finished. If you do, the record company inevitably ends up paying out more money if it wants to get the recording finished. Recording-fund deals can work for established artists, for those with their own recording facilities or more mature artists who can be relied on to make the recording without spending all the money on themselves. I have recently successfully negotiated just such a deal with a company in the EMI Group. The artist had a track record of making records and the manager was very experienced and respected by the record company. It's worked out well for the artist, as much of the recording was done in a home studio.

RECORD BUDGETS

If a record company is not offering a recording-fund deal and you've a development or exclusive recording deal, you'll need to have some idea of how much it's going to cost you to make the recordings. You need to know that the record company is committed to spending that amount of money. If you're doing a licence deal you'll usually have already finished making recordings, and so the issue is whether they will compensate you for the costs you've incurred.

The budget must take into account how much it will cost to rehearse the material, to do any necessary pre-production (preparation for recording, perhaps programming a drum machine or a computer to produce certain sounds), to record the material in the studio, to have it produced, mixed and edited. Some record companies include the cost of cutting or digitally mastering the recording in the budget. This can add £1,000 plus to the deal so, if the budget is tight, try and get them to pay for that separately. You also have to bear in mind the cost of hiring in specialist equipment and engaging the services of additional musicians and vocalists. The budget also usually includes what are called *per diems*, an expression meaning a daily expenses payment to cover food and drink and sometimes also transport to and from the studio (see Chapter 5).

The record company may commit to a guaranteed minimum spend on recording costs in the contract, but most are reluctant to do that. This is either because they're afraid they may get it wrong, or because setting a minimum figure means you tend to spend that amount of money whether it's necessary or not. On the other hand, you'll want to know the record company is committed to a particular level of spend so that you know that you can make the kind of record you want. Both sides have to be realistic. It's no good a record company thinking you can make an album for five pence, but neither is it any good you thinking the record company will let you have a blank cheque. This is where a decent recording budget is invaluable.

Recording costs are usually fully recoupable. There are, however, some elements of the recording cost budget that may be wholly or partially non-recoupable. A classic example is the costs of remixing. Mixing costs are very expensive. As I said, it's common to pay £10,000 or more to a well-known remixer. If you're on a tight budget these costs can take a lot out of the total. The record company may want to commission a remix that you don't think is necessary. Who is to pay for this and are the costs to be recoupable? Some record companies will agree that the first mix comes out of the recording budget as does any remix that you want to do, but if the record company wants to do additional remixes they pay that on top of the recording budget. So, you know what to do – make sure it's the record company that asks for the remix, not you. Steer them into suggesting it if necessary.

ROYALTIES

This could be the subject of a whole book in itself. No two companies calculate royalties in exactly the same way. This is an area where there is really no escaping the need for experience and legal advice.

Record company executives usually have guidelines as to what is or is not allowed. Certain top artists may have been given 'favoured nations' terms. This means that they have the best deal that the record company can offer on that particular point. If any other artist is offered better terms by that record company, the artist with the 'favoured nations' provision must also be given these better terms. As this has potentially huge financial implications for the record company, an executive crosses these boundaries at his peril. It may be impossible to do so and will definitely require agreement from someone high up the corporate ladder.

Retail versus dealer price

You need to know what price basis the record company is using to account to you. A 20% royalty on the retail price of a CD would be good, but 20% on the dealer price of the CD would be just average.

Until about seven or eight years ago, the majority of UK record companies calculated their royalties as a percentage of the retail price of the record in question. However, the retail price is not within the record company's control and varies considerably. Most UK companies have, therefore, moved over to using the dealer price of the record as the basis of calculation. Some, confusingly, use the retail price in some countries and the dealer price in others.

The record company will usually tell you what dealer price they charge for each type of record – vinyl, tape, CD and so on. If there isn't a dealer price available or the record company still calculates its royalties on a retail price basis and you want to make a comparison, then as a very general rule of thumb, in the UK you can work on the basis that the retail price is about 130% of the dealer price of an album.

Outside the UK and in particular in countries like Japan and the United States, they have very different methods of arriving at a dealer or 'wholesale' price basis. In order to make a proper comparison, you should ask the record company to give you the actual figures they are talking about so you can do what is sometimes known as a 'pennies' calculation. This means that you can calculate roughly what you'll get from each record sold. This calculation is essential when you're trying to compare offers from more than one record company. It's also important for a record company executive trying to make a deal to know how much he will have to pay in record royalties per record sold. He or his finance officer will need to calculate how many records will need to be sold before the advance they offer will be recouped. It has to make some kind of commercial sense even if the A&R man is so determined to do the deal that he wants to pay over the odds. At least he'll know what he has to aim at in terms of record sales.

Here is an example, of a pennies calculation:

Pennies Calculation

	Company A	Company B
	Dealer	Retail
Price basis		
Price	£8.49	£12.49
VAT	17.5%	17.5%
Percentage of Sales	100%	90%
Packaging Deduction	25%	25%
CD Deduction	20%	0%
Royalty Rate	18%	15%

Then insert figures into these calculations:

Company A:
1) £8.49 – 17.5% (VAT) (£1.26)   =   £7.22
2) £7.22 × 100%   =   £7.22
3) £7.22 – 25% (packaging) (£1.81)   =   £5.41
4) £5.41 × 18% (royalty)   =   £0.97
5) £0.97 × 80% (CD deduction)   =   £0.78 royalty per CD

Company B:
1) £12.49 – 17.5% (VAT) (£1.86)   =   £10.62
2) £10.62 – 25% (£2.66)   =   £7.96
3) £7.96 × 90% (% of sales)   =   £7.16
4) £7.16 × 0% (CD deduction)   =   £7.16
5) £7.165 x 15% (royalty)   =   £1.07 per CD

What percentage of sales?

Is the royalty calculated on all records sold or a lesser percentage? Virgin Records still calculates on 90% of sales and yet it's part of the EMI Group of companies that calculates royalties on 100% of sales. This is a hangover from the early years of the record business when records were made of acetate that broke easily. A 10% breakage allowance was built into the calculation. In these days of CDs and even online distribution, these allowances are clearly irrelevant. They are, however, still built into the way some companies calculate royalties. In working out if it's a good royalty, this difference must be taken into account. Again, a pennies calculation may help.

PACKAGING AND OTHER DEDUCTIONS

The most common deductions are packaging deductions, sometimes also referred to as container charges. This is a charge supposedly to cover the cost of making the cases or other packaging in which the record is sold. In reality, the actual cost is usually far less than the average packaging deduction and is a way by which the record company artificially reduces the royalty paid to you. These deductions must be taken into account in order to compare offers from different companies. An average packaging deduction for CDs is 20%, although many companies charge 25%. Other companies, such as V2, make a virtue out of having no packaging deductions. Their royalty rate may seem uncompetitive until you take this into account.

Other traps for the unwary are the reductions that some record companies apply to certain types of records. For instance, sales by mail order, through record clubs or at budget prices will be at a lower royalty rate. The principle behind all these deductions is that, where the record company gets less than the full price for a sale, it will reduce the amount payable to you on that sale. A record sold as a budget record will usually attract a 50% reduction in the royalty rate. A 50% reduction also often applies to records advertised on television, sold by mail order, or through record clubs. The reduction in the royalty for mail-order sales is important when you think that many companies will now offer mail-order sales over the Internet. If this becomes the established method of selling records then we ought to look again at whether or not a 50% reduction is appropriate (see Chapter 7).

A detailed exploration of all the royalty reductions is beyond the scope of this book. Your lawyer and accountant will be familiar with these. Most UK record companies usually apply the principles behind the reductions in a similar way, but the details will differ a great deal. For example, some record companies will pay you a full royalty on sales of compilation records they put out featuring one or more of your tracks, while others will only pay you 66% of the royalty.

WHAT IS A GOOD ROYALTY?

As a very general guideline, a basic royalty of more than 18% of the dealer price calculated on 100% of records sold with no reduction for CDs and a packaging deduction of no more than 20% would be acceptable. It's unusual to see royalty rates of more than 23% of the dealer price for new signings to exclusive record deals. However, royalties on licence deals could well exceed 23% on the above basis, because the record company is getting a finished recording and can assess the commercial potential up-front. The record company also hasn't taken any risk on the recording costs. On non-exclusive licence deals between record companies, the royalty may well be more than 23% of the dealer price with no packaging deductions, because they recognise the deduction for what it is.

NET PROFITS DEALS

Smaller record companies often offer these deals. You share the responsibility for costs such as manufacturing or promotion costs, which the record company wouldn't normally be able to recover from you.

Everything that's earned from all uses of the recordings is brought into account. This might include advances paid by overseas licensees. It will depend on the deal you do. All costs involved in the making of the recording are then taken out of that total income. As well as the obvious ones of recording costs and the costs of making a video, manufacturing, press and promotion costs are deducted as are, often, payments to music publishers and even legal and accountancy charges. There are many subtleties as to what may or may not be deducted that are negotiated on a deal-by-deal basis. Any net profits made after those deductions are then split between you and the record company. The usual division is 50:50, but it may go up to 55–65% in your favour and even to a 75% share to you of overseas profits.

At the outset, net profit deals can work quite well for the record company, as that is when costs are high. The record company still bears the risk on the costs initially, but it doesn't pay out anything to the artist until the deal goes into profit. Also, the record company gets to recoup costs it wouldn't normally be entitled to offset against you, such as manufacturing costs. You can still receive an advance to live on.

Where these deals start to become less attractive to a record company and much more attractive to the artist is when the initial costs have been recouped and ongoing costs are going down. If the record continues to sell well and you're on 50% or more of profits, you're doing considerably better than you would be if you were on a straight royalty basis.

RELEASE COMMITMENTS

Obviously, once you've got your album delivered and accepted you need to have some kind of assurance that it's going to see the light of day and not just sit on the shelf. You need a commitment from the record company to release your record in at least the home market and preferably also the main overseas markets. The release should usually take place within three to four months of delivery of the masters. If it doesn't, the usual remedy is to serve a notice telling the record company that if it doesn't release your record within another two to three months then you have the right to end your contract with them and not have to deliver any more masters. Even better would be if you could get a commitment from them to return your unreleased masters to you (perhaps in return for an override royalty until the recording costs have been recouped).

Some record companies don't want to do this, because they don't want to have to anticipate in advance what sort of deal they would want to do with you. They may also want to hold on to the masters in case another company has better luck in making you successful. They then have back catalogue material they try to release to cash in on this success. This is pretty daft because, although the tried and true fans will buy all records, there's no artist to promote the record so it's unlikely to go very far. Sometimes they hold on to the unreleased masters in order to try and sell it to your record company later.

Overseas, if your record isn't released within three to four months of the UK release you can serve another notice of 30 to 60 days; if there hasn't been a release you may have the chance to find a licensee and make them then license it to that company to release. They're unlikely to automatically give you your masters back, as they know it's difficult to make their overseas companies or licensees release recordings.

ACCOUNTING

You should get paid at least twice a year, possibly four times with smaller companies doing their own distribution. The accounts statements will be sent to you 60 to 90 days after the accounting date. If you've recouped all your advances the statement will have a cheque with it – yippee! If you aren't certain what the statement says, check it with your accountant. If he doesn't think it's right you should challenge it, but don't leave it too long as you probably can't object after a period of time, say one to three years. You have the right to audit (inspect) the books at least once a year. Send your accountants in to audit if you've had a successful period or at the end of a deal that has gone well.

NEW FORMS OF RECORD DEAL

Robbie Williams hit the headlines in 2002, not only in the tabloids but also in the financial papers, as a result of the new deal he struck with EMI Records. Much of the interest centred on how much he was going to get out of the deal (and my lips are sealed on that) but others were interested in what seemed to be a new type of deal that he had done.

The model for this new deal was one that had been used by Lord Lloyd-Webber in his Really Useful Group, but it had been applied to the particular circumstances of Mr Williams.

The basic idea is that a successful artist or entertainer makes money from several different sources. For example, an artist will make money from sales of his records, from use of songs and records, in films, ads and other audio-visual products, from live concerts and personal appearances, merchandising and sponsorship deals. The artist may also go on to have a successful career as a film or television actor, or as a writer, and he may successfully operate an Internet business. With this new type of deal the artist is asking investors to buy in to his overall success and to these various actual or potential income streams.

A new company is set up (or an existing company could be adapted if that is more tax effective). The company acts as the vehicle for all these income streams and the intellectual property rights attached to them. These rights could be assigned into the company or could be licensed for a period of time. The artist will also have to have various service agreements with the company agreeing to provide the company branding rights such as trademarks and domain names and the right to use his name and likeness. In return, the company may agree to pay him a fee for his services up-front and an ongoing royalty.

The new company invites investors to acquire a shareholding in return for a lump sum of money, which may be paid up-front or in instalments. Usually the artist will want that to be a minority interest, i.e. less than 50% and preferably less than 25%, which will mean he retains overall control of what is done with the company.

The investor could be an entertainment company or it could be a financial investor from the city or overseas. Once the investment is agreed, the company will pay through an agreed sum to the artist for the shares sold or issued, and some will be retained in the company as working capital.

The company will then be the vehicle used to do new recording, publishing, merchandising or sponsorship deals. Of course, the investor may be a record company and, as a condition of its investment, also get to do the record deal. There are also many variations on the terms. The company may only control some of the artist's services, for example, his live work, merchandising, sponsorship and Internet business. The record and/or publishing deals could be done quite separately as straightforward deals. There are also many variations on what can happen with the shares, whether the investor can acquire any more, how long the arrangement will last and what is to happen when it ends.

So why go to all this trouble? Well it's a question of leverage. If the artist is successful enough, he may want to increase the value of his talent and its products by selling an investor a piece of a number of income streams in one go. If the investor is a record company, it gets a piece of income that it wouldn't normally have a claim to, for example, to profits from live concerts. In order to get a piece of this, the investor will pay more up-front than it would for just an interest in recordings.

Now this arrangement isn't going to be on offer to every artist, even one who has a track record with record sales, as the other elements have to be successful and have potential for further growth or at least continued success. There are also problems attached. For example, if your record company has an interest in your other activities then there is a potential for conflict of interests. The artist also inevitably loses some control and has to get used to an investor looking over his shoulder. Still, if the financial benefits are large enough, no doubt these concerns can be overcome.

This has been a general overview of the main points of a record deal. In Chapter 11 on Band Issues, I deal with the parts of the record contract that cover what happens when a band splits up. Payment of mechanical royalties is dealt with in the next chapter on publishing contracts.

CONCLUSIONS

- There are three main types of record deal – licences, development deals and exclusive recording agreements.

- With each type of contract you need to work out how much exclusivity you're going to give and what territory the contract is to cover.

- Advances against royalties can include recording costs or these can be dealt with separately. Recording and personal advance budgets are useful in setting the level of the deal.

- Royalties can be calculated on the retail or the dealer price of the record. It's important to establish which, as it makes great deal of difference to the deal.

- Every record contract contains reductions in royalties on certain types of sale or method of distribution.

- Net profits deals work for the record company at the beginning but the scales tip in favour of the artist after the initial costs have been recouped.

- New types of recording deals are emerging which may work for you once you're established as a successful artist.

4: **WHAT IS A GOOD PUBLISHING DEAL?**

INTRODUCTION

In this chapter I'm going to look at what rights a songwriter has and what he can expect from the various types of publishing deals. As usual, I'm going to look at it mostly from the point of view of the talent, the songwriter, but I will also try to give the publisher's point of view. I'm going to ask whether you need to do a publishing deal at all. If so, whether, ideally, it should be before or after you've done your record deal.

Before we go into any detail about the contract, we need to look at how you find a music publisher, what a music publisher actually does, and what rights a songwriter has. You will not be surprised by now to learn that the doctrine of restraint of trade comes up here too. I'll look at some cases in this area, including a dispute between band members about who had written what.

HOW TO FIND A MUSIC PUBLISHER

Music publishers employ A&R people and scouts in the same way as record companies do. They're on the lookout for talented songwriters who either perform in a band or as a solo artist, or who mostly write songs for other people. Hopeful songwriters send demos to publishing companies in the same way as record companies.

You can find lists of UK music publishers in the *Music Week Directory* (see Useful Addresses). All the major record companies have well-established music publishing companies as part of the group. For example, there is an EMI Records and EMI Publishing. There are also independent music publishers that aren't associated with independent record companies, for example, PeerMusic or Bucks Music.

Your lawyer, accountant and manager can all refer you to publishers they think will be suitable for your style of songwriting.

WHAT DOES A PUBLISHER DO?

Have you ever wondered why we call them publishers? So have I. As far as I can work out, it comes from the early days of the music business when music was published in the form of sheet music in the same way as a book is published. Nowadays, of course, sheet music forms only a small part of the income that a songwriter and a publisher can make. These days the largest share of income comes from the use of songs on sound recordings (mechanicals) or with TV, film or other moving images (synchronisation). If digital distribution of music develops in the way we think it will online, the rights in a song may well be far more valuable than a physical sound recording like a CD or a cassette but, as we will see in Chapter 7 on New Media, there is a lot to be done in terms of establishing workable business models for this.

Publishers have three main roles. Firstly, they issue licences to people who want to use your music. Secondly, they actively look for ways to use your music – for example, putting it in an advert or on a film soundtrack. Thirdly, they collect the income from those licences and uses. The first of these roles is largely done in conjunction with the collecting societies (see Chapter 15), including the area of online uses where, after initially feeling their way, the societies have now begun to establish links with international societies and to get mandates from their members to grant commercial online licences. Some publishers are better than others in doing the second and third roles. Obviously, you need to be satisfied that they can do a reasonable job of collecting in the money for you. Whether you need them to be good at finding uses for your songs will depend on the type of songwriter you are (although most songwriters probably wouldn't turn down additional ways of making money).

So that people know whom to come to when they want to ask to use a song, and in order to track the money and collect it properly, the publisher has to register the songs with all the main collecting societies around the world. Sometimes this just requires that the songwriter fills in a form and files it with the society. Sometimes they also have to send in a tape and a written copy of the words and music, called a lead sheet.

If your music publisher is one of the major publishers, they will have their own companies in each of the major countries in the world. One or two of the independent publishers, most notably PeerMusic, have their own companies worldwide too. Most of the independent and smaller publishers don't have the resources to set up overseas companies. They appoint local publishers in the country concerned to look after their interests there. This is called sub-publishing.

Publishers will also now do some of the things that were originally only done by record companies. They will provide studio time for you to record demos. Some act almost like record companies, putting records out in limited editions as a way to attract record company interest. There are even some that will provide financial support for you when you're out on the road promoting your records, or extra funds for promotion or press coverage. These costs and payments are usually recoupable from your publishing income as and when it comes through. The main reason they do these things is in order to give you a bit of a boost, a head start, or to top up funding that may or may not be provided by your record company.

WHAT ARE MUSIC PUBLISHING RIGHTS?

Before you can have any rights in a literary or musical work[1] (i.e. in lyrics or music) you have to establish that the words and music are original and that they have been recorded in some way. This could be sheet music, with the words and music written down, or a demo of someone singing the words and music.[2]

HOW DO YOU PROVE THAT YOU HAVE COPYRIGHT IN A WORK?
There are a number of recognised ways of doing this.

You could put the sheet music or demo tape in a safe deposit box marked with your name and the date on which you wrote it and get a receipt.

You could send it to your lawyer and ask him to write back to confirm when he

---

1 Section 3(1) CDPA.
2 Section 3(2) CDPA.

received it from you. Some lawyers aren't happy about doing this. They don't want trouble later if they lose the tape in among the one hundred and one others in their office. Also, they can't really confirm something that they have no direct knowledge of. They don't know you wrote it or when you wrote it. They can only say that you sent a tape to them on a particular day.

The most popular way is to put the sheet music/tape/disc in an envelope addressed to yourself that you then post to yourself by registered/recorded mail (so you have a receipt) and which you then keep unopened in a safe place. The postmark and the fact that it's still sealed means that you've proof that that tape, sheet music or whatever must have existed some time before the postmark date. So, if someone copies the song illegally sometime later, you have evidence that your version was written before theirs.

WHO OWNS THESE RIGHTS?

The first owner of the copyright in a musical or literary work is the person who creates an original work and records it in a tangible form.[3]

There can be more than one writer or composer.[4] These are called co-writers. One person might write the words and the other the music, or the co-writers might all work on both elements.

Famous examples of successful co-writing partnerships are Elton John and Bernie Taupin, Andrew Lloyd Webber and Tim Rice and, more recently, Robbie Williams and Guy Chambers, although as I write this Mr Williams has parted company with Mr Chambers and one press report linked Mr Williams to writing with Elton John. Talk about swings and roundabouts. It's perfectly possible for two separate publishers to control parts of the same song. For example, Robbie Williams's current works are published by BMG Music Publishing (UK) Limited, while Guy Chambers is published by EMI Music Publishing Limited.

Where there are co-writers the song is jointly owned, and it's very important to record who owns what part of the music or lyrics. When you finish a new song and give it to your publisher, they fill in a form on your behalf called a Joint Registration Form. This is the form needed to record the details about the song, which is then sent to the collecting societies, MCPS and PRS (The Mechanical Copyright Protection Society Limited/The Performing Rights Society Limited). The form contains the title of the song, who wrote it, what shares of it they wrote and if there are any restrictions on what can be done with it. If you don't have a publisher and you're a member of PRS or MCPS or both, you should complete and file that form yourself.

Most publishing agreements will say that all songs are assumed to be written in equal shares by all co-writers unless the publisher is told something different when the work is completed and details given to them for registration. The whole question of who wrote what can be the cause of major arguments between co-writers, who are often members of the same band or the producer of the album. This can be the case even where not all members of a band contribute to the writing. Those members that do write resent those that don't. You definitely ought to sort these issues out at an early stage before you've made any money and it becomes a real issue (see Chapter 11).

---

3 Section 9(1) CDPA.
4 Section 10(1) CDPA.

A well-publicised 1999 case over songwriting shares involved the former members of Spandau Ballet.[5]

Spandau Ballet

Spandau Ballet was formed in 1979 and made up of the two Kemp brothers, Martin and Gary, together with Tony Hadley, John Keeble and Steve Norman. They were part of the New Romantic movement and, after turning down a record deal with Island Records, they set up their own label that they eventually licensed to Chrysalis Records. Their first single, 'To Cut A Long Story Short', went Top 5 in the UK. They released a couple more singles before having a Top 3 hit with 'Chant Number 1'. They released six albums plus a Greatest Hits compilation. The last album, *Heart Like A Sky*, was released in 1989. Ten years later they were in court arguing over song royalties. Martin Kemp was not involved in this case.

Everyone agreed that Gary Kemp had written the lyrics to all the songs. The dispute was over who composed the music. Gary Kemp's company received all the publishing income from the songs. He volunteered to give half of this money to the other band members, but stopped this arrangement in 1987. The other band members sued, saying that there was a legally binding agreement to continue to pay this money. They also argued that, if there was not a binding agreement, they were entitled to the money anyway because they were co-writers of the songs and therefore co-owners of the copyright. They said they'd contributed enough to the music to make them joint writers. The judge decided that there was no binding legal agreement. Gary Kemp was sole writer of all the music save for a song called 'Glow'. The judge also confirmed that to be a joint owner you have to have contributed to the song's creation, not just to its interpretation. So if a drummer just adds a short drum loop that doesn't make any material difference to the song, that won't qualify for a claim that he has co-written that song. A bassist who takes the melody line and just converts it into a part that is suitable for his instrument will also probably not have claim to being a co-writer.

DURATION OF COPYRIGHT

The copyright in a musical or literary work lasts for 70 years from the end of the calendar year in which the author dies.[6] If a song has been co-written, the rights last until 70 years from the end of the calendar year in which the last surviving co-writer dies.[7]

WHAT RIGHTS COME WITH OWNERSHIP OF COPYRIGHT?

The copyright owner of a literary or musical work (i.e. a song) has rights very similar to the recording copyright rights we looked at in the last chapter. The main rights are the right to authorise the reproduction of a musical or literary work with or without visual images (the mechanical and synchronisation rights mentioned above);[8] the right to authorise distribution of the work;[9] the right to rent or lend the work to members of the public;[10] the right to authorise public performance of the work or its inclusion in a cable

---

5 *Hadley and Others* v. *Kemp and Another* (1999) Chancery Division.
6 Section 12(2) CDPA.
7 Section 12(8) CDPA.
8 Section 16(1) (a) and section 17 CDPA.
9 Section 16(1) (b) and section 18 CDPA.
10 Section 16(1) (c) and (d) and sections 19 and 20 CDPA.

broadcast service[11] and the right to make an adaptation of the work or to do any of the above in relation to an adaptation.[12] As the copyright owner, you can allow or prevent someone from doing all or any of these things either throughout the world *or* in a particular country.

WHERE DOES THE MONEY COME FROM?

MECHANICAL LICENCES AND ROYALTIES

The biggest source of income for most songwriters is the issue of a licence to record a performance of a song. For example, if your record company wants to record a performance of your song, it has to ask permission from you or your publisher or the person who administers your songs. This may seem a bit strange. You've written a song that your band wants to record. It seems odd to have to ask permission from someone else to record your band performing it. But remember that different people are going to control the rights in the sound recording and the rights in the song. They are separate copyrights and the same people will probably not control both. The record company has to pay a licence fee to the owner of the rights in the song. Originally, when a recording was reproduced it was literally done mechanically, using mechanical piano-rolls. So the licence to reproduce the song on a sound recording is called a mechanical licence. The fee for this, the mechanical royalty, is either fixed by negotiation between representatives of the record and publishing companies in the country concerned or set by law or legal tribunal.

The present licensing system in the UK was the result of a referral to the Copyright Tribunal in 1992. The record and publishing companies couldn't agree on what was a proper licence fee. The 1988 Copyright Designs and Patents Act says that the solution in such situations is to refer the dispute to the Copyright Tribunal. The scheme approved by the Copyright Tribunal is operated by the MCPS on behalf of most of the music publishers in the UK. The current licence fee is 8.5% of the dealer price of the record or approximately 70–80p per CD album, depending on the dealer price. The MCPS can only licence the mechanical reproduction of a song if it's a straight 'cover', i.e. a faithful reproduction of the original by someone other than the original performers. If it's not a faithful reproduction then the MCPS doesn't have the authority to issue a licence and permission has to be asked from the original writers or the publishers.

Until recently, mechanical reproduction took the form of physical product such as a vinyl record, a cassette tape or a CD, with new formats such as DAT, DCC and Mini-disc added from time to time. New means of online reproduction have also been developed, with music being delivered via the Internet. The download of a computer file containing music on to an MP3 or similar player or a computer hard disc is still treated in the UK as a reproduction akin to a physical reproduction such as a CD. This is actually quite a difficult concept, although now accepted in the EU and governed by the EU Directive on Copyright in the Information Society

In 2002 MCPS/PRS started to issue blanket licences and, through its reciprocal arrangements, was offering these worldwide. The licence fee is based on a share of

11 Section 16(1) (e) and section 21 CDPA.
12 Section 21 CDPA.

revenue from the relevant site – between 8 and 12%. But because there is still resistance in some quarters these are one-year licences and are terminable on notice.

The MCPS also publishes guidelines for the licensing of other uses such as CD-ROMs, music in toys and in computer games. Some but not all publishers have given authority to MCPS to grant licences for these types of uses on their behalf, but because not all have, you have to check with MCPS for each song you want to use. An awful lot is still left to individuals to negotiate.

CONTROLLED COMPOSITIONS

Although in this book I'm mostly dealing with UK copyright and licensing schemes, the situation in the US is important as it can have a huge impact on publishing income coming from the United States.

In the UK we have a licensing scheme and a fixed rate that has to be paid for a licence. In the US the law also sets a fixed rate (about 6 cents a track) for the right to reproduce a song on a record, but in the US the record industry has an awful lot more power than the publishers. It lobbied the legislators and got a clause included in the law that allows a different rate to be set by agreement. Well, surprise, surprise, the record companies have insisted on a different rate. And is it higher? What do you think? The almost universal position in the US is that the record companies will only pay 75% of the fixed rate. This is referred to as a 'controlled compositions' or 'reduced mechanical royalty' clause. They are called controlled compositions because the compositions and what happens to them are under the control of the writer (who may also be a performer) or his publishers. Obviously, you can only agree to a reduced rate if you're the owner or controller of the song. You can't speak for anyone else. You'll be put under considerable pressure to agree to this 75% rate. This means that you're losing a quarter of your US publishing income from the reproduction of your songs on records. If you already have a publishing deal, you won't be allowed to accept this reduction without your publisher's agreement. Your publisher should fight on your and its behalf to get improvements on this rate. If you've a lot of bargaining power you can get a 100% rate. If you've medium bargaining power you can get them to agree to increase the 75% rate to 85% and then to 100% based on sales of a given number of records.

On a couple of occasions the UK record industry has tried to introduce a similar system here. So far they have not succeeded, but the publishers remain ever vigilant. The last big battle was over an appropriate rate for downloading music and, as we saw above, I would like to be able to put a sensible argument here on behalf of record companies as to why they do this with these US mechanical royalties. I *would* like to, but I can't think of a justification. The US laws have given them the opportunity to do it and they have taken advantage of it. End of story.

Most US record companies try to further reduce their liability to pay full mechanical royalties by limiting the number of tracks on a record that they will pay royalties on. This is usually no more than ten or eleven. So, if you have twelve tracks on your album, you won't get a mechanical royalty in the US on at least one or two of those tracks.

These controlled compositions clauses cause a lot of problems in every record deal negotiation. There are some improvements that your lawyer can try to get for you, but this is often the most keenly fought clause in the whole recording contract. A lot of money is at stake for both sides.

SYNCHRONISATION LICENCES AND ROYALTIES

If you're a songwriter who writes mostly music for films, adverts or computer games, then your main source of income may not be mechanical royalties but fees from the issue of licences to use your music with visual images. This licence is called a synchronisation licence, because it gives the right to synchronise music with visual images. The publisher also licenses and collects income from these licences. The fee for this use is called the synchronisation fee.

We can all think of artists who have broken into the big time via an advert or indeed where a flagging career has been boosted by a track used in a particularly good ad campaign or in a film. What about Wet, Wet, Wet and 'Love Is All Around Us' in the film *Four Weddings and a Funeral?* For the right music an advertising company will pay a lot of money – £100,000 or more as a synchronisation fee for the right work isn't unheard of. I should just say, though, before you all rush to get your music into adverts or films, that many advertising companies pay a lot less than this. Many also commission writers to write songs that sound like but aren't famous songs. Some songwriters make a career of writing jingles for adverts or in composing sound-alike songs. For some this is their main source of income. Others do it as a way to fund them writing their masterwork – that film soundtrack or concerto they otherwise wouldn't have the money to do.

In some countries there's a fixed rate for synchronisation licences. In most cases, though, it has to be fixed on a case-by-case basis. So this again is an area where your publisher or lawyer can get a good deal for you.

If you want to put one of your songs in a promotional video for one of your singles your publisher will probably give you a free synchronisation licence. If there is any chance that it will earn income commercially then they will want a separate fee for the commercial use.

If there is a synchronisation fee payable, there needs to be an agreement between the publisher and you as to how they are going to split that money. Will some or all of it go towards recouping any advances you've been paid? Will some or all of it be paid to you or kept by the publisher? Obviously, the publishers will want to keep their publisher's share of this income. For example, if you were on a 75:25 split of royalties in your favour, the publisher would want to keep 25% of the fee for himself. It's obviously in your publisher's best interests to try and use as much as possible of the remaining 75% to help recoup the advances it has made to you. You may not be in desperate need of cash and may decide that it would be sensible to agree to that. On the other hand, you may view it as some badly needed cash and argue with the publisher for at least some of it to be paid through to you. The publishing contract may spell out what is to happen or may say that it's up for negotiation on a case-by-case basis.

The situation may change if you're commissioned to write some music or a song for a specific project like a film soundtrack. Publishing contracts will often say that, even though they may have an exclusive arrangement with you, you can do these deals and keep the commission fee provided the synchronisation fee (which is also required) is paid through to them. Now, it doesn't take much intelligence to work out that, as a songwriter, you may want to increase the commission fee and decrease the synchronisation fee. The PRS rules also now require the publisher to use all reasonable efforts to find additional uses for a piece of music or song written specially for a film. So they have to try to get it recorded or used in some other way.

The MCPS has a mandate from most but not all of its members to grant synchronisation licences. Here again, however, there are difficulties in relation to new-media uses such as the Internet. Because many publishers have retained the right to license use of music with visual images, and because most uses on the Internet involve visual images, this means in effect that anyone wanting to use the music on the Internet will still probably have to deal directly with the publishers.

PERFORMING RIGHTS

We've looked so far at two main sources of publishing income – the mechanical licence and the synchronisation licence. The third significant source of income is the right to publicly perform a song. Public performance doesn't just mean live concerts – it includes the playing of music in shops, restaurants, and clubs; in fact anywhere that music is played in public.

Most songwriters who have had some success become members of the PRS or one of its overseas affiliates. The PRS is the only UK performing right society for the administration of the right to perform a work in public, and it's responsible for the collection of income generated by the public performance of the music. The income comes largely from licences taken out by broadcasters, shops, pubs and so on, as we'll see below. When you become a member of the PRS, the rules say that you have to assign your performing rights in your songs to the PRS. The PRS could have taken a licence of these rights or have been appointed as your agent, but it prefers to take an assignment. If you end your membership the performing rights are returned to you or to whomever you direct. The performing rights controlled by the PRS are the right to publicly perform a work, the right to broadcast it and to include it in a cable broadcast service, and the right to authorise others to do any or all of the above. So every time your song is played on television, radio, cable or satellite you'll receive (eventually) some income from that use of your song.

The PRS monitors use of music on TV and radio programmes by means of cue sheets. These are lists of music played on each programme, which the station producers complete after each show. The PRS has a random sampling policy for live shows. They couldn't possibly cover all live gigs, but do monitor the main venues and they keep the type of venues monitored under review.

So that there doesn't have to be a separate licence every time a song is played in public, the PRS has entered into licences with most of the broadcasters. They have done the same with major places of entertainment like clubs and restaurant chains. These are called 'blanket licences' because they cover all songs controlled by the PRS. If you've a blanket licence you don't have to worry about whether you can play a particular song provided you've paid the annual licence fee negotiated with the PRS.

Using cue sheets or samplings the PRS gets a good idea of what music has been performed and calculates the amount due under the various blanket licences. The share due to the songwriter members of PRS is paid out at regular intervals (four times a year) after the PRS has deducted its fee for doing the administration. The PRS rules require that at least six-twelfths (i.e. 50%) of the performing income is paid to the songwriter direct. It's not therefore going through the publisher's hands to be used to recoup any advances. This can be a very valuable source of income for an impoverished songwriter who is unrecouped and can't expect any royalties or further advances from his publisher for some time. The other 50% can be paid to a publisher nominated by you as having the right to publish your songs. This 'publisher's share' can be divided between you and the publisher. If they do share any of it with you, that share usually goes first towards recouping any outstanding balance on your account with your publisher. If you don't have a publisher you can collect 100% of the income yourself. Unlike music publishers, the PRS isn't there to go out and get your song played or performed for you. That is still mainly the job of your music publisher. The PRS is there to make sure that public places playing records do so under a proper licence scheme so that you can have a chance of earning some money from this use of your songs. If it were not there then each publisher would have to enter into separate arrangements with each broadcaster, shop, restaurant and so on. This doesn't make economic sense, so the music publishers, who are also members of the PRS, are happy to allow the PRS to do this job for them, provided, that is, that they don't charge too much for doing the job – there are periodical renegotiations of the collection fee.

PRINT

Although not as relevant these days, your publisher also has the right to issue licences to someone else for a song to be reproduced in printed form as sheet music or to do it themselves. Print income from sales of sheet music isn't a large source of income for a popular-music writer. For classical composers, however, it can be a very lucrative source of income. Included in this print category is the hire-out charge the publisher makes to orchestras wishing to have access to the 'parts' of the work, i.e. the sections written for the different instruments in the orchestra – £30–40,000 fees for the hire out of parts for a large orchestral or operatic piece aren't unheard of.

RECORD DEAL BEFORE PUBLISHING?

It used to be invariably the case that you did your record deal first and got a publishing deal later. Nowadays the publisher fills many of the same roles as a record company in finding you the right co-writers and producers, and even recording and releasing limited edition single records. The decision therefore becomes much more of a personal one. For some, it's important that they have got a deal, *any* deal. So if the publishers come courting first they will do that deal first. Others stick to the tried and true method of getting a record deal first and then hoping that that deal and the success of their first release will push the bidding up for their publishing rights. This can be a dangerous game as, if the first release doesn't prove to be a success, the publishing offers may dry up. You may be a writer who wants to hang on to your publishing rights for as long as you can, in which case you're going to be concerned to get a record deal that will give you enough by way of personal advances to live on for a reasonable period of time without having to go looking for money from a publisher.

If you don't have to do a publishing deal in order to get some money or other form of 'leg-up' you can become self-published. This way you fully control the copyright in your songs and how they are used. How do you do this? Usually by becoming a member of the various collecting societies like MCPS and PRS. The collection societies fulfil a lot of the administrative functions of a publisher, but a self-published songwriter still has to do a lot of work himself. The collection societies don't automatically notify all foreign societies of their interest in a particular song. The songwriter will have to track down where the music is being used and check if the song is registered locally and if the right amount of money has been paid.

Most creative people aren't known for being organised enough to do this, nor will they necessarily have the resources. This is one of the reasons that most new writers look for some form of support from a publishing company. If you're a more established songwriter, you may be more comfortable with this kind of arrangement or will appoint someone to administer it for you. Below I'm going to look at the three main types of publishing agreement and at some of the pros and cons of each. One of them will be the right one for you and, once you've worked out which it is, you can make your pitch to get it.

TYPES OF PUBLISHING DEAL

If you decide that being your own publisher isn't an option for you then there are three basic types of music publishing agreement that can provide outside support for you; the administration deal, the sub-publishing deal and the fully exclusive songwriting deal. Within the category of exclusive songwriting deals there is a sub-category where you just assign your rights in a single song. This is called the single song assignment.

THE ADMINISTRATION DEAL
Administration deals are popular if you're a songwriter who has a small but potentially lucrative catalogue or collection of songs. It may not be worthwhile for you to join the collection societies and be self-published. You may not have the necessary time, energy or organisational abilities to go tracking down the income yourself. You may prefer to employ someone to do it for you.

These types of deals also appeal to established songwriters. They may not need a publisher to try to exploit their songs. They may be disillusioned with exclusive publishing deals or want to own their copyrights. They may not need up-front advances against income and may relish the increased control that they would have if there were no publisher breathing down their neck. The same rules apply to these assignments as they do with sound recordings, so the comments I made in Chapter 3 (on What Is A Good Record Deal?) still apply here.

The administrator doesn't usually take an assignment of any interest in the copyright, but is granted a licence for a period of time. If an administrator asks to take an assignment of your rights outright, I would be very suspicious and would need to be convinced that there was a very good business reason to do it. If you assign your rights you aren't in a position of control. There isn't very much of a difference with an exclusive publishing deal, yet you're likely to see only small or no up-front advances. So what's the advantage? If it's for a licence term then the term can vary greatly from one year upwards. A three- to five-year licence term is common. Many are for much longer. I have recently concluded one that was for the life of copyright. I was still comfortable to do it, because the deal overall worked for that client – at least if it was a licence and things went wrong he wouldn't have to worry about getting his copyrights back, as he'd held on to ownership of them.

As the name suggests, the administrator administers the songs for you. You hand over the job of registering your songs with the various societies and of licensing others to use your songs. They also deal with the collection of the income from these licences and prepare accounts for you showing how much you've earned. It's up to you and the terms of the contract whether you give your administrator the freedom to issue whatever licences he thinks right for the songs, or insist that he has to come back to you for permission each time. This could prove a bit of a pain for you and for him, so you may want to say that the commonplace licences, such as the right for your band to record your songs, can be issued without coming back to you, but if someone wants to use your songs in an advert or a film you want to know about it first. Don't put too many restrictions on what licences your administrator can grant if you want to maximise what you can earn from your songs. By all means put a stop to something that you've a real problem with, for example, if you're a vegan you may quite rightly not want your work used in adverts for beefburgers, but think carefully before you block all uses of your songs in adverts, because you are cutting off a potentially very valuable source of income.

The administrator could be an individual, perhaps an ex-musician or songwriter himself, or it could be a company that specialises just in administration. On the other hand, it could be a music publisher who does administration deals as well as signing up songwriters to exclusive deals. Most of the major publishers and the bigger independent publishers will do administration deals in the right circumstances.

The administrator will usually charge 10–15% of your gross income as his fee. You wouldn't usually expect an administrator to pay any advances. You'll be paid only when your administrator has collected in some money. It's therefore very important to know how often the administrator will pay you. They should pay you at least every three months. It's also important to check out their reputation for efficient collection of money, particularly outside the UK. The administrator may be very good in the UK, but overseas he may not have the necessary resources or contacts. In which case, it's likely that all he will do is to collect what comes through collection societies overseas that are affiliated to the MCPS and PRS. If this is the case then you have to ask yourself whether it's worth it, because you can get this income yourself through direct membership of MCPS and PRS. You ought to be getting some kind of added value by having the administrator on board. It may be as little as taking the load off you, but it wouldn't be unreasonable to ask the administrator to try and track down unpaid licence fees or royalties on your behalf – and if he has a worldwide deal with you he shouldn't just limit his activities to the UK.

You often do an administration deal when you aren't too concerned about getting other uses for your songs. If you know people will either not want to put your songs in a film or advert, or if they do you're so well known you don't have to sell yourself, then you won't worry about someone going out and actively looking for these extra uses. Administrators will look after the administration side but won't be out there pitching your songs to advertising agencies or film companies.

THE SUB-PUBLISHING DEAL
The sub-publishing deal is a mixture of an administration deal and an exclusive publishing agreement. The owner of the copyrights sub-licenses some or all of these rights to a publisher. The original owner usually keeps the copyright, so it's normally a licence

rather than an assignment of rights. These types of deals come up in two very different circumstances.

You may be an established songwriter or a songwriter who wants to own or control your copyright, but you may want something more than a pure administration deal. If so, then a sub-publishing deal may suit. You may not need an advance or you may be prepared to do without an advance in return for keeping control of your copyright. That isn't to say that a sub-publisher won't pay any advance at all. They may pay modest sums in advances, but they may not be as big as you'd get under an exclusive publishing deal. Why? Because the sub-publisher doesn't get as much ownership or control from a sub-publishing deal as they would from an exclusive songwriting deal. You choose what song copyrights go through the deal and, depending on the deal, you may be free to have some of your work published by someone else.

If you do need someone to go and search out deals for you then you won't get that from an administrator, so a sub-publishing deal may work for you. You get someone actively looking for other ways of earning money from your songs and possibly spending some of their money to try and help that happen.

You may set up your own limited company to hold the existing copyrights and the copyright in any new works you write. This company then sub-publishes some or all of the rights to another publisher. In some cases the publisher will want an assignment of the copyright.[13] As you know, my advice is to avoid this if you can but, if you don't have much choice, then try and get them to agree that this is only for a limited period of time. This period is called 'the Rights Period' or 'the Retention Period'. The shorter you can make it, the better for you in terms of control of your copyrights. Bear in mind, though, that the shorter the period of time that the sub-publisher controls your copyrights, the fewer opportunities he has to make money from your songs and this may be reflected in the type of deal he offers. If you do get a publisher to agree a licence term then this could be as short as a year, but is more likely to be for at least three and possibly up to five years.

The sub-publishing deal also appeals to smaller publishers, ones that don't have their own established systems overseas. Instead of the cost of setting up their own companies in each of the main overseas countries, such publishers do sub-publishing deals in those countries. They keep the rights they have, but grant the overseas publisher the right to use some or all of those rights in their country for a period of time.

Whichever type of deal we are talking about, the sub-publisher needs to have the right to register the songs, to license some or all of the main publishing rights such as mechanical and synchronisation rights, and to collect in the income.

The sub-publishing contract will set out the extent to which the songwriter or small publisher has the right to grant licences to exploit the publishing rights. Don't be surprised if the sub-publisher presses for overall control and only wants to have to get your approval on certain very specific matters. You may have approval over alterations to the songs or over the grant of licences to include them in adverts for products that you may disapprove of. If you tie the sub-publisher's hands too much then they can't easily get further uses for the songs. You're employing a sub-publisher and paying them

---

13 Often this is in order to get 'market share', which is the measure of how many copyrights a publisher controls either in terms of numbers or, more often, in terms of how much income they generate. Market share is watched by the money markets and the analysts and is also keenly contested by the publishers themselves as a measure of how well they are doing.

a large fee to be pro-active on your behalf, so you need to balance the need for creative control against commercial realities.

How much you have to pay a sub-publisher will depend on a number of factors like how famous or successful you are, your bargaining power, how much the sub-publisher wants to control your catalogue of songs (whether for market share or income or to have the kudos of having you on their books), and how much you're expecting them to do. It's likely to be more than you would pay under an administration deal but probably a little less than under a fully exclusive songwriting agreement. A sub-publishing fee of 15–20% of the gross income received is common. If you expect a big advance then that may increase to 25% to compensate for the additional risk the sub-publisher is taking. The sub-publisher has paid out some money to you on the strength of what it knows about you and your potential. If you don't live up to that then that's the sub-publishers risk. The contract doesn't usually allow the sub-publisher to demand that money back from you.

What does a sub-publisher do?

Your sub-publisher should provide the same basic services as under an administration deal, including registering the songs, granting licences, collecting income and accounting to you on a regular basis. It's important to check whether there will be a delay in getting your money in from overseas.

Some larger publishers can account to you and pay you what you're due in the same accounting period that they receive the monies from overseas. For example, the sub-publisher grants a mechanical licence to reproduce your song on a record in the US. The record sales take place in the period between March and June 2000. The US record company will probably pay the mechanical royalty in the next three months, so it will be in the sub-publishers account by the end of September 2000. You may have a deal with the sub-publisher that says you are paid in September for income received in the period up to the end of June. On the scenario I have given, the income won't have come in until after the end of June. If the deal you have is that you'll get paid in the same accounting period, you'll get it in September. If it's not then you'll get it at the next accounting date, which would normally be March 2001. This is a six-month delay which, when you're first expecting your money from overseas, can seem a very long time to wait. If prompt payment and cashflow are important to you, and let's face it, they are to most of us, then you need to check this out carefully. Needless to say, the sub-publisher is the one earning interest on the money sitting in their bank account for six months and not you.

In addition to the basic administration services, the sub-publisher should give you something more for the extra money they're getting. This could be an advance, but the sub-publisher should also be more pro-active, going out and looking for other uses for the songs, suggesting co-writers, finding film projects or adverts and so on.

If you're a smaller publishing company appointing a sub-publisher overseas, you should be expecting them to act as if they were a branch of your company overseas. They should have a similar philosophy to you. I know this sounds a bit new-age, but it's important. You may have a reputation in the UK for signing up indie songwriters. Your overseas sub-publishers should also love the same type of music; otherwise they won't know what to do with it or how to work it.

If you're a songwriter with your own publishing company you may not notice any difference between what a sub-publisher does and what you'd expect from an exclusive publishing agreement. The sub-publisher will usually expect exclusive rights to sub-publish your songs and will charge a similar fee to an exclusive publisher. The crucial difference is that you retain the copyright in your songs and have much more control. Some songwriters set up their own publishing company solely for tax reasons and in such cases, although it's technically a sub-publishing agreement, it is to all intents and purposes the same as an exclusive publishing agreement.

THE SINGLE SONG ASSIGNMENT

The single song assignment is a bit of a halfway house. You don't do an exclusive publishing agreement. You're free to publish individual songs yourself or through a variety of different publishers. Unlike under a sub-publishing agreement, you assign the rights in a song to a publisher; you don't licence them. The assignment could be for the life of copyright or it could be for a shorter Rights or Retention Period. You may receive an advance, but it's likely to be small. The publisher is likely to get a fee of about 20–25% of the gross income received.

Deals such as these would be attractive to a songwriter who only writes a small number of songs on an irregular basis, or who wants to keep his options open. The publisher still gets the rights it needs in the particular song and market share in that song. Because the publisher controls the copyright in the song, it's in its interests to get as many other uses for the work as possible. The publisher will also carry out all the usual administrative functions and should account to you regularly. The same comments that I made above about accounting delays apply here. The song assignment will decide how much control you have over how your song is used. Because it's a one-off, you may not have as much control as with an exclusive deal for all your songs, but if you've enough bargaining power you should certainly be able to prevent major changes to your words or music and some control over the use of your song in films or adverts.

EXCLUSIVE PUBLISHING AGREEMENT

If none of the above options appeal or are on offer then there is the exclusive publishing agreement. For most pop songwriters this is the Holy Grail. Getting an established publisher behind them means that they've arrived, that someone else has faith in their work and is prepared to put money and commitment behind that conviction.

RESTRAINT OF TRADE

As we saw in Chapter 3, whenever there is an exclusive arrangement containing restrictions on what you can and can't do, there is an assumption that it is in restraint of trade. We also saw that the leading case in this area, *Schroeder* v. *Macaulay*,[14] had decided that this doctrine also applied to exclusive record and publishing contracts. We know that the contract was found to be an unreasonable restraint of trade and, as such, unenforceable, but so far I have not gone into any details as to what in the contract was found to be unreasonable. It was a publishing contract so I felt it was better dealt with here.

---

14 *A. Schroeder Music Publishing Co. Limited v. Macaulay* [1974] 1 WLR 1308.

Schroeder v. Maucalay

> The particular parts of the contract that led the court to decide that it was unenforceable were that it was an exclusive arrangement – it required absolute commitment from Macaulay, but there was no corresponding commitment on the part of the publishers to do anything with the songs. They could accept them and tuck the copies away in a drawer or put them on a shelf and forget about them. The term was for five years, but Schroeder could extend it for a further five years if more than £5,000 worth of royalties had been earned in the first five years. This was not a lot of money even then. Macaulay had had to assign the copyright for the life of copyright. Even though in those days this was 50 years after the end of the year in which he died not 70 years, it was still a long period of time to have a publisher controlling the copyright in his songs exclusively without having any obligation to do anything with them. The advance that he received was very low. It was £50 with further payments of £50 as each earlier advance was recouped. This was almost like putting him on a wage, but with no guarantee of when he would receive his next pay cheque. The court felt that, taken as a whole, the contract was an unreasonable restraint of trade.

As a result of this and later cases there has been a change in music publishing contracts. The length of the term is now limited and there is a maximum backstop – usually no more than three years per contract period. There is also usually a requirement that the publisher has to do something with the songs. For example, the contract will often say that if the publisher has not granted a mechanical or synchronisation licence for a song, or no sheet music has been printed of it or it has not been performed in public within, say, a year or two of the song being delivered, then you've the right to ask the publisher to do something with it. If nothing happens within another three to six months then you usually get the copyright in the song back.

WHAT IS IN A TYPICAL PUBLISHING CONTRACT?

EXCLUSIVITY

If you sign an exclusive publishing deal, you are usually agreeing that the publisher will own and control all your output as a songwriter during the term of that contract. In return for that exclusivity you can expect a commitment from the publishing company to do something with your songs. You can also usually expect that your publisher will be reasonably pro-active on your behalf.

Even though it's an exclusive deal, you can sometimes have exceptions to this. As I explained above, the exclusivity may not apply where you're commissioned to write a song or some music specifically for a film. The film company will usually want to own the copyright in that piece of music or song. Your exclusive publisher may agree that these commissioned works are excluded from your publishing deal. This could be agreed at the time the contract is done as a blanket exception or your publisher could agree to consider specific requests on a case-by-case basis.

If you're regularly commissioned to write music for films, your publisher isn't going to want to automatically exclude all these from your agreement. By not automatically agreeing that the film company can own the copyright, your publisher may gain some bargaining power with the film company to get a better deal. As the terms of the contract should say that you benefit one way or another from income from these deals, it should be in your interests for the publisher to argue on your behalf.

Occasionally a publisher will agree that the songs you write for a particular project are excluded from the deal. For example, you might write some songs for a largely uncommercial project that the publisher isn't interested in. Songs written for this project could be excluded from the deal. If you've a lot of bargaining power, you could insist that songs you write for another commercial project are excluded from the deal. Just bear in mind that the more songs you don't give your publisher control of, the more it is likely to reduce the deal terms on offer.

RIGHTS GRANTED

The publisher will expect to have assigned to it the copyright in all your songs already in existence that no one else has the right to publish. The assignment is usually of all rights in those works, subject to the performing rights that you may have already assigned to the PRS.

If you've done a publishing deal before, another company may still have the right to act as publisher of those songs. If the Rights or Retention Period of that earlier deal runs out while your new publishing deal is still running, the new publisher will expect to get the right to publish those songs too. If you don't think they should then you need to argue for this at the time the new publishing deal is done.

It's possible to grant a publisher some but not all of the rights of a copyright owner. I try to hold back rights to exploit music online from a few publishers, but it's true to say that they feel very uncomfortable about it and, now that there's a fledgling licence scheme in place, they are most unlikely to agree to exclude online rights. In other deals I've done I've given them the right to issue mechanical licences but not synchronisation licences. Obviously you can do this if you've the necessary bargaining power, but there's no point in doing it unless you can do something with the rights you've kept back. Remember also that the more rights you hold back the more likely it is that you'll get a worse deal from the publishing company.

TERRITORY

The rights that you assign could be for a particular country or worldwide. We saw in Chapter 3 that it was reasonably common to have one deal for the US and another deal for the rest of the world. Split-territory deals aren't at all common in exclusive publishing contracts. Depending on who the publisher is and what its overseas set-up is like, it may have sub-publishing deals in some countries. As a songwriter you should find out what the situation is overseas. You need to know that the sub-publishers are good, efficient companies and that there won't be any accounting delays.

RIGHTS PERIOD

You could assign rights for the life of copyright or for a shorter Rights or Retention Period, which runs from the end of the term of the publishing contract. This period can vary considerably from anything as short as two to three years to more than twenty years. At the time of writing (September 2002) the average deal on offer from the major publishers is twelve to fifteen years.

The Rights Period often gets shorter when there is a more positive economic climate and if there is a lot of competition to sign good songwriters. A few years ago I could get Retention Periods from some of the major music publishers as short as five years. This was when there were lots of good songwriters and a lot of money around. Publishers were going for short-term market share and weren't as concerned about hanging on to copyrights for any length of time. Many of the copyrights were for dance music songs and I guess they gambled that most of these would have a short life span. Now there's less money around, songwriters are expected to prove their worth over a longer period of time and it's difficult to get Rights Periods of less than ten years unless you've got a lot of bargaining power. There are, however, always the one-off crazy deals for one album or song at ludicrously high levels, but these are usually for short-term market share to boost a publisher's standing in a particular quarter.

TERM

The term of a UK music-publishing contract is usually shorter than that of a record contract. It's quite common to find a music-publishing contract with an initial period of one year and then options in the music publisher's favour for a further two or three option periods. Each contract period is usually for a minimum of twelve months, but can be longer depending on how long it takes you to fulfil the Minimum Commitment requirements that a publisher has for each contract period. For similar reasons to those given for record contracts, the options are in the publisher's favour not yours. The publisher has too much invested to allow you to just walk out the door when you want to.

Rolling contracts

Some publishers use a different basis for the term of the publishing contract. It's one that songwriters often like because it gives them more certainty up-front. What happens is that, instead of a term made up of a number of optional contract periods, the publisher fixes the term up-front and says it will run for, say, three or five years with no options. This is referred to as a rolling term. That fixed period may be extended until you've fulfilled the Minimum Commitment. Sometimes, but not often, there is no Minimum Commitment; the publisher just publishes anything you do in the fixed term. This is a big risk for the publisher to take. You may take the advance payable on signing the deal and then not write another thing. To offer this kind of deal, the publisher has to know you well and be convinced that you're going to continue to write good songs. For a songwriter this isn't only a great show of faith from your publisher, it's also a relief. You don't have to worry about fulfilling the Minimum Commitment or delivering songs to order.

With a rolling term you get an advance when you sign the deal and this is recouped from your earnings. When the initial advance has been wholly or partly recouped you're paid a further advance. This is called a rolling advance. The publisher won't usually pay you an advance in the last twelve months of the fixed term because it won't have enough time to recoup it before the deal runs out. When working out how recouped you are, to see if you should get a further advance, you should try to get the publisher to take into account as much of the income that's been earned from your songs but hasn't yet come through to its or your account in the UK. This is the 'pipeline income' that we came across in min-max formulas in record contracts.

MINIMUM COMMITMENT

There are a number of different types of Minimum Commitment. The simplest is where you're just required to write a minimum number of songs. If you co-write, your share of all the co-written works must add up to an equivalent number of whole songs. For example, if the Minimum Commitment is to write five new songs and you always only write the lyrics, so only control at best 50% of each song, then you'll have to write ten half-songs to add up to the five whole ones. This type of commitment works best for a pure songwriter who writes for others and doesn't perform and record his own material.

There may be an additional requirement that, in order to count towards the Minimum Commitment, the song must be exploited in some way, for instance commercially released as an A-side of a single or as an album track. This puts a greater burden on you if you're a pure songwriter who can't easily control whether anyone else will want to record your songs. The publisher usually insists on this when it wants to be certain there will be some form of exploitation (and hopefully some income) before it commits to any more advances or decides whether to exercise an option to extend the term.

There may be a requirement that you have to write a minimum number of the songs on an album. That percentage varies depending on the songwriter and the style of music. For a band, the requirement is usually that you have to write at least 60–70% of the songs on your own album. There is also usually a requirement that that album has to be commercially released. This sort of arrangement works better for a songwriter who also performs and records his own material.

A much less common commitment is one that you get when you have a songwriter who records some of his own material, writes to commissions from others, or writes for a number of different styles of music, for example, film, TV, classical and popular. The Minimum Commitment could be a number of 'points', with a different value being given to each type of usage, genre, format and so on. For example, two points for a ballet commission, five for a track on a popular-music album, with, say, 30 points in total required per contract period. The publisher is only likely to agree to this sort of commitment where you're already established in a number of these areas – these types of deals aren't common.

ADVANCES

It's usual under an exclusive publishing agreement for the publisher to pay advances. As we saw with record contracts (see Chapter 3), this is a pre-payment of your share of the gross income from the use of your songs. It's not a loan and isn't repayable to the publishing company if you never earn enough from the songs it controls to cover the amount of the advance. You usually don't have to pay it back, but if you take the money and run, never delivering a single song, your publisher may get a bit upset and may sue for return of their money on the basis that you've failed to fulfil your side of the bargain.

What size advance can you expect? This will change with circumstances. Your bargaining power, the number of co-writers there are, how much is your own material and how much is sampled from others will all help to determine the figure. It will also depend on how much the publisher thinks it's likely to earn from your songs on average. If the record deal has already been done, the publisher may take its lead from what it knows of the level of that deal. If that was a particularly 'hot' deal the publisher will know that it probably has to increase the overall terms of their offer. There are also financial models that help a publisher to decide how much they can realistically risk. Some publishers rely on these models, while others work on more of a gut instinct or a combination of the two. You also have to factor in market forces. If the publisher really wants to sign you up, whether to increase the profile of the company, for market share or just because the A&R man wants it, then that publisher will pay whatever it takes.

The higher the advance, the more the publisher will expect from you in return and the larger percentage of the income that the publisher will keep as their fee. The publisher will be more reluctant to give you a higher than average royalty if they've had to pay out a high advance – £50–75,000 for a writer for 80% or more of the songs on an album isn't unreasonable. Much higher figures can be expected if there is a 'hype' or if you have a proven track record. If the publisher knows that there is already some income out there from your catalogue waiting to be collected, or that you have a song on the next album to be released by a chart-topping act, they're more likely to risk paying higher advances.

The publishing deal is likely to recoup a lot faster than the record deal because, with a publishing deal, you only have to recoup the personal advances and maybe some money in demo costs or tour support – there aren't the additional recoupable expenses like recording costs, video costs and tour support. Also, the publisher pays through to you a much larger percentage of the income earned for the use of your songs than most record companies do with the income from sales of your records.

ROYALTIES

The publishing advance is recouped from your royalty earnings after first deducting the publisher's fee. For an exclusive publishing deal this will usually be about 20–25% of the gross income.

Royalties can be calculated in one of two ways, either 'at source' or on 'receipts'. 'At source' means that there have been no deductions made by anyone (after the collection societies, the VAT man and payments to any arranger or translator) from the gross income earned from your songs. For example, your publisher may have sub-publishers or their own companies overseas. These people have to be paid somehow and they could be paid out of the publisher's 20–25% fee. This is an 'at source' means of calculation. Or they could be paid off the top, off the gross before the income is paid through to you. Calculating your royalty on 'receipts' means you're paid after any such 'cut' has been paid to the sub-publishers.

Let me give you an example. €100 is earned in France from sales of recordings of your song. If you're on a 'source' deal then, as far as you're concerned, nothing gets deducted from that €100 by the sub-publisher in France before it's paid through to your publisher in the UK. The UK publisher would then deduct their 25% (assuming the VAT and taxmen have already done their worst) and pays through €75 to you. If you're on a 'receipts' deal then the sub-publisher in France would first take their 'cut' of, say, 15% (€15) leaving €85 to be sent through to your publisher in the UK. They then take their 25% of that €85, leaving you with just €63.

As a songwriter you should try and get an 'at source' deal. But your publisher may not have any choice. The deals done with their sub-publishers may mean they have to do deals on a 'receipts' basis in order to make any money out of use of your songs overseas. If you're offered a 'receipts' deal, the very least you should do is to try and limit the amount the sub-publishers can take off the 'at source' income. For example, you might want to say in the contract that the sub-publishers can't deduct any more than 15–20%. We saw in the *Elton John* v. *Dick James* case that the sub-publishers were spread all over the world and many were associated with Dick James and his UK companies. There was no limit on what these sub-publishers could take off the top as their cut. As Elton was on a 'receipts' deal he could have, and did in some cases, find himself in a situation where the sub-publisher took 50% or more, leaving small amounts to come into the UK, where a further percentage fee was deducted by Dick James – leaving very little over for Elton.

SYNCHRONISATION AND COVER ROYALTIES

Sometimes the publisher justifies taking a larger piece of the pie by saying that, in order to do certain work for you, it needs the incentive of getting more of a fee. Part of me says that this is a con and that getting 20–25% of your income should be enough for most purposes. The reality is that the business has accepted that publishers will get a larger fee for these types of work and it's hard to buck against the trend unless you have a great deal of bargaining power. What areas am I talking about? The two usual areas where the publisher takes a larger fee are synchronisation licences and covers.

I described a synchronisation licence earlier. For reasons that are obscure to me, the publisher seems to think that it should get a larger fee for going out and finding a film or TV project that your work would be suitable for. And there's me thinking that's what you were paying for in the first place. No, they need a further incentive. They usually look to get about another 5%, so if you were paying your publisher a fee on mechanical royalties of 25%, you would see that increase to 30% for synchronisation royalties.

If you find that the publisher won't move on this point, the best thing is to make sure that they don't get this increased percentage on projects that you or someone other than the publisher introduces. For example, if one of your mates from drama school brings a film project to you, you wouldn't expect the publisher to take a bigger fee because it didn't go out and find that work.

The same sort of rules should apply to a cover. As you know, a cover is a recording of a song done by someone other than the songwriter. So, for example, if a track were first recorded by U2 and is later recorded by Sinead O'Connor, Sinead's version would be the cover. Once again, the publisher will probably want an increased fee for finding other artists keen to cover your works. The answer is to make sure that something doesn't count as a cover unless the publisher has actually done something positive to get it. For example, if you bumped into an artist at an awards show and he was raving about what he thought he could do with your song, if he then goes on to cover that song, it hasn't happened because of anything the publisher has done. The publisher should not get an increased fee for that cover.

You have to be particularly careful where you're a songwriter who doesn't perform his own songs. Otherwise, you'll find that you're paying the higher fee for most of what you're doing, because the recording will always be by someone other than the person who wrote it, i.e. you. Everything will be a cover. In these cases I always push for all recordings to be treated in the same way and not as covers. The publishers are often very reluctant to do this, saying that getting anyone to record a song requires effort and that it's harder if the songwriter isn't the performing artist. You have to stand your ground on this. If you're a songwriter you'll be paying a publisher to find ways to use your songs.

You shouldn't expect them to increase their fee just because you aren't going to record your own songs.

PERFORMING INCOME
The PRS rules require that at least six-twelfths (50%) of the performing income has to go to the writer/composer. This is called 'the writer's share'. The other six-twelfths is called 'the publisher's share'. Depending on the deal you have, the publisher will either say that they intend to keep the whole of the publisher's share or they will agree to share some of it with you. You get to keep the writer's share and don't have to put it towards recoupment of your advances. Your share of the publisher's share will go towards recoupment of any unrecouped advance.

When you're dealing with contracts for the use of music in a film or TV programme, it's still common for the publisher to insist on keeping the entire 'publisher's share' and not putting any of it towards recoupment. TV and film publishing deals have lagged behind popular-music deals, where it's usual for the publisher to share up to 50% of the publisher's share with the songwriter.

ACCOUNTING
The publishing company will usually account to you every six months. You'll be sent a statement of what use has been made of your songs in the previous six months and how much income has been received. It should show the percentage that your publisher has kept as their fee and the amount that has been credited to your account. Your share of income will go first to recoup advances. After that your publisher should send a cheque with the statement for the royalties due to you. Even if the account isn't recouped, you or your representatives should check these accounting statements to see if they seem right and that the correct fee has been deducted. If, for example, you know that your music was used in an advert in the last six months but there is no mention of income from this in the statement, you should ask your publisher to explain. It also pays for you to audit the books of the publishing company from time to time. You don't want to be doing this every five minutes, but you may want to run a check after you've had a particularly successful time. You'll probably also want to think about doing an audit when the deal comes to an end, as that is going to be your last practical chance to check up on your publisher. Because it can be very expensive to carry out an audit (£10,000 plus isn't unusual), you only want to do it when you think there is a reasonable chance of getting something back from it. If the audit shows up serious errors in your favour, you should expect them to reimburse you the main costs of doing the audit as well as paying you whatever sums the audit has shown are due to you.

You shouldn't delay in raising any concerns you might have about an accounting statement, as the publishing contract will probably put a time limit on you doing so. Usually, if a statement hasn't been challenged for three years, sometimes less, then it's said to have been accepted and no objection can be raised to it after that time.

WHAT CAN YOU EXPECT FROM A PUBLISHER UNDER AN EXCLUSIVE PUBLISHING AGREEMENT?
We've already seen that there is a presumption that an exclusive songwriting agreement is in restraint of trade and it's up to the publisher to show that the contract, taken as a

whole, is reasonable to protect its interests and fair to the songwriter. As we saw in the *Schroeder* v. *Macaulay* case, a publishing contract should require the publisher to do something with your songs that it controls, and if the publisher doesn't manage to do so within a reasonable period of time you should be able to get those songs back. The publisher has to ensure that it does what it can to get the songs used, to maximise the income from all uses and to make sure the songs are properly registered, income properly collected and accounted through to the writer.

Your publisher should also take steps to protect your songs from unauthorised uses. Sampling of songs is rife and it's up to the publisher either to prevent such uses by court action or, if you and your publisher are prepared to allow the sample use, to ensure a proper amount is paid in compensation (see Chapter 13).

Open-ended contracts are likely to be seen as unfairly restrictive, as we see in the case of Holly Johnson and Perfect Songs Limited.[15]

Frankie Goes To Hollywood

This case came to court at the same time as the related case involving Johnson's record contract. Both the record and publishing companies were trying to get an injunction to bind Holly Johnson to the contracts, even though the band he was a member of, Frankie Goes To Hollywood, had disbanded. Holly Johnson argued that both agreements were unenforceable as being an unreasonable restraint of his trade.

When the court looked at the publishing contract, it found that it was potentially a very long contract, and that it was exclusive but there had not been equal bargaining power when it was entered into. It found that the restrictions in the contract were not reasonable and declared that the publishing agreement was unenforceable. The judge was concerned that Holly Johnson and his fellow band members had not had any choice in whether they did the publishing deal. It was offered as a package with the record deal. There was also no obligation on the publisher to do anything with the songs. There was no re-assignment of the rights in the songs if the publisher failed to exploit them in any way. The judge also thought that it was unfair that Perfect Songs had full control over what happened to the songs once they were delivered. The songwriters had little or no creative control. The judge considered what financial benefits the songwriters got out of the deal and found that the 35% fee retained by the publisher was too much.

Stone Roses publishing dispute

Another case that has had an effect on the form of publishing contracts is the Stone Roses publishing dispute.[16]

The Stone Roses were a Manchester band that had a hit with an album called *The Stone Roses*, released in 1989. They were signed to the Silvertone label, part of the Zomba Group. The members of the Stone Roses were also offered a package deal. They couldn't do the record deal without also signing the publishing deal. As we saw in the case of *Armatrading* v. *Stone,* it's very important that the songwriter gets independent advice from his own lawyer, someone who is familiar with the music business and its contracts. In this case, the songwriters had their own lawyer but he was not experienced in music contracts

15 *Perfect Songs Limited* v. *Johnson and Others* [1993] E.M.L.R 61.
16 *Zomba* v. *Mountfield and Others* [1993] E.M.L.R 152.

and made hardly any changes to the terms of the contract from the initial draft that the publishing company's lawyer gave to him. There was no equality of bargaining power. The agreement was an exclusive one and the rights were assigned for the life of copyright. There was a limited obligation on the publisher to do something with the songs under its control. After five years the Stone Roses could ask for the rights back in any of their songs that hadn't been exploited. The first contract period was linked to that of the record deal. The court found that the first contract period of the record deal was capable of being extended indefinitely. As the two were linked, this meant that the publishing agreement was similarly open-ended and, as such, unreasonable. The court also found that the advances were not reasonable and objected to the lack of artistic or creative control by the song-writers. Because Zomba had obtained an injunction preventing the band from recording for anyone else, they couldn't bring out any more records until this case had been decided. When it was they signed a big deal with US label Geffen. The band went on to release another album called, appropriately enough, *The Second Coming*, but split up shortly afterwards.

As a result of this and similar cases it's now common to have clauses in the publishing agreement making it clear that the publisher has to do something with the rights it has. Also that the songwriter should have some say on what happens to the songs once they're delivered. It's usual to say that no major changes to the music or any change to the lyrics can be made without the songwriter's approval. The criticism of the 65:35 split has led to the average publishing royalty rising to 70% in the songwriter's favour with the publisher keeping no more than 30%.

A more recent case involving a dispute as to ownership of a song is that of *Ludlow* v. *Williams*, a case between Robbie Williams and Guy Chambers and their respective publishers and Ludlow. The case technically turned on whether Mr Williams and Mr Chambers had copied a substantial part of a song published by Ludlow and is dealt with in more detail in Chapter 13 on sampling.

MORAL RIGHTS AND CREATIVE CONTROL
A songwriter may have strong views on what he wants or doesn't want to happen to his songs. For example, a songwriter may believe passionately that no one should be allowed to alter the words or music without his approval. This doesn't usually extend to straight translations. Those are taken to be a logical part of the exploitation process. But if, in the translation, the translator wanted to give the lyrics a different meaning and you objected to this, you should be entitled to prevent this happening. Obviously, I'm not talking about minor changes, but major ones that change the meaning of what you've written significantly. This contractual control overlaps with a songwriter's moral rights. Moral rights are described in more detail in Chapter 12. Where you're able to retain your moral rights then you should do so. The reality is that, because our copyright laws acknowledge these rights but allow you to waive them, all publishers have put clauses in their contracts requiring you to waive these rights. What we lawyers now do is to put contract clauses in to give you the same or similar rights to what you would have got from using your moral rights. So you might ask why we bother with this farce. Why don't we acknowledge that the songwriter has certain rights to object to what is morally being

done to his songs? Well, the essential difference is that the moral rights usually go a bit wider than what you get under your contract and a moral right is capable of being enforced by you even if your publishing company doesn't want to take any action.

A songwriter may want to reserve a song for himself or his band to record and won't want another artist applying for and getting a mechanical licence to record that song first. The publisher will usually agree not to issue a first mechanical licence to another artist where the songwriter wants to reserve it, but will usually require that there is a time limit of, say, six months on this. If it hasn't been recorded in that time then the restriction is lifted.

Finally of course, the songwriter will want to ensure he is properly credited.

WHAT TYPE OF DEAL SHOULD YOU DO?

How do you decide which deal is best for you? To some extent this may be out of your control. You may not be offered anything other than an exclusive publishing agreement. You may not be able to afford to keep control of your copyrights. You may be able to afford to do so but haven't got the organisational talents necessary to make sure that your works are properly protected and the income collected. In these cases the exclusive songwriter agreement is for you. But if you aren't bothered about getting an advance and you do want to control your copyrights, you may want to go for either a sub-publishing or an administration deal, depending on how much activity you require from your publisher.

CONCLUSIONS

- Decide what type of deal would ideally suit you.

- Decide if you need an advance and, if so, how big an advance – this will help you decide whether to go for a sub-publishing or an administration deal.

- You should try and do deals where your share of the income is calculated 'at source' – but if you have to have a 'receipts' deal then make sure you put a limit on what the overseas sub-publishers can deduct in their fees.

- If you're receiving more than 70% of the gross fees you're doing well.

- Look at the Minimum Commitment. Is it realistic? Can you achieve it within a reasonable period of time?

- If you're a songwriter who doesn't also record his own works, try not to agree to a contractual commitment that means your songs have to be exploited in some way, as this will be outside your control.

- If you're a songwriter who records his own songs, hold out for no reduction in the amount of royalty you receive on 'covers'.

- Make sure there's no delay in you receiving your money from overseas.

5: **GETTING A RECORD MADE**

INTRODUCTION

Just to make life easier for myself, I'm going to assume that you've signed a record deal and that the money for making your record will come from the record company, either as a separate recording budget fund or as an all-inclusive advance (see Chapter 3). At the end of the chapter I'm going to look at other ways of making a record, for example, where you're funding the making of the record yourself, and at new sources of funding.

PRODUCTION DEALS VERSUS DIRECT SIGNINGS

Before I go into the process of getting a record made, I need to look at two different ways of structuring a record deal. This has an impact on how the recording process is organised. We covered direct signings in Chapter 3; now we're going to take a quick look at the alternative, which is a production deal.

PRODUCTION DEALS

It's easy to confuse production with the process of producing a record by a record producer. I'll deal with the latter below. A production deal is one where someone (whether it's an individual, a partnership or a company) acts as a middleman between the record company and the artist. This middleman is the production company.

Sometimes a smaller label or someone who doesn't want a full-time role as a manager finds a talented artist. They may not have the necessary funds to make the record or, even if they can afford to make it, may not have the necessary clout to get decent manufacturing, distribution, marketing or promotion. The label or individual could sign up the artist and then look for a company with more resources to fund the recording and all aspects of putting out the record. In effect, they are selling on the rights they have to the artist's services, either by a licence of rights or an assignment of them.

In either case there is a contract between the production company and the artist called a production deal.

WHAT IS A PRODUCTION DEAL?

The contract may look very similar to a record deal. The production company could sign the artist up to record an album with options to make further albums. The number of options may be less than in a straight record deal, perhaps two options instead of four or five. The money available will often be less than with an exclusive record deal with an established larger record company and, in some ways, may resemble a development deal. The deal may be a 'net receipts' deal as opposed to one where the artist is paid a royalty on record sales. It will also probably say somewhere in the contract that the intention is to try to get another company involved with greater resources.

It's a little difficult to agree up-front what sort of deal will be done with the other company. I usually try to ensure the artist gets the chance to be involved in the negotiations with the third party. After all, the third party needs to know you're on side, so should want to co-operate with you. If the bigger record company is going to pay advances to the production company, you'll want to know that you'll get a decent share of them. Also, if you're on a 'net receipts' deal, you'll need to know that the royalty being paid is high enough when it's split between you and the production company. For example, if you're on a 50:50 net receipts deal and the royalty is 18% then you'll be on a 9% royalty, as will your production company. Maybe your percentage should be higher – 70% or 75% instead of 50:50. If you're the production company you should work out what's a good deal for you and should be looking at getting a clear profit equal to a 3–4% royalty.

WHAT'S IN IT FOR THE OTHER RECORD COMPANY?

The bigger company has the advantage of having someone else find and develop a new artist. By the time the project is brought to them they can hear what it's going to sound like. Some of the risk has been taken away. If they're licensing a finished record from a production company, they know exactly what they are getting. There's also a middleman to deal with the artist – who becomes someone else's problem. One downside for the recording company is lack of control. They need to be confident that the production company can deliver the goods, so they're more likely to trust someone who already has a track record.

WHAT'S IN IT FOR THE PRODUCTION COMPANY?

The production company has a much closer involvement with the artist. It has the thrill of discovering an artist early and of developing them. It gets another company to take the risk on manufacture, distribution and marketing costs, but at that stage it loses control. If the bigger company then fails in what it has to do, all the production company's work will have been wasted. For the production company it's essential they choose a bigger company with a good marketing department, or that the contract with the bigger company allows them to insist on outside press and marketing people being brought in if necessary. If it works, the production company get their costs and expenses repaid, the financial risk on the manufacture, distribution and marketing taken off their hands, and a decent royalty into the bargain.

WHAT'S IN IT FOR THE ARTIST?

If a production company is interested in you then it's a step up the ladder. If they know what they're doing, there will be a second chance later of getting a bigger company involved. There should also be greater artistic and creative freedom, unless the production team are control freaks. The downside for you is that, if you don't get the deal right, you could end up sharing a larger than necessary piece of the pie with the production company. You're also a further stage removed from the record company that's promoting the record, so it's that much harder to get your views heard.

FINDING A STUDIO

Whether you're signed direct or via a production company, one thing you'll have to do is to find a suitable recording studio. It could be as simple as the studio in your back bedroom or as complex as a full-blown commercial studio. Before you decide on a studio you should look at several – at the ambience as well as whether it has the necessary equipment. If equipment has to be hired in, it will add to the recording costs. You should listen to material produced in the studios and, if you can, talk to other artists who have used them. You should also talk to any in-house engineer or producer. How enthusiastic are they about the place and how it's run? If you have a record producer in mind or a favourite engineer, ask them what they think of the various studios on your shortlist.

You also need to think about where it is. Is it easy to get equipment in or out? Is it secure? You'll have seen stories in the press of recordings being 'leaked' from the studio. You don't want to risk that happening to your recordings. Does the studio keep tapes safe and secure, and who is responsible for this?

A studio can either be one that you go to day to day or a residential one where you stay in accommodation at or near the studio. Your own personal arrangements might decide which is better for you. If you have a young baby or are recently married, you might want to be at home regularly. Some bands respond best when they're immersed in the project in a residential studio. For others, the idea of spending 24 hours a day, seven days a week with the other band members is their idea of hell.

STUDIO PACKAGE DEALS

The recording studio may block out a period of time and the studio is yours for the whole of that time. These arrangements are sometimes called 'lockout' deals. Other deals are for a fixed eight- or ten-hour day. If you overrun, you may either find that the studio has been hired out to someone else or that there are heavy financial penalties. Some studios will give you discounts on their usual rate if you record at times when the studio wouldn't normally be in use, for example, in the early hours of the morning. This is called 'down time'. It's fine if you're on a very tight budget or if you just want to record some demo tracks. But if you're planning to use down time to record your whole album, you're putting very great limitations on yourself. It's mentally and physically tough recording an album without adding to this by having to record it all at two in the morning.

Some studios will offer a package deal that includes mixing and mastering of the finished recordings. There are two things to bear in mind here. First, the studio must have the technical capabilities to do a good job and secondly, the price offered should represent good value.

Your A&R man or production company representative is going to be an important source of information on where you choose to record. These people also have a vital role to play in giving you feedback on how the recording is going. It's far too easy to lock yourself away in a studio and become isolated from reality. You'll need feedback and constructive criticism. The A&R man won't be sitting at your shoulder all the way through the recordings, but he will want to visit the studio regularly during the recording process. Don't surround yourself with yes men – you'll need people who can be objective and whose opinion and judgement you respect.

Once you've chosen your studio you need to haggle on a price – or your manager, production company or A&R man will do it for you. Before you book the time, make sure that any people you want to help with the recording, like a producer, engineer or session musicians, are available. If you really want to work with a particular person then you may have to adjust your recording schedule to work around them. If they live outside the UK they may need a permit to work in this country. This can take time and has to be factored into the recording timetable.

Another key factor in the choice of the studio is whether you can afford it. Studio costs and fees to a producer usually make up most of the recording costs. You'll have to recoup these, so it's important that you keep an eye on them.

THE RECORDING BUDGET

When you were pitching for your record deal you may well have done a 'back of an envelope' calculation of how much it would cost you to record (see Chapter 3). Now you're going to have to do a much more detailed budget. You and your manager are going to have to work out how long you think you're going to take to record the album, how many days of studio time and what that will cost at the studio of your choice. You need to know how much your producer of choice will charge, how long a mixer will take to mix it and what he's likely to charge. If there are session vocalists or musicians who will need to be there for all or part of the time, you need to know how much they will charge per day or session. There are minimum rates set by bodies like the Musicians Union and Equity (see Chapter 15), but good people may want more than the minimum rate. If special equipment is required, you need to work out how much this will cost to hire and whether it's more cost-effective to buy it. It may be a piece of equipment that you'll need to have later when you're out on the road promoting the album. You may have an equipment budget as part of your deal or the cost may be built into the recording budget. Another possibility is that you'll have to buy the equipment out of your personal advance.

Don't forget rehearsal time. You don't want to spend expensive studio time rehearsing the songs until you're ready to record them. Do this before you set foot in the studio. Whether you do this in a professional rehearsal room or in a room over the local chip shop will depend on your budget.

Once you've thought of everything you should add 10–20% to it. This is called a contingency. It's to cover extra costs when you spend another day in the studio or on mixing or when you have to hire in equipment because yours or the studios isn't up to the job.

If you have a recording fund deal, your total budget should not exceed about 60% of the total advance to give you enough to live on. If you have a deal where you have an advance plus a recording budget, you'll have to keep within the maximum set by the record company and you'll have to take your finished outline budget to them for approval. Bear in mind that most record contracts say that if you overrun the agreed budget without first getting clearance from the record company, you'll be liable for the extra expense. It will be deducted from your royalties and possibly also from any further advances due to you under the deal.

MASTERING COSTS

These are a grey area. They are the costs that are involved in getting the final mixed recordings into a state ready to be made into records. I'll deal with the process in a little more detail below. The record contract will say whether these costs are to be included in the recording budget or not. Mastering can cost several thousand pounds, so it's important to know when setting your financial budget.

THE PRODUCER

The role of the producer has been described as getting the dynamics and emotion of the music on tape. The producer makes your material come alive. It's possible for you to produce yourself and many successful artists do. By the same token most artists, particularly when they are starting out, might find it difficult to get the necessary distance in order to hear how the music will sound to an outsider. The producer can be your external critic. You're going to be working closely together, so it's helpful if you have similar musical tastes and influences. You have to like working with them, respect them and have a common vision of how the music should sound.

Your A&R man can be very helpful in pointing you in the direction of possible producers. They can do a lot of the filtering process. They may play your demo to a series of different producers to see who's interested. They may invite producers to come to your gigs to get a feel for how you sound. Some vocalists need a little help in the studio in keeping in tune. A good producer will realise that when he hears you play live.

WHAT DOES A PRODUCER GET PAID?

Fee or advance
A producer will usually expect to be paid a fee per track that they produce. This could be a pure fee, which isn't recouped. It could be an advance against the producer's royalty, or it could be part non-recoupable fees and part advances. Good producers can charge £3–5,000 per track and many of those will expect some of it to be a non-recoupable fee. Whether they get that will depend on the negotiation. If it's being recorded in the producer's studio he may add on recording costs.

Royalty
The producers may just work for a fee, but they will often expect to receive a royalty calculated in the same way as your record royalty is calculated. A good producer may insist on a royalty of 4% of the dealer price or 3% of the retail price. They may ask for increases in the royalty if you sell more than a given amount. Producers who work with very commercial acts see themselves very much as key parts of the team and charge royalties accordingly. I have recently seen some such producers charging over 5% of the dealer price.

RECOUPMENT OF COSTS
Another big bone of contention is whether the producer receives his royalty as soon as he has recouped any advance he has received, or if he has to also wait until his royalty, together with your royalty, has also recouped the recording costs on the tracks he has produced. If he agrees to the latter, the producer may say that once that's achieved, his royalty is calculated as if he had been paid from record one after recouping his advance. This may be difficult to follow so let me give you an example:

A producer is to be paid a 3% royalty and has received a £30,000 advance. The recording costs on the tracks he worked on came to £200,000. Your royalty together with the producer's 3% is 12%. Say each record sold makes you £1.25. You'd have to sell £230,000 ÷ £1.25 = 184,000 copies of the record in order to recoup the advances. Say his 3% royalty earns him 31p. To recoup his £30,000 advance he'd have to sell £30,000 ÷ £0.31 = 96,774 copies. If he's on a deal where he's paid retrospectively he would then get paid on the number of copies sold between 184,000 and 96,774 copies, i.e. 87,226 × £0.31 = another £27,040. If you sell 96,775 copies, he recoups his advance and the extra £27,040 but if you don't sell more than 184,000 copies you don't recoup the recording costs and your producer gets no more royalties. So the producer is taking a risk, but if it pays off he gets a windfall.

In the US, the producer is almost invariably expected to have to wait until all recording costs have been recouped. Very rarely do US record companies accept that this should then be retroactive. In the UK it's much more common to have retroactive deals or, indeed, some deals where the producer doesn't have to wait until *any* recording costs have been recouped and is paid his royalty as soon as he has recouped his advance. This is very risky for the artist. You can only really do it if your record company agrees to advance you the cash to pay the producer. You're unlikely to be recouped as you've all the recording costs, video costs and so on to recoup first. This pushes you further into debt, so you're only going to want to agree to this if it's the only way you're going to be able to do the deal and get that particular producer. This is particularly the case with the 'hot' pop producers I spoke of above.

WHO DOES THE CONTRACT?

There is another important difference between UK and US producer deals. In the UK it's usually the record or production company that will do the deal with the producer. They will issue the contract and negotiate its terms. In the record contract it should say whether or not the record company has to get the artist's approval of the commercial terms. At the very least you should have approval of the royalty, because it will usually come out of your royalty, and of the advance, which will usually be a recoupable recording cost.

In the US the artist issues the contract and negotiates the deal with the producer – or his lawyer does. This is, of course, more expensive but does give the artist more control over the terms. It also means that the contract isn't with the record company, but between artist and producer. If the artist doesn't pay, the producer can only sue the artist, who may not have the money. In the UK the contract is between the record company and the producer, so if anything goes wrong the record producer can sue the record company not the artist. This puts the producer in a more secure position. The US record company will usually do the royalty calculation and, if asked, will pay royalties direct to the producer as a favour not as a legal obligation.

REMIX ROYALTY REDUCTION

The royalty to the producer usually comes out of the artist's royalty, so it's in the artist's interests to keep the royalty at a reasonable level. A good record mixer may also want to be paid a royalty. I try and get the record producer to agree that, if the mixer is paid a royalty, the producer's royalty is reduced by the same amount. Some producers will agree to this. Others are adamant that if they've done a good job of production there shouldn't be any reduction in their royalty just because the record company or artist decides to bring in another person to mix the records. If this becomes a real sticking point, it's sometimes possible to get the record company to contribute to the royalty for the mixer, perhaps by paying another 0.5%. The producers who are paid over a 5% royalty do usually agree to this being reduced by any royalty you have to pay to a remixer.

CREDITS

The producer will usually want to receive a credit on the packaging of the record. I haven't yet seen any producers arguing about what happens when the recording is digitally delivered online, but I'm sure that's only because it's not yet considered as a commercial medium. If artwork is also delivered online, as some are suggesting, then this would overcome that issue. If, however, it's a simple click and download of music then it's not easy to ensure that either the artist or the producer is credited. Perhaps it has to be part of the file that is downloaded or streamed.

Sometimes a 'name' producer will insist on having the right to remove his name from the packaging if his work is remixed and he doesn't like or wish to be associated with the end result.

STANDARD OF WORK

Whether it's you or your record company that's doing the contract, you'll want to know that the producer's work will be of a high standard. There will probably be instalment payments to the producer so that he isn't paid in full until recordings of the required standard have been delivered. So what is that standard? Well, just as we saw with record contracts, it's usually a question of whether the producer has to deliver technically satisfactory recordings or whether they have to be commercially acceptable. This is, of course, a very subjective test and the producer may well argue that he has no say in what the artist chooses to record, so it's not his fault if the finished recording isn't commercial. A common compromise is to say that it must be a first-class technical production and of at least the same high standards as the producer's previous productions.

RIGHTS

The producer usually assigns any and all copyright he has in the sound recordings he produces to the artist (US deals) or to the record or production company (UK deals). The recordings may have been made in a studio owned by the producer. In that case there is a possibility that the producer made the arrangements for the recording to be made. If so, the producer could claim to be the first owner of copyright.[1] The record company will want to make sure that it takes an assignment of any copyright the producer may have.

In the US they deal with it slightly differently. There the contracts will say that, for the purposes of copyright, the producer is employed by the artist. Under US copyright laws the artist owns the copyright in anything a producer creates where he is employed by the artist. This is called a 'work for hire'.

The producer may perform on the recordings. He may play an instrument or programme a keyboard. He may therefore have the same rights as any other performer.[2]

---

1 Section 9(2) (aa) CDPA and Chapter 3.
2 See section 191A ff CDPA for performer's rights and Chapter 3 for more details on what these rights are.

The record company will therefore want to know that he has given all the necessary consents to his performances being used. The fee or advance that the producer is paid will usually include any fees for his performances.

If the producer has made any original creative contribution to the writing or composing of the music or the words then he may have rights as a co-author of that song.[3] If the artist and producer agree on what each has contributed this isn't usually a problem. The producer's share may be published by a different publisher from the artist, so the artist will need to know that a mechanical licence will be available on standard industry terms so that his share of that song can be included on the recording. If the artist has agreed to reduced mechanical royalties in the US and Canada (the so-called Controlled Compositions clauses) then the artist should make sure the producer accepts the same reductions. He may, however, refuse to do this and there is no requirement that he do so.

If the producer co-writes a number of the songs on the album, this could affect the artist's ability to fulfil the Minimum Commitment requirements that you may have in your publishing deal. This must also be taken into account when agreeing what share is allocated to the producer. If a producer co-writes the songs, he will have moral rights in his work. The contract will usually require him to waive those moral rights (for more on moral rights, see Chapter 12). If he hasn't co-written any of the songs or isn't claiming any publishing rights, the contract will usually require him to confirm this.

PRODUCER'S DUTIES

In addition to making sure that the production is of the required standard, it's also the job of the producer to try to keep the recording costs within the budget and to let the artist/record company know if it's likely to run over budget. The contract may make the producer responsible for any overrun on the budget that is his fault.

He is responsible for getting all session musicians to complete the necessary consent forms, buying out their rights and getting all the necessary performers' consents. He has to deliver these signed forms to the record company with details of who did what on each recording. He also has to keep all recording tapes safe and deliver them up to the record company when asked to do so. This includes all outtakes, i.e. recordings that didn't end up in the final mix on the record.

One case in which these 'outtakes' then found their way onto a commercially released record involved Bruce Springsteen.[4]

The Springsteen Case

Bruce Springsteen had had agreements early in his career with a record company called Flute. Those agreements had been declared to be void from the outset in a previous court case. As we saw in other cases such as *Elton John* v. *Reed*, this was unusual. Most courts won't declare agreements to be void (i.e. as if they'd never been entered into) but voidable (i.e. could be set aside as to future rights). Because the recording and publishing agreements were said to be void, Springsteen argued that he was the owner of the copyright in all previous recordings, including any outtakes or other unreleased material. He couldn't

---

3 See section 9(2) (3) CDPA on authorship of words and music and section 10 on co-authorship. See also Chapter 4.
4 *Springsteen* v. *Flute International Limited and Others* [1998] Chancery Division.

produce any evidence in court to back up his claim that all copyrights had been reassigned to him, but the court accepted that he was the owner of the sound recording copyright and therefore could control what happened with them. The court decided he was within his rights to claim that CDs containing outtakes of his recordings released by Flute were an infringement of his rights.

While a record company is unlikely to risk upsetting an artist by releasing records containing outtakes while he is still under contract to them, they may not have any such qualms after the end of the contract. The producer will have handed those outtakes over to the record company, so the artist's agreement with the record company should cover what can or can't be done with those outtakes.

MIXING

This is the stage between production (i.e. the recording and capturing of the essence of the song) and mastering (when the recording is made ready for duplication).

The mixer selects from all the various recordings he has of a song those that will be mixed together to make up the final version. He also chooses which aspects to emphasise, for example a guitar part or a vocal might be brought into more prominence.

The producer might do the mix and, as he's been close to the recording process throughout, you'd think he would be best placed for the job. He may be, but very particular talents are required for mixing and sometimes a fresh 'ear' can hear things that the producer and the artist can't.

There are also mixers who take the finished, fully mixed recording and play around with it – maybe changing the rhythm or bringing in elements either sampled from the recordings themselves or from elsewhere. These are called remixers and the resulting recordings are called remixes. When samples are being introduced, you have to make sure that all necessary rights have been cleared and that the mixer has permission to include them (see Chapter 13). Remixes are often done to create a different sound for radio or to play in the clubs.

MIX CONTRACTS

The contracts for mixers and remixers are very similar to (and follow the same format as) producer contracts.

FEES AND ADVANCES

A mixer or remixer will usually only receive a non-recoupable, one-off fee for his work. This can be as much as £10,000-plus for one track to be remixed by a big-name DJ.

Big-name mixers can sometimes demand an advance, which is partly non-recoupable, and partly on account of royalties. The same comments apply here as with producer deals.

ROYALTIES

If a mixer has enough bargaining power, he can ask for and get a royalty of 1% or more.

This is usually calculated in the same way as the artist's royalty. As we saw with producer deals, the artist has to work out if there is enough left for him after producers and mixers have received royalties, whether the producer will take a reduced royalty, and whether a royalty has to be paid to a mixer or if he will take a fee instead.

The same issues apply to mixer deals: who does the contract, whether the mixer gets his royalty only after all mix costs have been recouped, and what standard of work is expected of him.

RIGHTS

As with producer deals, the record company will usually require the mixer to assign any sound recording copyright to the record company. There has been an increase in the last few years in remixers arguing for the right to retain a separate sound recording copyright in their mix. It's possible, if they have added enough original elements or have re-recorded the track as part of the remix process, to create a separate sound recording copyright. I think if I was the artist I would be nervous about some mixers owning a version of my track, and I'd want to have restrictions on what they could do with it. If they wanted to just put it on one of their own record compilations that might be all right. If I were the record company who had paid for the remixes, I think I'd want to own them and perhaps license rights back to the mixers for that compilation.

Mixers don't usually contribute to the creative writing of the song. Some remixers may claim that they have added enough original elements to create a new work. This may be true, depending on what they have done, but more likely they will be said to have made a new arrangement of it and can receive performance income on that version. This eats into the writer's performing income and most publishers will expect it to come out of the writer's share. The remix contract could ask the mixer to confirm he has no interest in the underlying song at all or, as we saw with producer contracts, if he is a co-author, that licences to use their part of the song will be granted without difficulties on usual industry terms.

PRODUCERS AND EXCLUSIVE DEALS

A development that was popular a couple of years ago involved a producer, who was also an artist, signing to an exclusive recording agreement as an artist. As we know, exclusive recording agreements usually allow an artist to perform on other people's records provided he isn't featured. This may not be wide enough for an artist to get as involved in another project as they would like. So they acted as producers not artists and signed producer deals that tied them exclusively as producers of an act. The deal looked very like a record deal and there was a very narrow line before the artist/producer put himself in breach of his record contract. The record contract may also put restrictions on whether an artist can be on artwork for covers, in videos and so on, which could seriously restrict what the artist could do with the other project.

If you're in any doubt at all it would be better to clear this project with your exclusive record company, even if you do end up sharing some of your royalties with them. Record companies are understandably very upset when artists they have signed exclusively and invested a lot of money in go off and help sell records for another record company.

MASTERING

This is part of the post-production process. Recordings have now been produced and mixed to everyone's satisfaction.

The next stage before the recording goes to be manufactured into records is mastering. It straddles recording and manufacturing. It's not just a mechanical process of ensuring all the right digital notes are in the right places. It's the means to give it a final 'tweaking' before the record is released. A person skilled in mastering can make the sound punchier, warmer, deeper or louder. He can bring out details not already obvious. Mastering is a separate process from the mix and needs a different set of ears. Some bands swear by a particular person mastering their records in much the same way as film directors have their favourite editors.

The mastering process helps the recording sound great no matter what medium it's manufactured in – CD, tape, vinyl – and whatever hardware it's played on. I'm sure you can think of albums that sound fantastic on CD but really 'woolly' in the tape version, or ones which sound fantastic played over headphones on your CD Walkman but awful on the car CD player. This could be a problem of the mix, but it's just as likely that someone didn't get the mastering process right.

When mastering a recording, equalising and compression of the sounds gives a consistency from track to track. Have you ever found yourself constantly having to adjust the volume between tracks on a compilation? It's either earth-shatteringly loud or so quiet you're straining to hear the words. That's an example of bad mastering. Radio really brings out the difference, as the radio process itself compresses the material. If a recording hasn't been properly mastered it can sound thin and weak.

When you've spent a small fortune on making a recording, you shouldn't spoil it for a few thousand pounds in mastering costs.

The person doing the mastering is engaged to do the job by the record or production company. He either provides the mastering suite and equipment or the company hires and pays for one. He is paid a fee for his work. The record company usually pays it and, depending on the contract, will either treat it as a recoupable recording cost or as a non-recoupable manufacturing cost. Some, but not all, artists credit the person who did the mastering, although the actual studios used are often referred to on the packaging.

DELIVERY REQUIREMENTS

There are a number of things that have to be delivered to the record company before you are said to have completed your side of the recording process.

As well as the finished, fully mixed and edited recordings, you will also have to deliver up all outtakes and all copies of the recordings. You may also have to deliver finished recordings of additional tracks to act as B-sides or second tracks on singles, and will definitely have to deliver up all signed session forms and clearances for any samples that have been used in the recording.

You'll have to deliver a list of all the tracks on the record in the order in which they appear (called a track-listing). You'll probably also have to provide 'label copy', that is all the information that has to appear on the label and packaging of the record. This includes things like who performed on each track, who wrote each track and who publishes those writers. If you've agreed to give credits to producers and mixers or a name check to the studio, then you'll have to give those details to the record company. This is also when you get to say thanks to particular people who have been helpful or supportive.

The contract will be very specific about what has to be delivered and to whom. It will also be quite technical about the form in which it wants the recordings delivered. It's very important that you do deliver all that is required of you. If you don't, then you'll find that all sorts of things don't happen. You won't get the instalment of advances due on delivery, the manufacturing process won't start nor will time start running for when the record company has to release the record.

You should try to get written confirmation from the record company confirming that everything has been delivered from the person identified in the contract as the person to whom delivery has to be made, for instance, the senior vice-president of A&R.

If you can't get that then you may have what is called a 'deemed acceptance' clause in the contract, i.e. if you deliver to the right person all the things you're meant to and they don't tell you they haven't accepted the recordings within a given period of time (about 30 days usually) then they are said to have accepted them and can't get out of it later.

If that isn't in your contract then you may have to just look at the circumstances. If you delivered all you had to by 26 March 2002 and they paid you the delivery advance on 5 April and mastered the album on 12 April then it's reasonable to assume that they'd accepted that delivery had taken place by 12 April at the latest and arguably by 5 April. However, I have had a record company try and argue that a record had not been delivered and had not fulfilled Minimum Commitment even after it had been released and had entered the Top 20 album charts. A swift notice of breach of contract quickly helped them to see sense.

ARTWORK

One key item that usually has to be delivered is the artwork for the cover of the album. Without the artwork the record can't be released, so it may be reasonable to assume (depending on the contract and individual circumstances) that delivery has not taken place until the record company has the finished artwork. The record company usually wants the artwork delivered in a specific format, which these days is often either online or on a computer disc.

Some talented bands do the artwork themselves. Some leave it to the record company's art department. Most hire someone else to do a design to their brief or specification.

If you're relying on the record company to do it, try to make sure you have final approval. If you're bringing in someone else, make sure they have a good, professional reputation for their work. Look at covers you admire, see who designed them. Interview a few designers and ask to see examples of their work. Do you get the feeling they understand what you want and what, if any, message you're trying to convey? Remember that if a potential customer doesn't know who you are, they may be attracted to pick up your CD over all the others by the striking artwork on the cover. You could use art students or friends to do it on the cheap, but then you could end up spending a lot of time supervising the work and would have been better off using a professional in the first place.

If you have a logo make sure it's on the artwork. This is all part of making the package look inviting and identifiably part of your image. You have to use it to rise above the masses; indeed, these days, striking artwork and logos repeated on your website and in any other marketing and promotional materials not only make the association easier – they also help to brand you and to make your work stand out from the crowd.

Once you've decided on a designer who you think can do a good job in the required time, you need to agree terms with them. You need a contract setting out what they are going to do, by when and for how much. If they are VAT registered they'll need to send you a VAT invoice before you pay them VAT on top. You may want to make payment in two instalments, one when they start work and the other when they deliver finished work that is satisfactory.

If photographs are to be used, you need to agree who is going to be responsible for supplying those and at whose expense. The record company will usually organise and pay for a photo-shoot, but it may not necessarily be with the top-name photographer you'd like to use.

Whether or not there are to be photographs, you need an agreement with the designer or photographer that confirms you're the owner of the copyright in the photographs and the copyright and any design rights in the artwork and graphics. There should be an assignment to you of any copyright or design rights they might have acquired. Ideally, you should have the right to do what you want then with those designs and photographs. However, designers and photographers are now wise to the fact that they can earn more money if you have to go back to them for permission to reuse their work. For example, they may now agree to license the artwork or photo to you for your album cover only. If you want to use it on a poster, T-shirt or other merchandise, or as a backdrop on your live stage shows, then you'll have to come back to the photographer or designer for further permission. If they give it – and they don't have to – then they will probably want another fee for it.

The cost of commissioning someone to create original artwork depends on who you use, but record companies don't usually want to pay more than about £2–3,000. The record company doesn't usually have any rights to use the artwork in any form of merchandise other than sales of the album, so they will only be interested in getting album cover rights. If you think you'll want it for other purposes, you'll probably have to pay for those yourself.

Whether you commission the designer or the record company does, it's usually the record company that pays and has rights to it – albeit if only for limited activities. The cost is usually non-recoupable and the record company will usually give you the right to use the artwork for other purposes, for example, for merchandising, if you repay to the company 50% of the origination costs. The record company may not automatically get this right off the designer, so you need to say in the contract that he must do so.

The value that attaches to a distinctive artwork design was highlighted by the application for an injunction made by Creation Records (Oasis's record label) against the publishers of various newspapers, including the *Sun*.[5]

---

5 *Creation Records Limited v. News Group Limited* EMLR 444 1997 16.

The Oasis Case

Oasis was going to release another album in the autumn of 1997 and decided that the photograph of it should be taken at a country hotel. Noel Gallagher, the lead guitarist and deviser of the band's artwork, had a particular idea in mind, a kind of homage to The Beatles and their cover of the *Sergeant Pepper* album. The hotel swimming pool was drained and a number of different objects were delivered to the hotel, including a white Rolls-Royce. This was lowered into the pool at an angle and Noel Gallagher supervised how the other objects were to be placed. A professional photographer took a number of photos from various angles so that the band had a choice of different images in different lights. Oasis thought it was essential that the plans for the photography were kept secret, and only a few people were allowed in on it.

Inevitably, perhaps, word leaked out and a couple of newspaper photographers turned up including one freelancer attached to the *Sun*. One of the photos he took was published a few days later in the *Sun*. It was very similar to the one chosen for the album cover, but had been shot from a different angle. The *Sun* offered copies of the photo for sale to readers in a poster form. Although other newspapers also published photos it seems none were very clear and none were offering posters of them for sale.

Creation got an immediate injunction restraining the *Sun* from publishing any more photos or from offering copies for sale. The judge then had to decide if that injunction should continue.

Creation Records were arguing that the freelance photographer had infringed their copyright or had breached confidence.

The judge rejected the argument that the way the scene was put together attracted a copyright as a dramatic work. He also rejected the argument that the *scene* was a work of artistic craftsmanship, a sculpture or a collage (those lawyers were trying hard, weren't they!). A film set can sometimes be said to be a work of artistic craftsmanship, but the judge decided that this was just an assembly of disparate objects without the necessary element of craftsmanship.

Creation Records and Oasis might have been thought to be on stronger ground in arguing that there was copyright in it as an artistic work of collage – being a collection of unrelated items. Their barrister argued that it should be put in the same category as the infamous Carl André bricks displayed at the Tate Gallery or Gilbert and George's living sculptures. The judge declined to follow that line of argument, as the assembly of objects didn't have the same degree of permanence – it was going to be dismantled after a few hours. This is a very restricted view of what would be entitled to copyright protection.

The judge did find that there was copyright in the photograph, but the *Sun* didn't copy that original – the freelancer took his own photograph of the same scene. Which was why Creation Records was trying to establish some kind of copyright in the scene.

So, having failed on all their ingenious copyright arguments, the lawyers then argued that the freelance photographer had breached confidentiality. Here they had more luck. The judge decided that any reasonable person would have assumed that, in viewing the scene, they were getting confidential information and so the freelance photographer was obliged not to photograph the scene. The *Sun* had admitted their photographer had to get around a security cordon to get the film out, so they must have known it was intended to be confidential.

On balance, the judge decided Oasis/Creation Records had more to lose if the *Sun* were to continue to be allowed to sell posters and continued the injunction on the basis of breach of confidence. If he had not then potentially huge sales of posters and other merchandise by the band and their record label would have been lost.

Once your artwork is delivered you should then be in a position to press for a release date for the album. This will depend on a huge number of factors, some of which I'll deal with in the next chapter, but once a provisional date has been set then the manufacturing process can begin and the whole marketing department should swing into action.

CONCLUSIONS

- Choose your studios well. Decide if they'll be residential or not.

- Set a reasonable recording budget and stick to it.

- Get the best producer and mixer you can afford.

- Don't skimp on mastering costs, but keep an eye on remix costs, as these can get very high.

- Check you've complied with the delivery requirements in your contract.

- Try to get copyright ownership of the artwork.

6: **MANUFACTURE, DISTRIBUTION AND MARKETING**

INTRODUCTION

Until about five years ago there was no serious viable alternative to the tried and tested method of distribution. You finished your record, it was mastered and 'cut' – literally cut into the vinyl or digitally mastered, (i.e. put in digital form in a computer program from which digital records such as CDs and DATS could be made). The only discussion or change here was digital versus analogue manufacturing methods. Once you had your physical CD, tape, vinyl record or whatever, you packaged it up and it was distributed out to the record stores on the back of a van.

This traditional method still accounts for more than 95% of record sales. In 1998 it was predicted that within five years there would be substantial growth in online sales and online distribution. The 'clicks and mortar' versus 'bricks and mortar' argument. The availability of music free over the Internet via digital distribution has undoubtedly had an impact in the commercial arena. It has led to considerable problems of piracy and, for some, a reduction in the value of music. However, as a viable alternative to physical distribution, it still has a long way to go. As we'll see below, online mail-order sales have increased significantly and perceived cost savings have resulted in an amalgamation of the warehousing and distribution networks of several of the major record companies. EMI pulled out of distribution in 2002 and it was estimated that it could save £10–20million a year if it pulled out of manufacturing and another £10million if it got out of distribution. Someone recently pointed out to me that by pulling out of these two traditional means of earning profits the record companies are focusing their money-making activities on the more risky aspects of the process, the marketing and promotion of artists and their records. So the stakes will be higher in future to get those expensive aspects right more often than they do at the moment.

MANUFACTURING

For at least the foreseeable future the compact disc is going to be around, although the annual sales growth has slowed to practically zero and, in the third quarter of 2002, album sales saw a year-on-year 15% drop in numbers. Cassette tape sales are declining, but the prediction of the death of vinyl was premature. It survives (albeit in a niche market), beloved by DJs and specialist collectors. There has been more of a struggle to establish the physical format of minidisc. It was first launched in the early 1990s but singularly failed to impress. However Sony, who had developed it, refused to let it die – in the late 1990s there was an attempt at a relaunch as more products became available in this format, and the price of players fell below £150. For all its portability and good sound quality, it still only represents a tiny fraction of the market in music sales. A potentially much more serious threat to the music business is the phenomenal increase in sales of recordable CDs (CDR). Originally intended as an alternative to the floppy disc, it's now being used to 'burn' copies of whole albums or favourite compilations. Many systems are being trialed to try and 'copy-prevent' albums to allow a maximum of one copy to be made, but it remains a big problem. These issues are discussed in more detail in Chapter 14 on piracy.

When the excitement over the Internet was at its height, social commentators argued that people would always want the experience of going into retail stores, of handling the product, enjoying the social interaction – if you can count being jostled in a queue for ten minutes as enjoyable social interaction. So far they've been correct, as retail record stores aren't disappearing – but they are evolving. Retail margins are very tight and with their high-rent high-street locations, retailers are responding to the pressure of the Internet, CDRs, MP3 files and all the other distractions from traditional record purchasing by becoming places that people want to visit, where the experience is pleasant and where the customer can get what he wants. There are already a number of stores that have machines in-store where you can select your CD or series of tracks that are stored digitally on a central computer server. The customer's selection is downloaded, together with appropriate artwork, and 'burned' on to a CD. The artwork is printed off and the customer has his very own CD to take away. What this might lead to is that no record ever goes out of stock or is deleted. As it can be stored digitally and reproduced on demand, it won't take up valuable space in warehouses and can be available within minutes. At the moment, though, it remains just a sales gimmick. The latest 'must-have' is the DVD – again, the result of greater availability of the players at an affordable price and more product. This product is still largely of film/TV series but there is a growing market for the music DVD, usually offering tracks or versions of hits not previously available.

For the purpose of this chapter let us assume that the record is going to be reproduced in a physical form, say as a CD. How do you go about this?

If you've paid for the recording yourself or via a production company then you won't have a record company to organise the manufacturing for you. You're going to have to go to specialist CD manufacturers and shop around for a deal. Lists of manufacturers can be found in the *Music Week Directory*. Before you decide on a manufacturer, you'd be well advised to gather together as much information on what is available as you can. You also need to make your arrangements with manufacturers at least four months before you intend to release your record, and even longer at popular times such as Christmas. This is to ensure that the manufacturing/pressing plant has capacity and won't squeeze your record out because a release by a big star is slotted in for the same time.

In addition to questions about their availability, you need to ask what service each company provides. Is it a full-service company that will produce a production master from which to reproduce the CDs, or will you have to find a company to make a production master for you and deliver that together with film or discs for the artwork to the manufacturer? If so, would it be cheaper, easier and quicker if you looked for a full-service company? You'll need to check the small print very carefully. What hidden costs are there? Do they charge you to deliver finished records to you?

What other services can they provide? Can they offer a distribution service or any marketing services like sales teams? If they do, is it better to use them for these services or to look for separate companies to do them?

Look at the quality of their work. Ask to see samples. Do they do everything in-house or is it farmed out? Who else do they work for?

Once you've narrowed down your choice you have to look at how quickly they can turn things around. They may have a minimum production run (say 5,000 copies). Is that all right for you or were you looking for a more modest 500 copies? To be honest, if you're going for a very short production run, possibly of a demo, you might be better off burning the CDs and putting the finished product together yourself.

Once you've decided on your manufacturer you'll need to agree a price, the number of units to be produced and a time for delivery. You ought to try to keep some of their fee back until you see things are running according to plan, but if you're a small unknown company they're likely to want cash up-front. Even so, keep an eye on things. Check the quality of the sound and of the artwork. Is the running order correct without any gaps in the songs? Have all the names been spelled correctly and correct credits given? If anything is wrong pull them up on it immediately. Don't wait until they've finished the run. This can also apply to major record companies. I learned recently of a release by one of the major companies that had the name of the artist on the back of the sleeve printed incorrectly. You'd think they'd know their own artist's name wouldn't you? Always check a sample of the finished product.

You also have to be sure that they can continue to manufacture repeat orders as your first batch, hopefully, sells out. You need to keep close contact between your distributor and your manufacturer so that you can put your repeat order in as soon as your distributor sees stocks are dwindling. This need for close co-operation is one of the reasons why some people prefer to keep production and distribution with the same company.

P&D DEALS

As you can probably guess, 'P' stands for production (i.e. manufacture) and 'D' for distribution. A P&D deal is one that combines both of these services in one contract with one company. Companies that offer P&D deals can often also offer marketing services like a telephone sales team (telesales), a strike force (a specialised team targeting record stores to take your records) or pluggers, who try to persuade radio stations to play your record. Whether you want these additional services will depend on your overall marketing plan and on the price and reliability of the service.

You should ask the same questions of P&D companies as you would of a manufacturer, but you'll also have to ask another series of questions about their distribution operation. Who do they supply records to? Is it just the small specialist stores or can they get into the major retail chain stores?

MAJORS VERSUS INDIES
Until recently, all the major record companies had their own distribution facilities. Mergers in recent years have resulted in some of those facilities being combined to save costs by pooling operations. Some independent distributors like Vital have also pulled out of distribution. Clearly, the risks are outweighing the possible profits from this activity. Without an efficient distribution system, all your talents and efforts in making the record and the marketing people's work in getting you noticed will mean nothing if the distribution company doesn't have the records in the stores for the public to buy.

All distributors have to also balance efficiency with a speedy response. If they can't meet demand quickly, your records won't be available, the customers won't be able to buy them and you won't get your chart position. Missing a week in the charts can be fatal.

The majors tend to manufacture their records locally and then shop them to a centralised depot, usually somewhere in Europe, and from there to local distribution centres in different countries. It doesn't take much thought to see how savings could be made by pooling the local distribution centres.

As well as dealing with their own artists' records, some of the majors act as separate distribution companies for other companies' records and other products, such as books and mobile phones.

Small companies are likely to either use specialist distributors or use the facilities of one of the majors. Other, bigger independent distribution companies, like Pinnacle and 3MV, are big enough to have their own warehousing and distribution set-ups. Contact details are in the section on Useful Addresses.

In the late 1990s it was thought to be a good marketing ploy for some 'credible' artists to be seen to be released on independently distributed labels. These distributors had their own chart and the artist could maintain the fiction that they'd not sold out to the majors. As the music business moved away from indie to more commercial pop music, this need to be seen to be on an independent distributor faded away, and the viability of independent distributors was severely tested.

If you aren't signed to a major or can't get a deal with a major distribution company, you may not have any alternative but to go to an independent distributor.

You also need to be aware that some smaller distributors are a bit like production companies and pass on the job of actual distribution to another company. You should ask if that's what your chosen distributor does; if it does you should try to find out how reliable and financially stable that other company is. As we'll see below, there are some things you can do to protect yourself by retaining ownership of the records until you've been paid.

CATALOGUE OR SINGLE ITEM DISTRIBUTION DEAL

You could do a deal for all the records you're likely to produce in the next year or so. These are called 'catalogue deals' and would be suitable for a small record label or production company. They would also work for a company that was going to license in rights to records by other artists, and also for an artist who has decided that he doesn't want or need the facilities of a record company and wants to distribute his own recordings. In recent months, some very successful artists have seriously considered bypassing record labels altogether and doing it all in-house. Management companies, such as the US-led The Firm, have made a splash in the UK by saying that they, as managers, will supply or outsource many of the facilities presently offered by record companies such as press, plugging and so on. If this were followed through to its logical conclusion, record companies would become little more than finance houses, possibly useful only for their initial set-up. However, it will take a 'name' artist to do this successfully before we could expect any more general changes to the system. There was a point in the Robbie Williams negotiation where it seemed that he wouldn't sign to a major but would set up his own label and do various deals around the world. It was reported in the press that his management had met with several manufacturers and distributors and had called in the major retailers to discuss plans for the release of the next album. However, at the end of the day he did re-sign to a major, EMI.

If you aren't doing a catalogue deal, you could just give distribution rights to a single track to a distribution company. You might choose this route if you were just seeing this release as a stepping stone to getting a record company interested in you. Just bear in mind, though, that if the distributor is only dealing with one track for you, you'll not have much bargaining power and will have to push hard to ensure that you get any kind of priority.

EXCLUSIVE VERSUS NON-EXCLUSIVE

Catalogue distribution deals are likely to be exclusive, but there may be one or two exceptions to the exclusivity. For example, you could have the right to put tracks on compilations to be distributed by another distributor or a major record company. Or you could have the right to distribute small quantities of the records yourself to one or two specialist outlets.

Non-exclusive distribution deals are less common, but might be used if you wanted to use one specialised distributor to target certain specialised outlets while keeping the right to also put your work with a more mainstream distributor or to sell records online over the Internet.

TERM
This is really only relevant for exclusive catalogue deals.

The distributor deals with all of your product over a period of time. This could be open-ended, continuing until one or other of you gives notice, usually three months at least. Other possibilities are a fixed period of one year with the distributor having the option to extend the term for another year, or the term could be for one year with further one-year extensions unless you give notice before the end of that time that you don't want it to carry on. You have to be careful with this one because, unless you're very good at remembering when to give notice, you might miss the relevant 'window' and find yourself locked in to another twelve months.

If you think you might want to move your label and catalogue at some point to a bigger distributor or major, the more flexible the term is and the easier it is for you to get out of it will be important. It could also be very important if you aren't sure how good the distributor is. On the other hand, the distributor might have greater commitment to you and be more inclined to give you priority if they know you're going to be with them for a pre-determined minimum period of time.

TERRITORY
The distribution deal could be a worldwide one, but is more likely to be for a limited number of countries, for example just for the UK or the UK and Europe. If you're a UK artist or label looking to distribute your records beyond Europe (say to the US) then you're much more likely to do it through licensing the rights to another record company with its own distribution set-up (see Chapter 3). It's possible to have deals where you ship finished records to them and they distribute them, but this is less common. They are sometimes referred to as 'consignment' or 'sale and return' deals.

There is a problem, though, with distribution deals for just one country, for example the UK, and that is imports or, more particularly, what is often referred to as parallel imports. What are these? Let's take an example. You have the rights to distribute a particular track in the UK. Another record company has the rights to distribute the same record in France. If the record is released in France first, the French record company could export the records into the UK, where you risk them taking your market from under you. You may think that wouldn't be allowed as they only have French distribution rights. Ah yes, that's right, but there is the principle of a common marketplace throughout the European Union (EU), which is meant to encourage the free movement of goods. So, within the EU, it's illegal for you to outlaw these imports. You can tell the UK distributor that he isn't to actively try and get orders from outside the UK, but it's very difficult to police it. How do you know who approached who?

It's easier, in theory, to prevent parallel imports coming in from outside the EU. For example, if you were giving one UK distributor European distribution rights and licensed the rights to a record company in the US for North America, your contract with the US record company could specify that they aren't allowed to ship records outside North America. The problem is that there are specialised exporting companies who also act as genuine domestic distributors. The US record label could legitimately sell records to such a company and then deny any knowledge or responsibility if that company then exports the records to the UK.

This is why there is a lot of pressure to ensure that a record is released simultaneously in as many countries as possible, or to ensure that there is something special about the release. For example, Japan, which has suffered badly from cheap imports, often insists that releases in Japan have extra 'bonus' tracks to make the records more attractive to the domestic market than the imports.

There is also pressure on price levels within the EU. The idea is that if the dealer prices are the same throughout the EU, there is less demand for imports brought in cheaper than the domestic product.

There are, of course, new issues to be addressed by distributors as a result of the possibility of buying records online. If this is ever to be a commercially viable market-place for the music industry then these issues will have to be addressed on a wider basis than the parochial, domestic solutions that have been the norm so far. The Internet is a global marketplace and one challenge is to try to find new ways of dealing with the fact that it's one big territory. Suppose you had a distribution deal with one company in the UK and another with a company in the US. Your licence deal with each would have to say either that it was open house on export sales and both could offer records for sale on their websites, for purchase anywhere in the world, or you could limit the territory to the UK/US and put it in each licence that they aren't to solicit offers or to fulfil orders from the other's country. For example, your email address is UK registered and you go online to try to buy a CD of an album that you know has been released in the US but isn't yet on sale in the UK. If you went to a US website to try to buy the CD they should refuse to accept orders for distribution outside the US. This solution is potentially off-putting for the consumer, which is the last thing anyone wants. Obviously, if you'd done a worldwide distribution deal with one company then that wouldn't be necessary. It may be that any solution to this territorial issue will have to be addressed by one-stop deals or reciprocal agreements between distributors in different countries. They could, for example, agree to pay each other a percentage commission for sales generated in the other company's territory. So far we're seeing some attempts at reciprocal agreements for licensing via MCPS and PRS, but international co-operation between record companies or distributors is taking longer.

Downloads off the Internet are another challenge to traditional distribution deals. If you store a recording in digital form on the Internet, there's no need for you to have large warehouses; the recording is made available to the consumer in the form of a computer file on demand. If there isn't a worldwide distribution deal in place then the same restrictions would have to be in place to stop a company accepting orders from customers outside their territory. Record companies and music publishers are now investing large amounts into systems called rights management systems that will police where a file is being downloaded to ensure that payment is being made, and which would also enable them to track whether a distributor was breaking the terms of his distribution licence but, as we'll see in Chapter 7, these systems have not yet delivered a fully workable solution.

RIGHTS GRANTED

If you're doing a P&D deal you'll be required to give the distributor the right to reproduce the sound recording[1] and the right to distribute and sell those copies.[2]

PRICE

The distributor will take a fee off the top of the price they get paid. So, for example, if the distributor gets paid £7.49 for each record sold, they takes a percentage of that as their fee.

The percentage can vary a great deal depending on how many additional services they provide, for example, a telesales service or a strike force dedicated to pushing your records. It can be as high as 28–30% of the dealer price if you're unknown or only have one track to distribute. Deals of 15–18% or less are available to successful independent companies with a high turnover of successful product. Major record companies will usually pay distribution fees in single figures. Sometimes the percentage the distributor gets as a fee goes down as the turnover increases. An average amount for a distributor to charge would be 20–23% to independent record labels or artist production companies.

The distributor will also usually have a discount policy. This is a sliding scale of discounts on the dealer price that have to be given to the various retail outlets. For example, major national chains like Woolworths or Virgin Megastores would be able to command a discount on the price because they order in bulk and are such important outlets for the music. Supermarket chains such as Tesco and Asda are also now in this category and, indeed, often undercut the high-street chains to their great consternation. You'll have little or no say in these discount rates, nor have a chance to change them. However, you should know what they are in order to check you're being paid properly.

PAYMENT TERMS

The distributor will often pay half of what is due within 30 days of receiving the payment from the retailers and the balance within 60 days. So if they get paid for a record sold

1 Section 17 CDPA.
2 Section 18 CDPA.

on 28 February, the label gets half of their money by the end of March and the rest by the end of April.

The distributor will probably keep back some of the money as a reserve against records that are returned. They usually have a fixed policy on this, but will sometimes negotiate the level of reserves. The reserve on singles is generally higher than for albums unless the album has been advertised on television. Retail stores may take copies of your record on a sale-or-return basis. So although the distributors have sent out, say, 1,000 copies, they don't know how many have actually been sold and won't include these copies as sales until they've been paid. They keep back a reserve against these returns and any other returns that appear to be sales (i.e. they've been shipped out but may be returned to the distributor for some legitimate reason such as being damaged or faulty). The distributor has to hold back money against such an eventuality.

The distributor won't usually take responsibility for bad debts. It also won't usually pay out before it gets paid, because that can lead to big problems. For example, a P&D deal is done with a local distributor who agrees to pay out on the number of records it actually sends out, less a reserve against returns. It ships out 1,000 copies of a record to the retail stores and pays you on 750 copies, keeping back a 25% reserve, before it has received payment of the 1000 sales. Months later, the stores return not 250 but 500 copies; the distributor is then out of pocket by 250 copies and will look to you to pay it back. Even worse for the label is the case where you do a deal with a local distributor who pays you on what they get paid. They do a deal with a bigger distribution company and ship records to that bigger company. The bigger company sells those records but, for whatever reason, fails to pay the smaller distributor, who can't then pay you (even though records have been sold) because they haven't been paid for them.

RETENTION OF TITLE

A way of protecting yourself when you're in a chain of deals like the one described above is to retain your title (your ownership) of the records until you've been paid. These sections of the contract have to be very carefully drafted in order to have a chance of working. Assuming the bigger distribution company has gone bust, the liquidator of that company will want to hold on to whatever stocks, i.e. records, that he can. He'll want to sell them to raise money for the creditors of the company, so he'll want to get around the retention of title if he can legitimately do so. Specialised legal advice is needed on this.

ADVANCES

Before I leave this section, I just want to touch on the question of advances. Will a distributor give you an advance? Well they might if you've got a good track record for finding hit records or have a catalogue that has a regular turnover. The advances for small independent labels or individual artists aren't likely to be high – possibly only a few thousand pounds. I have, however, seen advances of £20,000-plus for suitable small-label catalogues and, of course, if you were an established artist almost guaranteed to sell a million records, then the level of advances you can ask for is as significant as if you were doing a record deal. As with most advances, these sums aren't usually returnable if you don't sell enough records, but they are recoupable from monies you would otherwise receive from sales.

MARKETING

Once you've got a record mastered, copies manufactured and you've found a company to distribute it, another crucial step in the process is to let the public know about you and your record. The marketing process has many elements to it and it's an ongoing process. As soon as you've got something to sell – a record, live performance, merchandise – you need to let people know about it. This is often referred to as 'getting yourself heard above the noise'.

ARTWORK

Getting the right artwork for the record is crucial – it should form part of the whole campaign. It could be used as the backdrop to a stage show and on a poster campaign. It could appear on T-shirts and other merchandise. Make sure you own the copyright in the artwork and that there are no restrictions on what you can do with it.

PHOTOGRAPHS AND BIOGRAPHIES

You're going to need to have some decent photographs. They'll be needed for information packs, for the press, for letting overseas licensees or associated companies abroad know what you look like. Get the best photographer you can afford or that your record company will pay for. The costs the record company pays aren't usually recoupable or repayable by you unless you want to use the photographs for merchandising, for example on a T-shirt or poster, when they may expect you to repay half the costs.

The record contract will usually give you approval over which photographs of you are used. It will also usually give you approval of the official biography that is put together about you. This is a bit like your life history – how your life so far is presented to the outside world. If you're sensitive about any part of your past or of giving your true age, it could be useful to have approval. It also ensures that a consistent message or image is presented of you, which forms part of your brand, as we'll see in Chapter 8 on branding. I have a client who has a life-threatening illness and, while happy to campaign for greater awareness of the condition, doesn't want it to be the only message that is sent out. For people like this the question of approval is very important.

If you give the record company photographs or biographical details they will assume you've approved them, so make sure you're happy with them.

IN-HOUSE OR EXTERNAL MARKETING

Most big record companies will have in-house marketing and press departments. These are staffed by dedicated marketing and press people, one or more of whom will be allocated to marketing you. You need to be sure that these people understand the gameplan and, preferably, that they love your music. At the very least they should like it, because otherwise they won't sound convincing when they try to sell you to the press, radio, TV and so on.

If your marketing is to be done in-house it will normally be paid for by the record company on a non-recoupable basis.

The position changes if you're with a smaller company without its own in-house marketing departments, or when you just can't get on with the in-house people and insist on using outside specialists. The costs are then usually partly or wholly recoupable from your record income.

Whether it's being done in-house or with a number of outside specialists, the whole campaign has to be co-ordinated.

The sales force and any special strike force have to be primed with artwork, photographs, biographies and campaign details. Promotion packs have to be sent out to any exporters, to clubs, DJs and to some retail outlets.

The fact that your record is being released has to be notified to the music press, to the chart compilers and to MCPS/PRS to get the relevant mechanical licence and details registered for when the record is performed publicly. Each release has to have its own catalogue number. I once acted for a label called Produce Records and their catalogue identity was MILK 1, 2, 3, etc.

Each record released also has to have a barcode to enable it to be scanned through checkouts in the stores. The barcode is also used to register sales for purposes of compiling the charts. The BPI (see Useful Addresses) can give you information about how to go about getting a barcode.

If you're going to do special promotional items to accompany the records sent out for promotional purposes, these have to be designed and manufactured well in advance. There have been some very innovative and just plain cute gimmicks produced. EMI handed out lemon-shaped squeezy toys to promote a single by Pocket Size called 'Squashy Lemon Squeezy'. It sits in my desk drawer and is a great stress-release toy.

The adverts for a co-ordinated advertising campaign will have to be designed and approved well in advance so that they're ready for distribution at the same time as the promotional packs, posters, promotional items and so on.

The strike or sales force goes into action several weeks before the release date, trying to get orders from the retail shops. These are called the 'pre-sales'. Everyone is interested in getting these figures, as they're a good indicator of how well a particular record is being received. It will help determine the chart position, it tells the marketing people how much more work they have to do, and pre-sales can give you some information to pass on to your manufacturer and distributor to help them assess how many copies of the record will be needed. The figures may also tell you in what areas of the country the record is selling best, so the distributor can know to make more copies available in those areas. If the release is by a big artist, the retailers may be invited to a preview run-through of the album (called a 'playback') to excite their interest.

The aim is to get the campaign to run as a seamless whole. You'll be needed to do interviews until you're bored of the sound of your own voice. Your press people should be setting up reviews of your records and any live dates that you're doing to promote the record. You may be doing personal appearances and perhaps performing a couple of numbers, either live or mimed to a backing track.

TV ADVERTISING

Part of the marketing campaign might be to advertise your records on television. This is an expensive business. A basic television campaign in four ITV regions can easily cost between £60,000 and £100,000. The record company is only going to want to spend this money if they think they will earn it back in extra record sales. To keep their risk to a minimum, the record company will try and recoup some or all of these costs, either as a further advance or by reducing the royalty payable to you. How this works is that the record company reduces by 50% the royalty they would otherwise have had to pay you on sales of your records until they have recouped (from that reduced royalty) 50% or more of the costs of the TV ad campaign.

We lawyers try and get you the right of approval over whether an advert is made but have to fight for this, as record companies know if you get the right of approval you'll only give your approval if you get a better deal on recoupment. Then they don't recoup so much of the cost. If we can't get you approval we try to limit the ways in which your income is affected, either by restricting the reduction to sales in the country where the campaign is run, or limiting the time over which they can recoup the costs from reduced royalties, or both.

Don't rule out the idea of a television campaign without carefully looking at the proposals. A good, targeted campaign could be what it takes to lift your record into the Top 20 albums chart, which could make all the difference to you being a megastar or just an artist who once had a record out. However, be aware of the cynical attempt to reduce royalties to you when your record has been particularly successful by rushing out a cheap TV campaign in the same accounting period as your album was released and achieved most of its sales. By doing this they can halve royalties on *all* sales in that accounting period even if they were before the ad campaign. Don't think this is fanciful. One of my colleagues found that a major record company was trying to do this with an artist who had had a very successful debut album. A TV campaign wasn't needed and the lawyer and manager had to fight hard to get a deal whereby the royalties were not artificially reduced.

TV AND RADIO PLUGGERS

It's absolutely crucial to the success of a record that it gets exposure on radio and TV. Unless your record gets a decent number of radio plays, it's unlikely to enter the charts. A Top 20 chart position can get your record on to programmes like *Top Of The Pops* and included on multi-artist compilations.

The people who decide what is played on Radio 1, Capital Radio, Kiss FM and other pivotal regional radio stations are very powerful, and some feel that the records chosen for the playlists are towards the commercial pop end of the market. There was a big problem a couple of years ago when 27-year-old artists were being thought of as too old! Now, however, Radio 2 has stepped into the gap, picked up many of the ex-Radio 1 DJs who had been influential opinion-formers and given them shows. Those who had grown up with these people gravitated to Radio 2, which has become much more the station of mainstream commercial releases by older artists as well as middle-of-the-road tracks by younger artists. Now, ironically, for many releases failure to get on the Radio 2 playlist is a kiss of death.

The TV and radio pluggers who have the tough job of trying to get records playlisted are either employed in-house by the record company or are from outside agencies who specialise in this work. Their costs are dealt with in similar ways to press agents (see below).

WHAT DO YOU PAY EXTERNAL MARKETING AND PRESS PEOPLE?

There are many different ways of paying for external marketing and press work.

Remember, if you aren't using in-house people, some or all of these costs will be down to you.

Retainers
Press people and pluggers could be on retainers. These are regular, monthly payments that are made to keep them as your press agent, constantly having an eye on press opportunities for you. When you aren't actively doing any promotion, for instance when you're in the studio recording the next album, the level of retainer could be quite small. It would then increase when press/promotion activities rise around the time of the release of the record. However, as the economy slows down and competition among these companies hots up, the incidents of people on retainers has declined and now many are only paid when they actually do some work.

Bonuses
If someone is on a retainer or a fixed fee they may be paid a bonus for achieving certain targets. For example, a press officer could get paid a bonus for every front page/cover he gets that features you.

A plugger might get a bonus if a record goes into the Top 30, 20, 10 or whatever.

Fixed Fees
Marketing and press people could be on a fixed fee, possibly with bonuses linked to success.

Royalties
Press and pluggers could be on a retainer or a fixed fee with bonuses. Good pluggers and those in great demand (usually the same ones) can insist on 'points', i.e. a royalty (usually 0.5–1%) on each record sold. If you want the best you may have to pay this. It will either come out of the artist royalty or be paid by the record company, or a combination of the two.

WHERE DO YOU FIND THEM?
The usual ways – word of mouth, those companies already on a retainer arrangement with your record company, those companies known to your manager as doing a good job in this area of music. The *Music Week Directory* carries a list of press and promotions companies, but it would be a good idea to get a recommendation from someone in the business before you choose one.

DO THEY WANT A CONTRACT?
If they're on a fixed fee they will probably just invoice you for the fee when the work is done. If you've agreed they'll undertake something out of the ordinary, or you're putting them on a retainer, you'll probably want a simple contract. If they're being paid a royalty you'll definitely need a contract setting out how that royalty will be calculated and when it will be paid. The simplest thing is to do this on the same basis as you get your royalties under your record deal.

VIDEOGRAMS

Promotional videograms are an essential part of the marketing process. A good video can get your record played on TV music stations like MTV, which is powerful in making a record a success. There are also Breakfast TV and Saturday morning TV programmes that look to play videos, as well as all the cable and satellite channels.

However, videos are very expensive to make and there's no point in making one if your record doesn't get radio plays or TV airtime. It will be a waste of money. The video has to fit in with the overall marketing plan. You'll end up paying some or all of the costs, so be careful you don't overspend or make a video unnecessarily.

The creative elements such as what the story is going to be (the storyboard), who's going to produce and direct it, and when and where it is to be shot will probably be agreed between you and your record company. Depending on your contract, you may have a final say on some of these things and the record company on others. There's a significant increase in the use of DVD as a marketing tool, using extra elements from the normal CD or promotional videogram; possibly an interview with the artist, footage from the last tour or of the making of the album. The costs of these and how recoupable they are are normally dealt with in the same way as for long-form videos, but there can be complications if some of the elements are owned by the record company and others are owned by the artist or a third party (for example, live footage, photos, interviews). In such cases I can only recommend you get specialist advice.

RIGHTS

The record company will usually expect to own all rights in any audio-visual recordings of your performances. There are complications where they haven't paid for or don't own the copyright in all the elements on the video or DVD.

If you have a lot of bargaining power, you can limit the rights you give them to audio-visual rights on recordings you make for them under the record deal. Most major record companies won't give you this, as they want to know that if someone makes a recording of your live set they can't then put it out as a competing record or video. You might have to agree that you won't do that with any recordings of your performances without their approval.

LONG-FORM VIDEO

This might be a compilation of your best promotional videos or it might be a specially made 30-minutes-plus video, maybe of you out on the road touring, or live performances intercut with interviews and so on. DVDs are a good example of how to combine excellent visual elements with sound and the convenience of digital recordings for the consumer.

The record company may have the exclusive right to make long-form videos, or they may have the first option to bid for the right to make one, or the right to match an offer that someone else may have made to make one.

The cost of making a long-form video is usually mutually agreed between you and the record company and a separate account is set up. You usually get to dictate, or at least approve, all the creative aspects of the long-form video.

The royalty rate will be similar or slightly higher than that for promotional videos. There may be an advance payable for the long-form or the record company may have had to match any offer made by a third party. The advance and the costs should only be recoupable from the royalties on this long-form video. Income from records or any commercial use of promotional videos should not be used to recoup these costs.

EPQs

This is the name given to electronic press packages. That is pre-recorded interviews, photos and biographies, together with promotional clips of your latest single release, that are put together by your in-house or external press officer. These take the form of videotapes or DVD and they're sent out to reviewers, press reporters, DJs, radio station controllers and so on as an additional means to promote you. Some companies are now sending them out as file attachments to emails. Most new record contracts contain a clause that says that the record company can put one of these together and that you'll co-operate with them. There seems to be no reason why you wouldn't want to agree to the compiling of an EPQ, but you might want some creative control and you'll need to agree whether some or all of the costs can be recouped.

CONCLUSIONS

- Decide on whether you need separate manufacturing and distribution deals.

- Check the returns and discounts policy of your distributor.

- Try to retain ownership of your records until you've been paid.

- Get your marketing campaign organised well in advance.

- Agree whether your press and plugging is to be done in-house or by outside agencies.

- If outsiders are doing press or promotion, try to get the record company to agree that only 50% of the cost is recoupable.

- Get approval of any photos and biographies.

- Get approval, if you can, of any television advertising campaigns for your records – particularly if your royalty will be reduced.

7: NEW MEDIA / E-COMMERCE

INTRODUCTION

By the time the first edition of this chapter was published most of it was already out of date. The area was developing so quickly it was impossible to keep up. Respected new-media publications such as *Revolution* moved to weekly issues and still struggled to keep pace. However, the craziness of the early years of music online has calmed down and developments aren't as swift as they were three years ago, as the area settles into a more established pattern. As we'll see below, many of the early predictions have not come to fruition and many problems still remain to be solved.

OVERVIEW

The whole area of exploiting rights online opened up a potential new marketplace and a number of new distribution and marketing opportunities for artists and labels.

It also brought potentially far-reaching changes to how we view music and whether it should be made available free of charge. It has also given the lawyers a number of knotty legal problems to sort out. Some of these, such as the issue of protection of copyright online, are being addressed by the major nations, but the problem of piracy and territorial issues remain problematic.

As I sat down to write this chapter in 1999, Time Warner had announced its merger with America Online (AOL). This was seen as a revolutionary yet, at the same time, obvious move because Time Warner had the content through its various music, film and TV companies, and the bandwidth through the cable companies it owned. AOL was meant to bring to the deal its vast customer base and access to enormous numbers of potential purchasers of this content, with a brand name that had consumer trust and loyalty. When it was announced, some analysts started talking about this being the deal that finally burst the over-inflated bubble of Internet stock prices.

As we now know, the whole area of e-commerce and Internet business suffered a painful reality check with the withdrawal of venture capital funding and the subsequent collapse of the stocks. It was, however, a reality based on a mirage. While a few canny souls made money and got out with actual cash, most were paper millionaires. On the ground many lost their high-paid jobs and have retreated back into the jobs they had before the dot.com boom or into re-education. With industries which grow rapidly and then suffer a setback, it's the businesses with an innovative idea, a solid business plan and a good management team that survive. I don't believe Internet businesses are any different; they've just had to learn to survive in more difficult circumstances than they might have imagined in the early, glory days when money seemed no object.

In June 2001, Music Business International featured an article on EMI and other record company mergers. It showed a picture of Eric Nicoli and Ken Berry of EMI reporting 'pleasing' 2001 results. Within six months Ken Berry was out and in the last twelve months EMI's share price has fallen to dramatic lows. MBI itself didn't see the year out.

Other players instrumental in the growth of online businesses, such as Thomas Middleton at BMG and Messier at Universal, have themselves lost their jobs. Their roles in some of the more innovative developments in the business are discussed below.

Companies other than EMI have emerged as vulnerable. Vivendi, who acquired Universal, is heavily burdened by debt and looking to off-load assets – not including its music assets at the moment, but it may only be a matter of time. BMG have just negotiated their way through what was an expensive option deal with Clive Calder of the Zomba group, which would make Calder even more wealthy but is supposedly also paving the way for a German stock-market listing for BMG. Whether that will happen in the current market conditions seems doubtful. The feted AOL/Time Warner merger has also hit the buffers, with record losses, share prices tumbling and investigations into alleged accounting irregularities.

Middleton's fall from grace was dramatic, and it's a measure of how one's perceived successes can turn on you that in 2000 he was being lauded for doing a deal with the peer-to-peer file sharing company Napster. As we'll see, two years later Napster was declared bankrupt and BMG was denied the right to purchase the assets by a US court.

Three years ago there were three main areas of concern: the effect on existing 'bricks and mortar' businesses, piracy, and making money from the new media. These areas have been addressed with varying degrees of success, but all remain of concern.

REPRODUCTION AND DISTRIBUTION

Let's look first at how the Internet has brought us new ways to reproduce and distribute music. As we saw in Chapters 5 and 6, until very recently the only way of doing things was to make recordings of an artist's performances (now mostly in digital form), which were then mastered and distributed as physical copies, tapes, CDs and so on. The phenomenal growth of the Internet as a means of making music available in download-able form has led to us thinking more and more that non-physical means are the way forward. There was a belief that the traditional forms of tape or CD would quickly be replaced by computer programs and the downloading of computer files containing music to our PCs. It hasn't happened that swiftly, but gradually music is becoming available through our home entertainment systems in our living rooms through the remote control. Burning favourite tracks on to blank CD-Rs is another worrying trend for the industry (see Chapter 14 on Piracy) and the huge capacity of DVDs may be the next challenge for both the film and music industries. Domestic recordable DVDs at an affordable price were made available in the stores at Christmas 2002.

The process of digitising sound recordings and then compressing them, using technologies like those associated with the MP3[1] format, makes it possible to distribute a near CD-quality digital sound recording online over the Internet. Depending on the equipment, it takes just a few minutes to download a single track on to your PC. It still takes an unacceptably long time to download an album and up to 5 hours for a film but, as compression technology[2] and bandwidth[3] improves, so the quality will also improve and the download time will shorten considerably. At the moment, few want to tie up a computer and, more importantly, an expensive telephone line for the time it takes to

---

1 MP3 = MPEG 1 layer 3 compression technology.
2 MP4 is already with us and telecommunications companies are busy developing other compression formats.
3 Bandwidth is the 'pipe' down which the digital signals are sent to the personal computer.

download a whole album. It's not yet a friendly consumer experience and until it's quick, user-friendly and reasonably priced it won't take off commercially. For the time being, therefore, it remains a reasonably small market dominated by pirate products. When telephone charges are cut and technology improves so that an album can be available quickly, then there will be a potential commercial market for this material.

In 1999/2000 there were a great deal of gloomy prophecies about the end of the retail sector, of the high-street shop, the 'Mom and Pop' store as the Americans call them. The major retail chains were very concerned about this perceived threat to their business. Respected analysts such as Jupiter predicted about 5% of the retail business would be done online. Although this was still only a very small percentage, it was enough for the retailers to foresee their own demise. In fact, although the retail sector has suffered pressure on its profit margins, this is largely as a consequence of wider economic issues and not as a result of online sales stealing their market.

The online sales market represented 10% of UK album revenues in 2001.[4] Companies like Amazon, which are still making huge losses but are supported by their investors, offer music and video as a key component of their marketing, but the prime method of sale isn't the digital downloads that the retailers feared but traditional, mail-order sales. There is still significant consumer resistance to buying online. As we shall see below, there are serious difficulties of piracy that act as a block on the development of a market in legitimate downloads, and companies are struggling to make money out of them.

There has been consolidation in the retail and distribution sectors. The major record companies have pulled out of distribution, striking deals with distribution specialists like THE. Even independent distributors such as Vital have pulled out of distribution, concentrating instead on their sales service. Retail chains such as 'Our Price' have re-emerged as V-shops. HMV, which was an early adopter of in-shop kiosks for burning CDs, have quietly withdrawn from that as an area for current development.

As the growth of Internet-driven sales has come from mail order not downloads, the expected savings in warehousing/storage costs have not been as big as had been anticipated. The regulators put brakes on potential mergers, preventing some of the cost savings that many company bosses hoped these mergers would bring. The record companies who now use third parties to distribute their records may have made some savings, but these have not so far filtered through to the artists. Instead, deductions now include 'back-end fulfilment charges', to cover matters such as credit card fees and anti-piracy methods.

There was also talk that the savings that companies would make by making music available online would lead to savings for the consumer. This also hasn't happened. CD prices remain as high as ever and, as yet, record companies are struggling to get consumers to take up their online offerings in big enough numbers to make them viable.

PIRACY

Three years ago, the second area of concern was that of piracy and that remains a very serious worry. Piracy has always been a problem for the music business with CD, tape

4 BPI Market Information June 2002.

and video copying a huge business in the Far East and former eastern bloc countries (see Chapter 14 on Piracy). While people appreciated that the Internet facilitated easy large-scale copying, the industry had almost accepted that they would have to deal with that type of piracy in the same way as they had to throw resources at preventing physical-format piracy and at strengthening international copyright and anti-piracy treaties.

What was not immediately appreciated by many was the impact of the Internet on home copying and small-scale illegal copying. Most European countries have, for some time, permitted limited home copying and many have various forms of taxes and levies on blank tapes. In the US, the Home Audio Recording Act also permitted limited copying, but encouraged record companies to include devices to prevent multiple copying. These activities were not seen as threatening to business.

MP3
The potential scale of home copying was not brought home to the record companies until compression programs became readily available. There were several types of these, but the one that became the best known was MP3. Michael Robinson, the founder of MP3.com, capitalised on the new technology by setting up systems that allowed customers to copy their CDs in MP3 format to be downloadable either to play at home or on MP3 players for use in mobile players or in-car. MP3.com was sued by all the major record companies and several artists, was found to have infringed copyright and ordered to pay significant amounts in damages. Ironically, the last of the major companies to hold out for a settlement was the Universal Music Group (UMG). In July of 2001, UMG bought MP3.com and continues to run it as part of its core music business, despite the departure of Messier, the charismatic UMG chief executive behind the acquisition. It has, however, expanded the marketing aspect of its activities and is still looking for a satisfactory business model.

NAPSTER
Another major problem was Napster, Inc. File-sharing software was made available on a central server that enabled users to see which other user had music in MP3-compressed form that they wanted to hear, thus enabling the two to link up and share new music. This became known as peer to peer (P2P). At its height Napster had up to 60 million users a day and was thought to represent a huge threat. The relatively harmless home copying by individuals was now available on a massive scale. The Recording Industry Association of America (RIAA) on behalf of the record companies as well as some artists, issued proceedings and obtained a preliminary injunction suspending the activities of Napster until it could satisfy the court that it had removed all material that was not authorised for copying. They were found to have facilitated illegal copying by the individual users. They were subsequently ordered to pay significant amounts in damages. In the meantime, Thomas Middleton, the Chief Executive of BMG, did a deal to invest $85 million in Napster, Inc., to create a legitimate subscription-based model. Since, as we've seen, Mr Middleton has also now lost his job, the parallels with MP3.com are clear. The difference is that Napster didn't survive the damages award; the suspension of their services drove people who were used to being able to easily swap music for free to switch to other P2P services like Gnutella and Morpheus, which had developed systems that didn't rely on a central server, making it much more difficult to attach liability to one source. Napster,

Inc. was declared bankrupt in 2002 and the court prevented BMG from buying its assets. In November 2002 an offer by Roxia, a media software company in which EMI has an interest, to acquire the intellectual property, such as its patents, but not, significantly, the liabilities of the company, is under consideration by the bankruptcy court.

ANTI-PIRACY DEVICES

As their well-publicised actions against MP3.com and Napster showed, RIAA and the music industry generally took the view that attack was the better form of defence. Many believe that in doing so they alienated consumers. Indeed, there was some initial evidence that Napster-style file sharing led to an increase in legitimate sales of music. In the last year, however, the UK has seen a 15% drop in the value of music purchased and worse is feared. Several methods have been used to try to either control the problem or to harness it to make money.

Considerable resources have been put into anti-piracy devices such as watermarking and ways to track the copying of music to control it or ensure proper payment. In the 1990s, the Secure Digital Media Initiative (SDMI) was hailed as an industry-backed secure system to control illegal copying. In fact, the creators of the SDMI system offered a reward to anyone who could crack it. Predictably, such is the power of the Internet to harness resources and minds, some computer programmers did so within 48 hours. The SDMI has quietly disappeared from view. Other ideas included a system of permanent and temporary 'passwords' on computer files, which only allow one copy of a file to be made and played on a legitimate player. Making one copy destroys one of the passwords and if you then try to copy it again, the copy won't play because the player can only find one of the required two passwords. Other systems are in development as the feeling is that, while computer whizzes and organised pirates will always find ways of bypassing these systems, the average consumer prefers to have legitimate material. Whether this will hold for under-20-year-olds brought up on Napster and free music isn't yet known.

LEGAL DEVELOPMENTS

On the legal side, laws have now brought us firmly into the 21st century in confirming beyond legal doubt that the rights of a copyright owner extend to duplication or broadcast online. In Europe this was confirmed by the European Copyright Directive, which should be implemented into UK law in 2003. In the US it was done by the Digital Millennium Copyright Act 1998. Both pieces of legislation were the subject of intense lobbying. Internet service providers (ISPs) sought, and largely got, protection from liability for illegal material not within their control. In most cases the ISP is now only obliged to do something once it's brought to their attention. Until it has been given notice it has no liability. This was at least in part to deal with the result of a German case against an ISP.

The CompuServe Case

In an attempt to try control the content of a website, a court in Germany brought a criminal case against the general manager of CompuServe in Germany for unlawfully allowing pornographic material to be available on a website hosted by CompuServe.[5] He

---

5 *Bavaria v. Somm 1998 (unreported).*

was convicted in May 1998 on the basis that as controller of the ISP he was responsible for the content of the websites using that ISP. Naturally, this was of concern to those people who ran ISPs, who were afraid that they might be laying themselves open to a criminal charge. They said that it was impossible to monitor the content of all the websites on their ISP. In practice, what they will usually agree to do is to close down a website if a lawyer or a court has told them officially that the site they are hosting contains pornographic or other unlawful material.

Concern has also been voiced as to how you treat 'transient' copying, i.e. technical copies or reproductions made as a side effect of say, sending an email from computer to computer around the world. Again, the EU Directive confirms that this copying isn't a 'reproduction' and therefore not an infringement of copyright.

To support the efforts of the anti-piracy brigade, the legislation makes it an offence to circumvent, or make available the means to circumvent, devices intended to protect copyright. The details are quite subtle and how, precisely, they will be implemented in the UK is still not known, but a concern is that this will prevent access to non-copyright, public-domain material or prevent the use of copyright material for fair dealing purposes, for example, legitimate uses for education, comment or criticism. The freedom of speech lobby continues to be very vocal on the subject.

NEW BUSINESS MODELS

RECORDING ROYALTY EQUIVALENTS

One of the consequences of the easy availability of free music has been a devaluing of music and its creativity to the point where the young are unwilling to go out and buy music. This has meant that it's very difficult to find business models that work financially for both the consumer and the copyright owner. We've seen a number of different types: micro-billing, where download costs are added to your phone bill; per-download, pay-per-listen charges, which are still popular with some of the majors; and, the most popular, some kind of subscription system, where a regular payment secures delivery of music to the subscriber online.

However, there is severe price-resistance to setting the subscription fees at a level that still makes sufficient money for the record companies. As we'll see below, there are also concerns about how the artists are to be accounted for for these uses, as most record deals still don't envisage this business model and older record deals didn't touch on this at all. This is still a developing area, with most major record companies moving to accounting to the artist on a percentage of what they receive from these uses net of costs. Percentages as low as 30% and as high as 70% have been seen, with many settling on a 50:50 split. Some record companies are still working on a royalty basis, using the price they receive as the price on which they calculate the royalty. These companies are the same ones that try to cover some of their R&D costs as well as the online equivalent of packaging charges by deducting back-end-fulfilment charges. Royalty rates of 14–16% have been quoted. This could result in significantly less money for the artist than a percentage of net receipts, depending on the percentages of course, so a calculation of how much the artist will get in his pocket will be useful for comparisons.

There are also still serious concerns as to how to track the uses so that the artist gets paid properly. In order to win over the artists, there will have to be a transparent tracking system so that the artist feels comfortable that he's getting paid for these uses where the record companies are getting a payment. It's still a very small source of income at the moment, but this is precisely why it's worth getting it right now before it becomes big business and methods get too entrenched.

The challenge for us lawyers will be to see how we can ensure a fair balance between what the record company or the website company gets to keep and how much is paid through to the artist.

PUBLISHING INCOME

So far I've looked mainly at sound recordings. Songs are, of course, also a very valuable aspect of online usage of music, so there should also be a payment for the right to reproduce the underlying song. As we'll see in Chapter 15, where details of the new licence schemes are given, it's clear that the collection societies are trying to be flexible in their attitude to this new medium, and are trying to strike a balance between encouraging a new source of income and obtaining a fair return for the use of their members' copyrights. The trouble is that it took a long time to get these systems in place and, in the meantime, people were having very creative ideas but were unable to deliver them legally because the licensing system wasn't there. Some went ahead without a licence, thus making it now quite difficult to police. One godsend for the publishers is that, in fact, most of these businesses have not survived the dot.com crash.

All these arrangements will probably be subject to frequent review until the new medium matures into an established method of selling music. Most of the licences are terminable at short notice. Also, international deals are only in place in principle at the moment between the various collecting societies to enable a one-stop service. If you're broadcasting a webcast that can be received in more than one country, you'll have to check whether you have to get a licence for each country until truly reciprocal arrangements are in place.

ACCOUNTING SYSTEMS AND TAX

So far I've touched on questions of security and how payment is being made for copying, distributing and communicating music to the public. What about collecting the money? At the moment, various companies are looking at tracking systems for accounting worldwide, but no internationally acceptable system is yet in place.

The whole question of how e-commerce is to be taxed is also fraught with difficulties, which are, thankfully, outside the scope of this book. If you intend to venture into online distribution you should take specialist tax advice.

MORAL RIGHTS

Another issue, which may gain in importance with digital copying or distribution online, is that of moral rights (see Chapter 12). If a song or a recording can be digitised it can also be digitally manipulated, possibly by the end consumer or by the record company. Some artists are very sensitive about their work being altered in any way, and for these artists lawyers have to be careful to try to protect the integrity of that work as far as we can. One of the ways is, of course, through the assertion of moral rights. These rights are often waived or excluded in contracts, so it's therefore important in this area to make sure any moral rights that are waived are replaced as far as possible by contractual protections.

MARKETING ONLINE

OFFICIAL WEBSITES

The Internet has proved to be an excellent means of marketing the 'brand'. Brands that are Internet-savvy can link their online marketing efforts with those of their record company and their own efforts in terms of live work. We've seen artists like Robbie Williams successfully sell out a concert in minutes when tickets were offered for sale on his website. This activity enabled him, with permission, to create a database of committed fans keen to learn more about what he was planning. He had a ready-made mailing list and, in some cases, provided new customers for the inner sanctum on his website where selected information and exclusive tracks or visuals are made available for a small fee. Other artists use websites to communicate directly with their fans.

A couple of years ago we were very concerned to ensure that artists retained ownership of their domain names and official websites. The major record companies were seen as the bad guys, trying, unfairly, to exploit the new media for their own profits. This issue still exists in that record companies still have to convince some of us that they should automatically have rights to distribute music online when they don't even seem to have a gameplan in place for how to use them. However, the low level of legitimate sales by record companies online and the sensible attitudes of the majors to how these websites have been used have calmed some of the fears. Many major record companies now don't insist on ownership of all variations of the artist's domain name and, even where they do, they provide links to the artists or fan-club sites. Most will now agree that their ownership and controls only last during the term of the record deal and will make arrangements for transfer of names at the end of the deal.

Record companies have in some, but not all cases, proved that they have the resources and skills to create interesting, even dynamic websites. Sometimes they are better at this than the artist. Artists sometimes insist on ownership of domains and websites and then do nothing with them, or are initially enthusiastic but then don't maintain and update the website. This can do more damage than not having a website at all.

A well-linked campaign, on the other hand, can be very effective. If all promotional material contains a website address and that website is vibrant and informative, you create a receptive audience for the marketing material you want to get to potential consumers.

SMS

Another area of marketing that was in its infancy three years ago and has now taken off is SMS (short message services) text messages on mobile phones. Text messages to fans are now a key point of many artists' marketing plans. Mobile ring-tone downloads are also a popular form of generating revenues, but as the technology improves so too do concerns of piracy and illegal downloading of copyright materials. One point to note on this is that they have not taken off in any significant way in the US, where mobile phones aren't as popular as in Europe. In the US marketing is still focused on PC or hand-held computer devices so, until these are combined with mobile phones, a global marketing campaign needs to take these cultural differences into account.

WEBSITE DESIGN RIGHTS AND COPYRIGHT

An artist may decide to employ someone to design his website. The website is likely to be made up of many different elements, all of which could be the subject of copyright or other legal protection.

The website will have words that, if original, could be a literary work with its own literary copyright.[6]

The website will no doubt have visual images or graphics. These could be still photographs, moving images, or film. Each of these could have its own copyright.[7]

The website will be made up of a number of computer programs. Computer programs are also protected by copyright.[8]

The designer will have copyright in the original design drawings. He may also have a design right.[9]

In this area of the music business, there was a tendency in the late 1990s (particularly in the US) to register a patent in a particular aspect of a website or an innovative use of computer or compression technology. If you feel you've created something that could be capable of patent protection you should take advice from a specialist patent lawyer.

When commissioning someone else to design a website, you have to make sure that all rights have been cleared for use in the site design, so that you have all the rights you need to do what you want with the website. You also need to find out whether these rights have been 'bought-out' for a one-off payment or if there is an ongoing obligation to pay for the use. It's possible that in order to use the music or a sound recording you'll have to pay a royalty or further fee.

If the person commissioned to design the website is your employee then you'll own the copyright in their original work,[10] but the other rights may still have to be cleared.

If you ask someone who isn't employed by you to design the website, you must make sure that you take an assignment from them of all rights in the website. You could make this a condition of the commission fee, or it could be the subject of a separate fee, or occasionally a royalty. The designer may grant the right to use the work only on the website and not, for example, to print design elements from the website and sell them separately as posters or otherwise as part of a merchandising campaign (see Chapter 8 on branding). These additional uses could be the subject of a separate fee.

Assignments of copyright should be confirmed in writing.[11] A written agreement also establishes what rights you have and on what terms. It should contain a confirmation from the designer that he has all the necessary rights from third parties for the use of any or all elements of the design.

---

6 Sections 1(1) (a), s 3(1), 1(1)(b) and 5(1) CDPA.
7 Sections 1(1) (a), 4(1) (a) and (2) CDPA.
8 Sections 1(1) (a) and 3(1) CDPA.
9 Sections 1(1) (a), 4(1) (a) and Part III CDPA.
10 Section 11 (2) CDPA.
11 Section 90 (3) CDPA.

HOSTING AGREEMENT

Once you have the website, you need to find a way to make it available to others via the Internet. You could become your own ISP, set yourself up with the necessary Internet capacity to launch your own site and provide that service to others. This isn't, however, the way that most artists get their website on the Internet. More usually, they arrange to have the website site 'hosted' by another ISP. Anyone going down this route should have an agreement with the host ISP setting out the kind of service that will be provided and at what cost. These agreements are called 'hosting' agreements.

If you're trying to establish yourself as having a website to which your fans and potential customers return over and over again, you need to know that the host will supply a reliable service. We all know of systems where the hardware on the server 'goes down' on a regular basis. These sites get a reputation as being unreliable and people are less likely to go back to them. Fans, or potential fans, won't bother to go to a website that's never available or which is difficult to use. The first is the fault of the server, the second that of the designer – both are your problem.

The hosting agreement should insist that the server will be functioning properly for at least 95% of the time. It should provide compensation if the server is 'down' for more than an agreed percentage of the time or for more than a maximum agreed number of hours a day.

If the website is to be used to sell merchandise online, you'll need to know that any credit card payment facility is 100% secure. The ISP should guarantee this in the hosting agreement.

The ISP should also be able to supply a reasonable amount of 'back office' support. These are the support staff who are there to process orders, keep the databases up to date and provide technical support. These are also sometimes referred to as the fulfilment centres.

The ISP should agree in the hosting agreement to provide regular, detailed information on the number of 'hits', i.e. visits that are being made to the website. This is the information you need to establish who your fans are and who's likely to want to buy records, merchandise, concert tickets and so on.

The website becomes your one-stop shop window on the world. Its design and reliability will say a lot about you. A good website will enable you to target your likely market with greater precision.

DATA PROTECTION

It's important that you try to retain control over the website and of the domain name (the address) that leads people to the website. If it's owned by your record company during your record deal make sure you have a say over what it contains and whether you can have your own site alongside the record company's official one.

The band name is a key element in the branding of the band (see Chapter 8). Successful branding means that you not only get to sell more records but also merchandise, membership of your fan club and tickets to your concerts.

Obviously, the record company has an interest in the sales of your records. As we saw in Chapter 3, the record company is likely to be either owner of the copyright in the sound recordings or at least an exclusive licensee of the copyright, with similar rights to those of a record company with exclusive sound recording rights.[12] It therefore makes sense for you to co-operate with your record label and their ISP. The website could be linked to other websites by artists on the same record label and vice versa, or with the label's own main site. It makes sense to co-ordinate efforts.

If you're putting together data on people electronically, you have to register with the Data Protection Register (details are in Useful Addresses). You can't do what you want with the data you collect. You have to get permission to use it for a purpose other than that for which it was collected. You'll have seen this in magazine adverts for a particular product. If you send off for that product you'll be asked to fill in a form with your details. The product owner may want to try to sell you other products that he has in his range, or to sell his list of customers and their product preferences to another company. He can't do this without your permission. There is often a box on the form that you have to tick if you *don't* want your information to be used in this way. This 'negative' consent technique is lawful, and is being adapted for online use, although the Data Protection Registrar is apparently in favour of you having to tick a box if you *do* want more information rather than the other way around. You'll often find a box that has to be checked or unchecked to block your information being used in other ways. If you're compiling a database and you don't comply with the rules on passing on information you can be fined.

The Data Protection legislation extends to information held in hard-copy form as well as electronically. The Data Protection Act 1998 came into force on 1 March 2000. The Act also implemented the Database Directive.[13] A key tenet of the Directive is that information held on an individual should not be sent to a country that doesn't have adequate protection in place to keep personal information confidential.

If, however, these data protection hurdles are overcome, a database of consumer profiles and information is a valuable asset. If you own your domain name then, subject to anything to the contrary in the hosting agreement, you'll own the data collected in relation to that website.

HOW DO YOU MAKE IT STICKY?

One of the big challenges of marketing online is to make sure that fans come to a particular website and, once they have found it, come back to it over and over again. Phrases are bandied about as to how you get more 'eyeballs' (visitors) and whether the website is 'sticky'. The design of the website is, of course, crucial. It should be eye-catching and user-friendly. The text used in it should be designed so that it features prominently in the first twenty websites that come up when key phrases are used to search for information using one of the search engines like Yahoo, MSN or Excite. This is an art form in itself and specialist web designers should be used.

The website should be regularly updated. The ISP host should be able to provide regular access to a webmaster who can help to put the latest news online.

The website should be easy to view. The key information should be available without having to go through several 'click through' layers. It should all be on the home page – the first page a visitor to the website sees.

12 Section 180 CDPA.
13 European Union Directive on the Legal Protection of Databases.

The website should be different – it should have something that will raise it above the general 'noise' online. It's all very well if you're David Bowie or Prince making your records available online. Just by saying you're doing it, your name (or brand) is well known enough to guarantee you press interest. If you're Joe Bloggs trying to get noticed, you have to be more innovative.

BEING DIFFERENT

In October 1999 I received my first e-demo. The band put together a package that consisted of a brief biography of the band members and a sample of their latest demo. It was simple and to the point. It also had the advantage of being the first one I, and perhaps many others in the UK music business, had received. If for no other reason, that made it memorable.

REACHING THE FANBASE

The Internet is a great means of reaching your fanbase. Someone jokingly said to me that, in future, bands might call themselves the equivalent of Elvis.com to make themselves supremely marketable in this new medium. Well, it's already happened. In autumn 1999 the band Marillion released an album called Marillion.com which is apparently the same name as their website/domain name.

The Internet can give you a profile of your fans, of where they live and what about you and your website interests them in particular. This may, in fact, surprise you and make you change your marketing plans. If you're doing a countrywide tour you could email your known fans in each town that you're visiting to drum up support and ticket sales beforehand. You could use the local fans to spread the word for you among their e-pals. They'll probably be delighted by the personal involvement with you.

CONCLUSIONS

- Artists should try to own their own domain name.

- Piracy is a major problem.

- While the Internet is a very valuable marketing tool, the commercial opportunities are still in their infancy.

- If you commission someone to design your website, make sure they give you ownership of all the various elements of it.

- There is no standard set as yet for what artists should receive in income from online sales of sound recording. This means the whole question is open to negotiation on a case-by-case basis.

8: **BRANDING**

INTRODUCTION

In this and the following chapter I'm going to look at the whole area of branding: first by looking at merchandising deals, at how you get a trademark and at the benefits of building up a reputation in your name; and then, in the next chapter, by looking at sponsorship deals.

Branding is the way in which you use your name, logo and reputation to build up a particular image in the public mind. You may think that this isn't relevant for an artist just starting out in the business. It's true that new artists are going to be more concerned at getting that first record deal than in worrying about their 'brand'. However, you only have to look at many of the boy and girl bands, and at the image-making that surrounds TV artists such as Hear'Say, Liberty X, Will Young or Darius and some of the more successful US artists like Britney Spears, to be able to see that putting a bit of thought into branding even at its simplest level can pay big dividends. Not everyone can be or wants to be the next Gareth Gates, but all artists should think about getting some of the basics of branding right from the beginning. It can be as simple as getting a good, memorable name and registering it as a domain name. With those two small and cheap steps you've already started to establish a brand.

Branding is big business and becoming bigger. The growth of online activities on the Internet has added to the commercial outlets for the brand. The proliferation of 'reality' TV series means that getting your image or brand right assumes an even greater importance. At its most straightforward, building up an artist's name and reputation helps to sell more records and concert tickets. At its more sophisticated, a name, reputation and public image can help to sell other things, not necessarily ones that involve music. Artists like The Spice Girls used their names, likenesses and the 'girl power' image to sell everything from crisps to soft drinks and sweets.

This idea of branding isn't anything new. All successful companies have invested a lot of money in the company name and logo and in establishing name recognition for their products. Think of Heinz, Sainsbury's, Coca-Cola or McDonald's. Companies such as Virgin turned branding into an art form. Sir Richard Branson realised the value in the Virgin name, in the fact that the consumer immediately recognises it and the familiar red and white colours. By putting that recognition together with a reputation for being slightly anti-establishment, he got consumers to buy into almost everything that the name was linked with. A healthy dose of self-publicity from Sir Richard himself kept the name and the brand in the public eye.

With nine out of ten new artists failing to make a significant mark on the record-buying public, the strike rate of the record business is appalling. The record companies rely on excellent marketing to achieve one or more hits, and some more moderate hits to keep them going. Getting the marketing campaign right is therefore crucial if you're to have a chance.

Since writing the first edition of this book, there's been an explosion in the number of bands that have been put together as a result of TV competitions and auditions on programmes such as *Popstars,* which spawned Hear'Say (who did well initially but in October 2002 announced they were splitting up). The runners-up on that programme were Liberty, who, as a result of an unsuccessful court case (see page 5) had to change their name to Liberty X. They continue to enjoy international success. Then there was the *Pop Idols* phenomenon, where the public had to telephone in to vote for their favourite contestants. The final had a remarkable audience of about 8 million voting for Will Young and Gareth Gates. Who cares who won? Both have gone on to No. 1 chart success and have toured with other finalists, including Will Young singing a number at the Queen's Jubilee concert at Buckingham Palace.

As I write, a new programme is airing on BBC1 called *Fame Academy,* which is a cross between the reality TV programme *Big Brother* and a *Pop Idol*-type talent contest. I'm sure the first track has already been written by one of the stable of writers. That is, in fact, the other aspect of these shows. In most cases the contestants, or at least the finalists, are required as a condition of their participation to sign up to recording contracts and often also to sponsorship and merchandising contracts. The TV production company takes a piece of all this income. In some cases the TV company is in business with a manager who has an option to manage some or all of the successful artists. The artist is offered these contracts at a time when they have relatively little bargaining power and, although there can be some tinkering around the edges, the basic deal is usually already set and non-negotiable. Of course, once the artist is successful renegotiation becomes a possibility. The other thing to watch out for is the fact that the manager must not be in a conflict of interest and should not be receiving management commission and profits from the same source of income. Most decent managers involved in these types of programmes are aware of the potential problems (see Chapter 3).

These programmes are now taking off in the US with the first series *American Idols* being a big success and making TV celebrities of judges such as Simon Cowell.

Other shows, such as *Popstars: The Rivals,* which aims to pitch groups against each other, have done deals with partners such as McDonald's, Littlewoods Leisure and Lycos UK to offer online enhancements to the programme, such as online voting, mobile text messages with news updates, special ring-tones and themed games. This shows some of the benefits of cross-media branding.

Other cross-media marketing initiatives include the streaming of live radio in a deal between Freeserve and Virgin Radio, with the partners splitting advertising revenue and sharing revenue based on the amount of traffic each partner directs to the site. That said, Virgin appears to be looking primarily to the promotional aspects of the deal as opposed to looking for significant commercial success.

This is where you see the shift in emphasis from dreams of the Internet providing brand new, lucrative revenue streams to the reality of it being primarily a promotional, branding opportunity. A classic example of this is a proposed campaign for a new Sony Walkman, which is to be Internet compatible and which is being advertised by a network of video screens in bar toilets across London.

As I said earlier, some well-known artists do use their websites to promote what they're up to in quite creative ways. Some aim to get closer to the fans and try to find out what they want. Occasionally they can be used to correct some of the misinformation on the Internet by acting as an official information site. Sometimes the artist can be prevailed upon to write a behind-the-scenes diary of what he's up to on the road or while making the new album. The more sophisticated sites make this information only available to fans who sign up to a special area of the site that gives the fan something different and the artist a targeted mailing list – provided he complies with Data Protection rules of course.

BRANDING OF ARTISTS

Many artists are now recognising the value in the name, the 'brand', and are actively trying to put themselves into a position where they can make some money out of that brand. They may not have followed exactly in the footsteps of The Spice Girls, but do pick and choose the products they wish to be involved with, for example, clothing shops or ranges.

To a greater or lesser extent, a successful artist is always going to be a brand, in the sense of being a name that people recognise. The more successful the artist is, the more likely it is that the name, likeness and image will be recognised by members of the public. If they like or admire that artist's reputation, they'll want to know more about him and will buy things that tell them more about him like books, magazines and records. They'll buy products that have his name or likeness on it such as calendars, posters, screensavers, T-shirts or other items of clothing. They'll also buy products that he's associated with – food, sweets, drinks and so on. Part of this branding process involves doing merchandising deals for these products. If you have taken steps as early as you could afford to protect your brand then you will have the means of stopping others from cashing in on your name without your approval.

Cross-media branding is becoming increasingly important. It has been shown that consumers are spending more time online, reading and researching as well as being entertained. No branding strategy should ignore online uses, particularly as it has been shown that marketing online generates disproportionately high returns.[1]

There's also the possibility of more focused marketing and direct communication with the consumer or fan.

It's usually a good idea to use the same name, tag-line/slogan – which could be the title of the new album or the name of the tour and imagery – across all forms of marketing. This ensures a consistent message and enhances the brand. Make sure that all media carry your name and contact details. Check that any online links between sites work well and link to a website that carries a consistent message.

If you're considering linking up with other sites with a view to drawing traffic to your site and theirs, then you may agree to share revenue with that site. For example, if you link to a video-games site and customers come from that site to yours and buy your latest record, you might agree with the video-games site to pay them a percentage of the value of the sale as a kind of referral fee. Figures of 1–3% aren't unheard of.

If the name, likeness or logo is one that can be trademarked, you can apply to register a trademark or marks. Not all names are registrable. If it's too common a name or it's descriptive of something, the Trade Mark Registry won't let you register it.

Even if you haven't got a trademark registered, if someone tries to pass themselves off as you in order to cash in on your reputation and this results in loss or damage to you, you have the means to try and stop them. This is called an action for 'passing off'. Below are some examples of court cases involving allegations of passing off.

If a company wants to use your name to promote their product they will do a sponsorship deal. You lend them the use of your name and may agree to provide some other services, such as recording a single or performing in an advert, and they give you money and sometimes goods or services such as airline tickets or cars in return (see Chapter 9).

If your fans are looking for information about you, or where to buy your records, say, they will look under your name. They aren't usually going to start looking under the record company name. In fact, many fans may not know or care what label your records come out on as long as they can find copies of them in their record shop. When you look at the Internet you can see why the record companies are so concerned to own, or at least control, artists' websites and domain names. A fan is going to search for the artist's name. If you wanted to find information on Robbie Williams on the Internet you would search under 'Robbie' rather than under his record company, EMI. There *are* record company websites and they are getting better. At first they tended to be corporate affairs where the services and information provided was intended for other companies or businesses; now they're generally more of a magazine format where news on all the major artists on the label is brought together in one place. Some have links to specialised websites, many of which are owned and put together by the artist or his management team. These links open up many new possibilities for marketing an artist.

Is branding a good idea? There are some that thought the ubiquity of The Spice Girls, *Pop Idols – the Rivals* and so on are taking the idea too far. While I believe we can never underestimate the public's interest in the inside story and behind-the-scenes glimpses of artists, you do have to be careful to avoid overkill. Indeed, some believe that the TV series *Fame Academy* is the last of this particular genre. If they are right it will probably re-emerge in a hybrid form. To some artists the whole idea is anathema. Most artists know that they have to work on building up a name and a reputation in order to sell their records. Most also like the trappings of fame. Some, though, think that they're somehow selling out if they put their name to other products – selling their soul as it were. It's obviously a personal thing.

Some artists, particularly those boy or girl bands with a relatively short shelf life before a new favourite comes along, do embrace branding in order to make as much money as they can as quickly as they can. Others are content to limit their branding activities to tour merchandise or sponsorship deals to help support a tour that would otherwise make a loss. It all comes back to the gameplan (see Chapter 2).

I've also worked with artists who take the sponsor's or merchandiser's money and put it into charitable funds rather than spending it on themselves. Some make a point of telling the public they have done this, others keep it quiet.

Is it a sell out? I don't think it is. If it's not right for you, don't do it. But before you come over all credible and refuse to entertain any form of merchandising or branding, just remember that you're already doing it to some extent when you use your name to promote sales of your records or tickets to your gigs.

There are many artists and bands whose image doesn't easily lend itself to selling loads of posters, T-shirts and so on. If that is you then fine, don't waste time or money on it. You also don't have to have your name associated with every product that comes along. Indeed, it's probably not wise to do so, as the public will quickly tire of you. The products you choose to associate with should be selected with the overall gameplan in mind.

If you do decide to do merchandising deals for your name, logo or likeness, you also need to decide how far you're prepared to go in protecting that merchandise from the pirates who will inevitably come along and try to steal your market, often with inferior products. Even if *you* don't do merchandising deals, you may find that the pirates do. I know of artists that have decided, for example, not to do a merchandising deal for calendars, only to find that unofficial versions appear in the shops anyway (see below).

MERCHANDISING DEALS

In its simplest form a band is involved in merchandising when they sell tickets to their gigs. The band name attracts the fans that have bought the records and now want to see them perform live. The ticket to the gig is bought on the back of the band name. If the band's core business is performing live then the band name is being used to sell records or other goods like T-shirts and posters.

In the entertainment business, merchandising has been big business for years. People can buy the T-shirt, the football strip, the video game and the duvet cover bearing the name and image of their favourite cartoon character, football team or pop group. Disney and Manchester United Football Club are good examples. They know that there's a lot of money to be made from maximising the use of the name and likeness.

HOW DO YOU GO ABOUT GETTING A TRADEMARK?
Before you can begin to use your name to sell merchandise outside your core business of selling records, it's essential that you have a name or logo that's easily marketable and that you have or are starting to get a reputation that people can relate to. If your gameplan is to do a fair amount of merchandising, you should think of a distinctive name and logo from the beginning. We all know how difficult it is to find a name that no one else has thought of and we saw in Chapter 1 how to check this out. The same thought must go into making your logo as distinctive as possible.

If you're going to have any chance of holding off the pirates, you need to protect your rights in your name and logo as far as possible. If you want to prevent others jumping on the bandwagon and manufacturing unauthorised merchandise to satisfy market demand, you'll need to have your own house in order.

It's important to get trademark protection as early as possible. Elvis Presley's estate was not able to protect the use of the Elvis name for merchandising as a registered trademark in the UK because it waited until ten years after his death.[2]

---

2 Elvis Presley Trade Marks [1997] RPC 543.

The Elvis Presley Case

In 1989, Elvis Presley Enterprises Inc, the successors to the Estate of Elvis Presley, filed UK trademark applications for 'Elvis', 'Elvis Presley' and the signature 'Elvis A Presley'.

The UK trademark applications were accepted by the Trade Marks Registry but were then opposed by Sid Shaw, a trader who'd been marketing Elvis memorabilia in the UK since the late 1970s under the name 'Elvisly Yours'. He opposed the registration of the marks by the Elvis Estate on the grounds, among others, that they conflicted with Sid Shaw's own prior trademark registrations for Elvisly Yours. The Registry upheld the Estate's applications; Mr Shaw appealed to the High Court, which allowed the appeal. In a judgement which was quite critical of character and personality merchandising in general, the court decided that the public didn't care whether Elvis Presley memorabilia was approved by the Estate of Elvis Presley or not. The Estate took the case to the Court of Appeal.

The Court of Appeal refused the Estate's appeal and refused registration of all three trademarks. The court concluded that the trademarks were not in themselves distinctive and, as there was no evidence produced by the Estate of any use of the marks in the UK which might have indicated that the marks had become distinctive of the Estate of Elvis Presley in the minds of the public, there was therefore no reason at all why the marks should be registered.

The Wet Wet Wet Case

The courts have shown that they aren't prepared to interpret the Trade Marks Act too narrowly in favour of someone who has registered a trademark in a band name. One example is a case involving the band Wet Wet Wet: the Bravado and Mainstream case.[3]

Bravado had rights in a trademark in the name Wet Wet Wet. Bravado asked for the Scottish law equivalent of an injunction to be ordered against Mainstream to prevent it from infringing that trademark. Mainstream was publishing and marketing a book entitled *A Sweet Little Mystery – Wet Wet Wet – the Inside Story*. Mainstream argued that they were not using Wet Wet Wet in a trademark sense, but rather that it was used to describe the subject matter of the book. They also said that they weren't suggesting in any way that it was published by Bravado and, as such, somehow 'official'. Bravado argued that if they couldn't prevent this use then it would be meaningless having the trademark, because they couldn't then stop it being used on other merchandise relating to the band.

The court decided that the words *were* being used in the course of trade but refused to grant the injunction, because it said that would be interpreting the meaning of the Trade Mark Act far too narrowly. If it were so interpreted then any mention of the group name could be an infringement of the trademark.

HOW TO APPLY FOR A TRADEMARK

You don't have to be already rich and famous to register a trademark in your name or logo. In fact, as we saw in the Elvis case, there are dangers in waiting too long to apply for a trademark. As soon as you can afford to, you should think about doing it. You can apply to protect your name or that of your brand worldwide, but this would be expensive.

---

3 *Bravado Merchandising Services Ltd v. Mainstream Publishing (Edinburgh) Ltd* [1996] F.S.R. 205.

To start with, I usually advise that you apply to register the name in your home market, for example the UK for a British-based band, and then in other places where you have, or hope to gain, a market for your records and other merchandise, for example the US, Europe or Japan.

Each country has its own special rules for registration of a trademark and, in many cases, an application to register a trademark in one country can help you with applications in other parts of the world. For example, the rules at present allow you to backdate an application for a trademark in the US to the date of your UK application provided you apply within six months of the UK application. So, if you apply for a UK trademark registration on 1 July, you have until 31 December to apply in the US and still backdate it to 1 July. Just making the application itself can trigger trademark protection. Even if it takes a year or more to get a registration, the trademark, when and if it's granted, will be backdated to the date of the application. It also gives you priority over anyone else who applies after you to register a trademark in the same or a similar name or logo. This is, however, a specialised area and you should take advice from a trademark lawyer or a specialist trademark agent. Your lawyer can put you in touch with a trademark agent and a good music lawyer should have a working knowledge of trademark law. While you may be happy to leave all this to your manager to sort out for you, do remember that the name should be registered in *your* name and not that of your manager or record company.

Once you've decided the countries that you'd like to apply for a trademark – finances permitting – you have to decide what types of product or particular goods you want to sell under the trademark. In most countries, goods and services are split for trademark registration purposes into classes and it's important to make sure that you cover all relevant classes of goods and as soon as possible. You can add other classes later, but then you run the risk of someone selling goods with your name in a class that you haven't protected. For example, you may have applied to register a trademark for the class that covers records, but not the class that covers printed material such as posters. In theory, someone else could apply for a trademark in that area, but then you get into the whole area of passing off. It's also not usually as cost-effective. You get a costs saving by applying for several classes at a time.[4]

A registered trademark has distinct advantages over an unregistered mark. Actions to stop infringements of registered trademarks are generally quicker and more cost-effective than when you're relying on unregistered rights. A registered trademark puts the world on notice of your rights. A registered trademark is attractive to merchandising companies, as it gives them a monopoly over the goods for which the mark is registered and gives the merchandising company more of an incentive to do a deal with you.

PASSING OFF

If you haven't registered a trademark then, in the UK, you can try and rely on the common law right of 'passing off' in order to protect your name and reputation. Before you can do this you'll have to prove there is goodwill in the name. This may not be the case if

---

4 In the UK there are 42 classes for goods and services. Some common ones used in the music business are Class 9 for records, Class 16 for printed material such as programmes and posters and Class 25 for clothing.

you're unknown and haven't yet got a reputation or any goodwill in the name. You have to show that someone else is trading on your reputation by passing themselves off as you, using your reputation to confuse the public that they are you or are authorised by you. As well as having this goodwill or reputation, you also have to show that this has actually caused confusion in the mind of the public resulting in damage or loss to you. For example, a band using the same name as yours, or one confusingly similar, might advertise tickets to a gig in the same town as your planned gigs. Fans might buy those tickets thinking they're coming to see you. This loses you ticket sales and might possibly damage your reputation if the other band isn't as good as you. You have to have established a reputation in the name in the particular area in question. If your name is associated with records and someone trades under the same or a very similar name in the area of clothing, where you don't have any a reputation, there is less likely to be confusion in the mind of the public.

One famous passing-off case involved the pop group Abba.[5]

The Abba Case

A company called Annabas was selling a range of T-shirts, pillowcases, badges and other goods bearing the name and photographs of the band Abba. The band didn't own the copyright in any of the photographs and Annabas had obtained permission from the copyright owners of the photographs to use them. The band had to rely on a claim for passing off. Abba lost their application for an injunction preventing the sale because they were unable to show they had an existing trade in these goods or any immediate likelihood of one being started. The judge also went on to say that he thought that no one reading adverts for the goods or receiving those goods would reasonably imagine that the band had given their approval to the goods offered. He felt Annabas was only catering for a popular demand among teenagers for effigies of their idols. These words have been often repeated in later cases.

It's clear from this case that you have to establish that you already have a trade in the area in question that could be prejudiced, or that there was a reasonable likelihood of you starting such a trade. If you're seriously thinking about doing merchandising you should do so sooner rather than later, and should be setting yourself up ready for starting such a trade (for example, by commissioning designs, talking to merchandise companies or manufacturers, applying to register your trademark) well in advance of when you want to start business to get around some of the pitfalls highlighted in the Abba case.

The Beatles Case

In the same year as the Abba case, another one, involving two former members of The Beatles – George Harrison and Ringo Starr – came to court.[6]

It was a case against a record company who planned to release recordings of interviews given by The Beatles interspersed with Beatles songs. George and Ringo's copyright had not been infringed nor was there any breach of confidence, so they could only bring an action on the basis of passing off. They argued that anyone buying this record would think

5 *Lyngstad v. Annabas Productions Limited* [1977] FSR 62.
6 *Harrison and Starkey v. Polydor Limited* [1977] FSRI.

it was an official release endorsed by The Beatles. The court refused to grant them an injunction because it felt that anyone buying the record *The Beatles Tapes* would know that there was no implication that The Beatles had endorsed or authorised the release.

OTHER REMEDIES

If you can't rely on either a trademark or the remedy of passing off then you'll have to see if there's been any infringement of copyright, for example in a design, or possibly if there's been a false description of goods that might be unlawful under the Trade Descriptions Act 1968.

CONCLUSIONS ON PROTECTING YOUR NAME

Clearly, getting registered trademark protection is the best way to go about protecting your brand, but when you're just getting started you probably won't have the money to spend on protecting the band name. A balance has to be struck. If you're ultimately successful and haven't applied for a trademark you may end up kicking yourself if others cash in on your name and market unauthorised products. If you apply late you may be too late, as in the case of Elvis. On the other hand, it's often not at all certain whether an artist is ultimately going to be successful enough to justify the expense. A sensible thing to do would be to register a trademark in just one or two classes, including records, of course, and perhaps only in one or two countries at first and then add more countries or classes as things develop.

It's also worth bearing in mind that a record company may advance you the money to make the trademark applications. If you don't want your record company to own your trademark, make sure the application for the registration is in your name not theirs, even if they offer to register it on your behalf.

As we've already seen in the area of e-commerce, there's also a great deal of mileage to be had from registering your domain name. Among other things, it gives you control of the doorway to official information on you and what you have to offer. Registration is cheap and quick, but please don't forget that it will need reviewing every couple of years. One record company, who shall remain nameless, arranged for all the reminders for domain-name registrations to go to one email address. The owner of that address left the company and no one seems to have thought to check the mailbox or redirect the mail. At least one domain name registration lapsed at a crucial marketing moment and had to be bought back on the open market.

UNAUTHORISED, UNOFFICIAL MERCHANDISE

The line of arguments that we saw being developed in the Abba and Beatles cases was expanded on in a case involving The Spice Girls.

The Spice Girls

The Spice Girls applied for an injunction against an Italian publisher, Panini, of an unauthorised sticker book and stickers entitled *The Fab Five*. At this time the Spice Girls had no trademark registrations and, in fact, it probably wouldn't have helped them if they had, because Panini had been careful not to use the name 'Spice Girls' anywhere in the book or on the stickers. So The Spice Girls were trying to use the law of passing off to protect the band's image. They argued that even though the words 'Spice Girls' were not used, the book was clearly about them. The book didn't carry a sticker that it was unauthorised so, they argued, this amounted to a misrepresentation that The Spice Girls had authorised or endorsed the book.

The judge was not swayed by arguments that it made a difference whether the book was marked 'authorised' or 'official'. He refused to grant an injunction. As a consequence of this decision, if a company puts out an unauthorised calendar featuring pictures of an artist or band then, provided it is made clear that it's not a calendar that has the official blessing of the band and it doesn't reproduce copyright words/lyrics or photographs without permission, then that wouldn't be a passing off nor a breach of copyright rights. The judge decided that even the use of the words 'official' wouldn't have made this a case of passing off, because the product clearly indicated it was not approved by the artist. In this particular case, The Spice Girls had a trademark application pending, but it hadn't been registered so they couldn't rely on arguing that there had been an infringement of their trademark. This is a good example of why it's important to have a registered trademark if you're going to try to put a stop to the sale of unauthorised goods.

You might be forgiven for thinking that all these cases involve millions of pounds and are only of interest to the megastars that can employ people to do all this for them. Well, it's true that it's usually only the big names that have the inclination or the money to bring cases to court, but protecting your name can start at a very low level – like preventing the pirate merchandisers from selling dodgy T-shirts or posters outside your gigs, or stopping another local band from cashing in on the hard work you've put into starting to make a name for yourself.

HOW DO YOU GO ABOUT GETTING A MERCHANDISE DEAL?

You may start off by producing a small range of T-shirts that you sell at your gigs. You can get these printed up locally, put up a temporary stall in the foyer of the venue and sell them from there. If it's clear that you can sell enough to make money then you might approach a merchandising company about doing it for you on a larger scale. The merchandising company could be a big multi-national company or a small independent company. You can get names of merchandising companies out of directories such as *Gavin* or *Music Week*. You can also get recommendations from your mates in other bands, your lawyer, accountant or manager.

If you're starting to sell out the larger venues and are a regular on the gig circuit, merchandising companies may approach you. If they do, you could try them out with your concert or tour merchandise before deciding if they're right to do your retail or mail-order merchandising as well.

THE MERCHANDISING DEAL

If you have a registered trademark, this will increase your appeal to a merchandiser. However, merchandise companies will still be interested in you even if you haven't got a registered trademark if you're sufficiently well known for them to run the commercial risk of producing merchandise for sale. The merchandise company will take a view as to whether yours is the sort of image that will sell particular types of merchandise. They will know if your image will sell T-shirts or posters at gigs and if it will also sell either the same merchandise or a different range of products through retail stores.

Even quite small acts can often shift reasonable numbers of T-shirts to fans at the gigs or through mail order. If there's a steady turnover, a merchandiser will be interested in doing a deal. Obviously, if you only sell two T-shirts a month, and then only to your close family, then getting a merchandise deal is going to be a non-starter. In that case you should be looking to do it yourself. Why would you want to do this? Well, obviously, the more that you keep to yourself the more of the profit you get to keep. There is, however, an awful lot of work involved in mailing out the merchandise to fulfil orders and in ensuring that you've enough products to sell at your gigs.

If things start to go only moderately well you'll probably need to employ someone to look after that side of things for you. You'll also need to do a deal with a company to make the clothing or other products for you to your design. You'll have to be responsible for selling it either by mail order, through selected retail outlets such as local record stores, and at your gigs. You'll need to be able to keep a check on the quality of the product being produced, to be a salesman, to be able to market the goods and to distribute them. You'll need to make sure that the orders are fulfilled promptly and that the accounts are properly kept. This is quite a tall order, even if you do get to keep the lion's share of the profits. No wonder, then, that many bands find a specialist merchandising company to do this for them.

WHAT IS IN A TYPICAL MERCHANDISING DEAL?

Obviously, each merchandise deal will be different and, once again, it's important for you to use a lawyer who is used to doing these sorts of deals. There are, however, some points that are an issue in every merchandising deal.

Territory

You can do a one-stop, worldwide deal with one company for all your merchandise needs, but this is still comparatively rare. It's more usual for you to do a series of deals with different companies for different types of goods. For example, you could do a deal with one company for merchandise to sell at your gigs like T-shirts, sweatshirts, caps and so on. This deal could be limited to the UK or Europe. You could then do another deal for the US, probably with a company who specialises in the US marketplace. If we are talking about merchandise in the wider sense of marketing your name or likeness on sweet packages or crisp packets, then you'll do your deal with the company that manufactures those goods. That deal could be a worldwide one or for specific countries. If you're going to do a worldwide or multi-territory deal, make sure that your merchandise company has the resources to look after your interests properly in each country. Find out if they sub-contract the work and, if so, who to. Is the sub-contractor reliable?

Term

If you're doing a series of concerts, you could do a merchandise deal that was just linked to those dates. If you were doing a world tour with various legs, it's likely you would do a deal with one merchandise company that covered the whole tour. However, you could do a deal with one company to cover the period of the UK or European legs, and with another company or companies in other parts of the world. This isn't as common, as it's difficult to administer and police. The term of the contract would be the duration of the tour or of that particular leg of it.

If you're doing merchandise deals to sell goods in shops or by mail order then the term is more likely to be for a fixed period of time, probably a minimum of one year and up to three years or more.

The more money the merchandising company is investing in manufacturing costs and/or up-front advances, the longer term they're likely to want in return. The longer the term, the better their chances will be of recouping their investment.

Some merchandising deals are linked to recoupment of all or a proportion of the advance. The term of the deal runs until that happens. This can be dangerous if sales don't live up to expectations or if the merchandising company isn't as good as you would like them to be. The best thing to do with these types of deals is to have the right to get out of the deal after, say, a year by paying back the amount of money that is unrecouped. This will give you the flexibility to get out of a deal that isn't working and into one that might.

Rights granted

The deal will usually be a licence of rights in your name and likeness for a particular period, not an assignment of rights. The rights granted will be the right to manufacture, reproduce and sell certain products featuring your name and/or logo. If you have a registered trademark you'll be required to grant a trademark licence to the merchandising company to use the trademark on specific goods.

The rights granted could be for particular products or for all types of merchandise. These days the trend is towards limiting the granting of rights to particular products. You could grant the right to use your name or likeness or your registered logo on T-shirts and keep back rights to all other products such as calendars, posters, sweets and so on.

You might grant the right to use your band name and/or logo for some particular types of a particular product and keep rights back to other forms of the same product. For example, you could grant a licence for ordinary toys and keep back the rights to use your name on musical toys. You could then do merchandising deals for all or any of those types of toys with one or more other companies. If your music is going to be used in the musical toys then you or your publisher will license the right to include the music for either a one-off 'buy-out' fee or for a fee and an ongoing royalty (see Chapter 4).

Quality control

Once you've decided what goods are going to feature your name, likeness or logo, you have to make sure that the goods are of the highest possible quality. If you don't keep a tight hold on quality control, you could do potentially serious and possibly irreversible damage to the reputation of your brand. If a T-shirt featuring your name and logo falls apart, or the colours run on the first wash, then that is going to reflect very badly on you.

The fan that bought the T-shirt won't care that it was another company that made it – they'll blame you and give you a reputation for selling shoddy goods.

The contract will usually say that the merchandising company must submit samples of designs for you to approve. If they're making the goods to a design you've given them then they should make up samples to that design. Only once you're satisfied with the quality of the sample should you authorise full production to go ahead. Even then, you should have the right to inspect the product at short notice and to insist upon improvements if the quality has dropped to an unacceptable level. The contract should contain a guarantee that the product will be of at least the same quality as the sample you've approved.

It's also important that the merchandising company makes sure that what it manufactures complies with all local laws. Toys and other children's products in particular have very stringent safety standards. You may want to insist that the manufacturer takes out product liability insurance. Be careful also if the company sub-contracts any of the processes. The sub-contractor must also stick to rigid quality controls and ensure product safety, carrying insurance against any damage caused by the product.

If the design is one created for you, either by the merchandising company or a third party, make sure they assign the rights in that design to you. If you don't, you may find that the designer comes knocking on your door for more money.

Methods of distribution

The rights you grant can't only be limited to certain types of products, but also to certain methods of distribution.

You might grant mail-order rights only or limit the rights to selling merchandise to retail shops or at your gigs. There are specialist companies who are good at doing tour merchandising but aren't as good at selling goods to retail shops, and vice versa. It's important that you find the right company for the right method of distribution.

Depending on the means of distribution the basis on which you're paid may also change.

Advances and Guaranteed Minimum payments

You can usually expect to get an advance against what you're going to earn from sales of the goods. This advance is recoupable from those earnings but, as we've already seen with other types of music business deals, the advance isn't usually returnable if you don't sell enough to recoup the advance. One exception is if you're doing a merchandising deal for a live tour and you don't do some or all of the concerts. Then you can expect to be asked to repay some or all of the advance. Some tour agreements also say that advances are repayable in whole or in part if ticket sales at the concerts don't reach a particular level. For example, you may get a fixed sum, sometimes called the Guaranteed Minimum, that isn't repayable unless you cancel the whole tour. Then there are other payments that are made which are dependent either on you doing a particular number of big, stadium-type concerts or on you selling a minimum number of tickets over the whole concert tour. If you don't do those gigs or don't sell enough tickets then you don't get those further payments.

There's also another catch with tour merchandise agreements, which is the one that I touched on above. The contract may say that the term continues until you've earned enough from sales of the tour merchandise to recoup either the whole advance or the Guaranteed Minimum. If you aren't certain that you'll be able to do this within a reasonable time, then you'll want to have the option to get out of this by paying back the unrecouped amount. If you don't have this option and your tour isn't a big success then you could be stuck with the same tour merchandising company for the next tour, without the prospect of any more advances. If you can get out of it, you can try to find someone else to do a deal for the tour merchandise for the next year's tour, and may even get them to pay you another advance.

The advances could be payable in full when you sign the deal, or in a number of instalments linked to concert appearances or sales of product with, say, 25% of the total being payable on signature.

Royalties and licence fees

You'll usually receive a percentage of the sale price of the goods as a royalty, which will go first to recoup any advances you've already had. This percentage will either be calculated on the gross income or, more usually, on the net income after certain expenses are deducted. Deductions can include VAT or similar sale taxes, the cost of manufacture and printing of the goods, and all or some costs of their distribution and sale.

When you're doing a tour merchandising deal, commissions or fees are often payable to the owners of the concert venues for the right to sell merchandise on their premises. It's usual for the merchandise company to deduct this payment from the gross income. Some companies will also try to deduct other expenses, including travel and accommodation costs for their salesmen and other unspecified expenses. I'm not convinced that these should be deducted and it's a good rule with all these deductions to look at them very carefully, and to ask for a justification for the deduction if necessary.

Obviously, if you're being paid a percentage of the gross income it will be a much smaller percentage than if it were a percentage of the net. A fee of 20–30% of gross would be equal to about 60–70% of the net income, depending on what is deducted from the gross. For example, if you had a gross income from sales of T-shirts featuring your name of £10 per T-shirt, a 20% royalty would be £2.00. If you had a net income of £2.00, then a 60% royalty based on the net income would be £1.20.

Accounting

Accounts are usually delivered for retail or mail-order deals every three or six months. Obviously, from your point of view you'll want to be accounted to as quickly and as often as possible. You should have the right to go in and inspect the books of account regularly – at least once a year. You should also be able to go in and do a stock check from time to time.

Merchandising deals for tours are different. There is usually a tour accountant who will check the stock and the sales sheet on a daily basis. He will expect to be paid within a very short period of time, preferably within 24 hours of each gig or, at the very latest, within seven days.

Trademark and copyright notices

If you have a trademark registered, the contract should confirm that they will include a trademark notice on each product and a copyright notice for each design.

Termination rights

As with all contracts, the merchandising contract should say in what circumstances the deal can be brought to an end. These should include a persistent failure of quality standards, failure to put the product into the marketplace by the agreed date, and other material breaches of contract, for example, if they don't account to you when they should. If the company goes bust or just stops acting as a merchandise company, you should also have the right to end the deal.

Enforcement

This could be the subject of a chapter in its own right. The contract should say who's responsible for tracking infringements of your rights. There's usually a requirement that the merchandising company reports to you any infringements of your trademark or copyright that they come across on each product. It's as much in their interest as yours to keep pirate activities to a minimum.

There are civil and criminal remedies to stopping infringements. You can also enlist the help of Trading Standards Authorities and Customs & Excise. Often, these authorities are prepared to seize unauthorised products bearing a name that is a registered trademark. Even without a registered trademark, Trading Standards Authorities are sometimes prepared to rely on the Trade Descriptions Act in order to make seizures and bring prosecutions. In my own experience, the Trading Standards Authorities are an invaluable help in clearing the streets of counterfeit products. It's possible to provide Customs & Excise with trademark registration details to assist them in identifying and seizing unauthorised products entering the country at ports and airports.

CONCLUSIONS

- Merchandising is the use of your name and reputation to sell goods.

- Not everyone will want to do lots of merchandise deals and not everyone will be in a position to. You have to build up a name and reputation.

- Consider registering a trademark in your name and logo.

- If you haven't got a registered trademark but you do have a reputation, you may be able to stop people trading on your name through the laws against passing off.

- Make sure you own the copyright in any designs you commission.

- Make sure you have the right to use the design featured in your album artwork.

- Think about limiting the territory and the rights you grant.

9: **SPONSORSHIP**

INTRODUCTION

This subject really fits into the whole area of branding. We saw in the previous chapter how an artist or a band protects their name by registering trademarks or through taking advantage of the laws of passing off and of copyright.

Having protected the name, your brand, you can choose how far to exploit that brand. You can decide to only use it to sell your records and videos and to promote your live performances. Many artists choose to do just that and don't really go outside their core area of activity at all. This is fine. No one is saying that you have to. But you may need to look at some kind of merchandising deal to bolster your income from live work. Many tours would make a loss if they weren't underwritten by merchandising deals and often by sponsorship.

Sponsorship is a kind of extension to a merchandising deal. The sponsor uses the association between you and their product to increase awareness of the product and to encourage more people to buy it. The sponsor provides sponsorship money in return for the right to trade on your importance to a particular sector of the market. For example, a sponsor of a soft drink might look for a sponsorship deal with a pop artist who would appeal to teenagers. An alcoholic drinks manufacturer, on the other hand, would want to sponsor an artist that had an appeal to over-eighteens and, in particular, those in their early twenties.

Pepsi has been a keen sponsor of artists in recent years. The Spice Girls released a track as a Pepsi single and featured that track in a Pepsi ad on television. Robbie Williams has done sponsorship deals with Lloyds Bank, for his Royal Albert Hall concert, and several deals with Smart Cars, including the premiere of his film, where a fleet of Smart Cars was available to ferry celebrities to the premiere. The Corrs have also been associated with Lloyds Bank in television ads.

Sponsorship deals are often done for concert tours. You'll often see the name of a sponsor on the ticket. For example, 'Band X sponsored by Carling'. When you arrive at the gig, you'll find that there are banners and posters from the sponsors. There may be more than one sponsor. You could have a main sponsor (the title sponsor) for the tour, another for the programme and the tickets, another for the soft drinks on sale at the venue and yet another for the alcoholic drinks. Venues often restrict the extent to which they will allow outside sponsors to plaster their brands all over the venue (see Chapter 10).

HOW DO YOU FIND A SPONSOR?

There are a number of ways to get a sponsor. You might be surprised to know that it's possible for a band to approach a designer or company to ask for sponsorship. The shoe company who makes Doc Marten boots has, on at least one occasion that I know of, sponsored an artist following a direct approach from the manager. Companies want to promote themselves as supporting and encouraging youth culture of which, of course, music plays a huge part. Such sponsorships by clothing companies are not common.

AN ENDORSEMENT DEAL

What is much more common, though, is for clothing companies to loan clothes for photo-shoots or live appearances in return for a suitably prominent name-check. If you're lucky, you sometimes get to keep the clothes. Diesel and other similar 'youth' brands have looked at sponsorship in the past, and up-and-coming new designers or those trying to break in to the UK market may be keen to do a deal. A number of designers have really made their name by having a 'star' seen out and about in their clothes. If the star mentions the designer's name in press or TV interviews then so much the better. These kinds of deal are closer to what I would call endorsements than pure sponsorship. You let it be known that you support or endorse a particular product. For example, you might mention in an interview that you do all your shopping at a particular shop in fashionable Notting Hill. Suddenly all the wannabes are queuing at the door of that shop, partly in the off-chance that you'll be in there, but also to try to copy your look.

SPONSORSHIP AGENTS

Apart from the direct approach, another means of getting a sponsorship deal is to approach a specialist agent who either represents one or two big companies looking for suitable projects to sponsor, or who will act for you and go to potential sponsors on your behalf. There are lists of these agencies in the *Music Week Directory* and magazines like *Audience*. There is also the tried and trusted word-of-mouth recommendation from friends or other contacts in the business. If you're sufficiently successful to have a brand that a sponsor might be interested in, they or their agents are likely to approach you or your manager direct. As with all these things, don't feel you have to grab the first thing that comes along. If you're desperate for some funding to underwrite a shortfall on a tour then by all means do a deal, but keep it short and see how things work out before you get in too deep.

What do they charge?

If you employ an agent to find a sponsorship deal for you then they will usually take a percentage of the deal they do for you. This percentage can vary between 5% and 15% of the gross sponsorship income. For example, if the agent brokers a deal for a drinks company to sponsor your next UK tour and the drinks company is prepared to offer £100,000 for the privilege, the agent would take between £5,000 and £15,000 of that as their fee. If the sponsorship is made up partly or wholly of goods rather than cash, the agent will expect to get their percentage in the cash equivalent of the value of those goods. So if the drinks company were to offer £80,000 in cash and £20,000 worth of free lager to give away to your fans, then your agent on a commission of 15% would still want their £15,000 in cash.

The money is usually paid to the agent at the same time as you're paid. If you're paid in two instalments, half at the beginning of the deal and the rest when you finish the tour, then your agent would get 50% of their fee upfront and 50% when you get the balance of the money. They have a vested interest in you completing the tour and if the amount of money is large enough, they may decide to insure you against you failing to complete the tour.

The agent may want to be exclusively employed as your agent for a period of time. This is usually for a year but could be longer. During that time you wouldn't be able to use any other sponsorship agents, so you have to make sure that they are good enough first. The advantage you get from an exclusive arrangement is the incentive that the agent has to bring deals to you as opposed to anyone else. The disadvantage is that you can't go to anyone else if they don't get you particularly good deals. If you can get an agent on a non-exclusive basis, that will give you more flexibility.

If the agent gets you a deal for some tour sponsorship and that sponsor comes back to you to sponsor your next tour, then some agents insist that they should also get commission on that repeat work, even if they are no longer your exclusive agent by the time of the second tour. The logic is that they made the initial introduction and so should benefit from any follow-up. I can see this logic, but obviously other factors also play a part in you getting the follow-up offer for the next tour, such as the professional way you dealt with the first deal, the benefits that the sponsor saw that came from your efforts and your increased fame in the meantime. So while it might be acceptable to agree to pay the agent for a short while after the end of your relationship with them, I would try and draw the line at, say, six to twelve months. This is all subject to negotiation when you take them on.

The agent could be your only agent worldwide and be solely responsible for getting you sponsorship deals around the world. As many sponsors are multi-national companies, this may not be such a bad thing, but if you think your agent doesn't have the necessary overseas connections you might just agree that they can act for you in the UK and decide to use other agents overseas.

If the agent is representing a company that comes to you with an offer of sponsorship, you wouldn't expect to have to pay him a fee for brokering the deal. In those circumstances he should be paid by the company concerned. If he also looks to you for payment you would be right to be suspicious.

INTEGRITY

No, don't worry, I'm not going to go all serious on you and talk about your moral values – well actually, I suppose I am a bit. What I want you to think about is whether you'll accept sponsorship from *any* company that offers it and the more the merrier, or are you going to select who sponsors you on moral or ethical grounds?

When you decide on your gameplan to look for sponsorship deals, you have to think about what effect that will have on your brand and your reputation. There is a narrow line to be drawn between using sponsorship by selected companies to enhance the brand and of being accused by fans of 'selling out'. The products you choose to be associated with must complement the image you've established for yourself. For example, if you're aiming at the teenage market you may alienate them (or perhaps the parents who supply the pocket-money) by being associated with alcohol or tobacco. On the other hand, if you cultivate a bad-boy image you won't want to be associated with cuddly toys. The exception to this would be if your plan is to reposition yourself in the marketplace. For example, if you wanted to move out of the teen or pre-teen market, you might choose sponsors of adult products to show you're growing up. You should also consider the moral sensibilities of your fans. You could alienate a large proportion of them if you had manufacturers of GM foods or a fur company as your sponsor.

Don't forget that the companies that you're being sponsored by will also expect things from you. They won't want you to do anything that will bring their brand into disrepute or show them up in a bad way. Bear this in mind when negotiating your sponsorship deal. You need to be careful that you keep an even balance between your and their expectations. If you feel at all uncomfortable about what you're being asked to do then that should give you a signal either to try and change it a little or to pull out of the deal.

Your public is a very fickle thing. It's very difficult to know whether they will accept what you're doing as par for the course and what they expect from you. If your fans think you're selling out then you and your press people are going to have quite a bit to do to redress the balance.

The other issues you need to think about are whether you want to be associated with companies that are involved either directly or indirectly in activities or causes that you disagree with. For example, if you're a committed vegetarian you may not want to be involved with a company that has a subsidiary that is in the business of raising battery hens. If you've a strong aversion to anything to do with cruelty to animals or animal testing, you wouldn't want to do a sponsorship deal with a company that had a French sister company that ran laboratories that used animals to test their products. If these things matter to you then you need to have an ethical check made on the company to make sure that they aren't in any way involved with things that would be unacceptable to you. Remember that, although they are using their association with you to benefit their business, you're being associated with them too, and with the sort of things that they stand for.

SCOPE OF THE SPONSORSHIP DEAL

The sponsorship deal could be for a particular tour or for a series of tours. For example, it could be just for the UK or European leg of your tour or could be for the whole world tour. It could also just be for a particular project. A company could sponsor you for a particular event, for example, a one-off concert, or they could expect some personal endorsements of their product. They may want you to do personal appearances or to give private performances at their company sales conferences to rally the troops. They may want you to write and record a song especially for them that they may want to release as a promotion or as a proper commercial release. I'm sure you'll have seen special offers where you get a single or album by your favourite artist if you collect a given number of ring-pulls, packet tops or special coupons. If you have an exclusive record deal, you can't do these deals unless you first get the record company's agreement to waive their exclusivity. They may agree to this if they think that the publicity will help sell lots more records, or if the sponsoring company has access to markets in parts of the world that your record company can't break into without spending a lot of money. For example, some of the soft drinks companies have a huge market in parts of South East Asia or in South America. By being associated with them in those countries, you're getting a huge amount of exposure that should help to sell lots of your records. This exposure could be much more valuable than any amount of marketing money that your record company may be prepared to put into launching you in those areas. Obviously, it makes sense in these cases for there to be a considerable degree of co-operation between what your record company is planning, what you're doing in terms of live appearances and what the sponsor intends to do. If you can dovetail these plans then your chances of world-domination come a lot closer.

Whether it's a tour sponsorship or an individual event sponsorship, it's a reasonable rule of thumb that the more a sponsor expects from you the more you can expect to be paid.

EXCLUSIVITY

You could only have one sponsor at any given time or you could have a series of sponsors for different products. If you're only going to have one sponsor then, in return for that exclusivity, you should get a lot more money.

If you're going to look for a number of different sponsors for different products then take care that you don't narrow down your options too much. If you're going to have a drinks sponsor, then limit the extent of their sponsorship to alcoholic or non-alcoholic drinks, depending on what you're looking for from another sponsor. For example, if Pepsi or Coca-Cola was looking to sponsor you, you might limit their sponsorship to soft drinks. You couldn't have another soft drinks sponsor, but you could have a sponsor for alcoholic drinks. If you have a food sponsor, try and limit it to their particular product, for example biscuits or crisps or whatever. This would leave you with lots more food products to find sponsors for. Be careful what you agree to do in return for the sponsorship money or you could find yourself in trouble.

The Spice Girls v. *Aprila*

An example of this is a case brought by The Spice Girls against an Italian scooter company.[1] The Spice Girls were suing the company for payment of the balance of the monies they said they were due under a sponsorship deal that they'd done with the scooter manufacturer. The scooter manufacturer had produced a series of scooters, each in the colours that were associated with each member of The Spice Girls. For example, they'd produced a bright orange version as the Geri Spice Scooter, Geri Halliwell being otherwise known as Ginger Spice. Geri Halliwell had, however, left the group shortly after the deal was done. The scooter company refused to pay and counter-claimed that The Spice Girls had misled them, because at the time they did the deal they knew that Geri Halliwell intended to leave the group. In February 2000 the court decided against The Spice Girls and found that they had misled the scooter company, who didn't have to pay them the balance of their sponsorship money. Furthermore, The Spice Girls were ordered to pay damages to the scooter company for the losses they'd suffered.

WHAT'S IN A TYPICAL SPONSORSHIP DEAL?

THE SERVICES

The first thing you have to establish is what they want you to do or what event they expect to be sponsoring. Remember to keep the scope of their sponsorship as narrow

1 *The Spice Girls Limited v. Aprila World Service BV* Chancery Division, 24/2/2000.

as you can, without them reducing the money on offer, to allow you the possibility of getting other sponsors.

If the sponsor expects you to do a series of things, for example, writing a new song, doing a live concert tour, making a television ad or a TV special, then make sure that you aren't overcommitting yourself. By taking too much on you may not be able to do it all properly and professionally. If you agree to do too much, you'll end up either not doing it or doing it badly. This will reflect back on you and could do you more harm than good. If you fail to deliver the goods the sponsor could decide to sue you.

EXCLUSIVITY

Once you've agreed what they are going to sponsor and what the product is that will be associated with you, you have to decide if you're going to have one exclusive sponsor or whether you are going to give them exclusive rights for a particular product or type of product, and still have the option to take on other sponsors for other products.

TERRITORY

Next you have to decide whether the deal is a worldwide one or if it's to be limited to particular countries. You could do a deal for just the US or the Far East, depending on the type of sponsorship. For example, one company that is 'big' in that area of the world but not so well known in other parts of the world could sponsor the Far Eastern section of your tour. You could then switch to another sponsor for the US or Europe.

CREATIVE CONTROL

If the sponsor intends to feature your name and likeness in any way in the campaign, whether on packaging, adverts or otherwise, you'll want to have prior approval of those uses. You may want to insist or ask for a special photo-shoot with a photographer of your choosing. You could then submit to them a number of examples of photos that you like and agree that they can have final choice.

If you're writing a special song then you ought to have some say in what it sounds like, even if the sponsor does give you a brief to work to. If you're recording a song for them that has been specifically commissioned, you'll want to know whether any particular lyric or theme is to be featured and whether you're comfortable with that. If you're being asked to record a new or special version of an existing song, or to allow a particular track to be used in the campaign, you'll need to know whether they intend to change the lyrics or music. If they do, you'll probably want some control over that and to have final approval. Bear in mind, also, that that approval should extend to any co-writers or composers of the original work, and that your publishers and record company may have to give their permission to you making the recording of the new version. You may also want to check the context in which the song is being used in case you find that offensive.

The American singer-songwriter Tom Waits has a consistent policy not to endorse products or do adverts. He has taken at least two, if not more, legal cases against companies that used sound-alikes to imitate his distinctive 'gargling with razor blades' voice. One case[2] involved a US advert for Doritos snack chips, which used a singer to

[2] Entertainment Law Review 1992 (3(6) 208).

imitate Waits's voice and the way he sang a particular song used in the advert 'Step Right Up'. Waits sued and received $2.6 million in compensation for appropriation of his voice.

TERM

You have to agree how long the deal is to last. If it's for a specific event or a tour then the sponsorship deal will run from the lead-up to the event, which could be weeks or days before the tour, and end shortly after the event or tour has been completed. The sponsor may occasionally have the right to use up printed materials or products they have already manufactured, but this wouldn't normally be for more than three to six months and they shouldn't manufacture more of the product in anticipation that the deal was about to come to an end. Obviously, during the time that they're allowed to sell off the product, any exclusivity they had would end so that you could go off and look for a new sponsor. If it's a general sponsorship deal for a particular product then you might agree that it runs for a year, perhaps with an option to extend it by mutual agreement. You would normally only agree to an extension if you got paid a further sum of money. You'll want to make sure that any remaining stocks are sold off as soon as possible at the end of the deal, as it could interfere with either the sponsorship deal for the next part of the tour or a new sponsorship deal for the same type of product.

You should also bear in mind that the longer your name becomes associated with one company for a particular product, the more difficult it will be to get a deal with another company. For example, if the public has come to associate your name with Pepsi for soft drinks, Coca-Cola is less likely to want to sponsor you. Some of you might be saying, 'I wish I had this problem,' at this point.

BANNER ADVERTISING AT VENUES

If the sponsorship is for a tour or part of a tour, the sponsors will usually want to have their name on banners in each concert arena. They may agree that these only go up in the foyer or they may want them in the concert hall itself. Most artists insist on no banners over the stage and, if the sponsor's name is being projected on to the stage backdrop, that this stops several minutes before they go on stage. Whether you want to insist on these kinds of restriction will depend on your own views as to how closely you want to be associated with the sponsor, as well as your bargaining power. I don't think it's unreasonable, though, to ask that the banners aren't so intrusive that they detract from your own performance.

If your sponsorship deal involves publicity for the sponsor at the concert venue, you have to be careful that you don't run foul of any restrictions within the venue itself. The venue owner may already have given the drinks concession to another company. For example, Coca-Cola may already have the right to have their soft drinks on sale at the venue to the exclusion of all other competing brands. If that is the case, the venue won't take it too well if your sponsor, Pepsi, then drapes their banners and logos about the place. That doesn't mean that you definitely won't be able to do the sponsorship deal, just that you'll have to be aware of any restrictions and make sure you don't agree to do anything in the contract that you can't put into effect on the ground. Any sponsor will want to have the opportunity to put a stand in the foyer. You shouldn't guarantee that they can do this, as there may be venue or local authority restrictions. Any permissions required and fees payable should be the sponsor's responsibility.

MEET AND GREETS

Whatever the type of sponsorship deal you do, it's likely that the sponsor will require you to be involved in some kind of 'meet and greet' sessions. These are where the sponsors, their key customers and possibly competition winners get to meet you. This may be before or after a concert or at specially organised events. Bear in mind that a live performance can be very draining. You may not want to meet a lot of people beforehand, and afterwards you may need time to come down from the adrenaline rush of performing. Don't over-commit yourself. I know of some bands that share the meet and greet sessions out between them. It's the job of your manager to make sure that your sponsors don't get over-eager and expect or even demand too much of you.

FREEBIES AND PROMOTIONAL ACTIVITIES

No, not free goods for you – I mean things that the sponsor will expect to get for nothing as part of the sponsorship fee. They will usually want a guaranteed number of free tickets to your concerts. They will always want more than you'll want to give. There will need to be a compromise. You may offer more tickets at bigger venues and less or none at all at smaller ones.

The sponsor may want you to attend press conferences for product launches or to make personal appearances. These should always be subject to your availability and to the other professional commitments that you have. If you're on a concert tour in Europe, you don't want to find yourself committed to having to return to London for a press conference. You should also try and limit these appearances to a maximum number of days over the term of the deal.

Take care before you guarantee that you'll do a concert tour in a particular region. You may not be able to deliver this or, if you do, you may lose a lot of money. However, the sponsor may agree to underwrite all or part of such a tour if it's important to them that you perform in those parts of the world.

If the sponsor wants to feature you in adverts, they need to specify how many, whether TV or radio, and the extent to which you have to be involved. You should have rights of approval. It's unlikely that you'll be able to limit the number of times they can repeat the adverts unless you've considerable bargaining power. If you do then you should aim to allow them a reasonable amount of repeats without it getting to the stage that every time you turn on the television there you are. There's nothing more off-putting than that. The sponsor shouldn't want that either, but sometimes they need to have the brakes applied for them.

TRADEMARK LICENCES AND GOODWILL

I discussed in the last chapter the advantages of registering a trademark. If you have a trademark either pending or registered in your name, or a logo, then in your sponsorship deal you'll be expected to grant a licence to your sponsor to use that trademark. You should limit the licence to the uses covered by the sponsorship deal and the licence should end when the sponsorship deal does.

PAYMENT

I bet you were wondering when I was going to get to this. What are you going to get paid for all of this work? The amounts can vary widely depending on what you're expected to do, the size of the company, your fame and the length of the deal and how exclusive it is. Each will have to be negotiated on a case-by-case basis. The sponsor or the agent will usually come to you with a figure for what the sponsor thinks it's worth and, after due consideration, you may want to accept that or try to push it higher.

The sponsorship contract won't only spell out how much you'll get paid – it will also say when you will get the money. The sponsorship fee could be money alone, or cash and goods, or occasionally just goods (although in that case it's more of an endorsement deal). It's not usually recoupable or returnable. There are exceptions, though. If you break your side of the bargain, for example by not doing the tour, or if it's a case of misrepresentation as in the case of The Spice Girls, then the contract may say that you're required to repay some or all of the money. Or you may get sued for its return. You may also be required to return some of the money or to pay compensation if you bring the sponsor's brand into disrepute.

When you'll be paid will also usually be some kind of compromise. The sponsor will want to hold back as much of the fee as they can until they're sure you're delivering your side of the bargain. On the other hand, you'll be actively promoting the sponsor's product (well, you will, won't you?) and you'll want to be getting some, if not all, of the sponsorship fee in the bank. At the very least you'll want to be paid as soon as specific things have been achieved, for example some of the money should be paid when you sign the deal, some when you start the concert tour and the balance at the end of the tour.

You should also be clear what is included in the fee. If you're doing a recording of a song, remember that there will be mechanical royalties to be paid to your publisher and any co-writer (see Chapter 4). If you have an exclusive recording deal, your record company may want payment in return for releasing you from that exclusivity. If an advert is going to be put together with visual images for television, for example, a synchronisation fee will be payable to your publisher and to the publisher of any co-writer. These can be significant amounts of money. Who's going to be responsible for these fees? Are they included in the sponsorship fee so that you have to sort it out with the publishers? Or is it the sponsor's responsibility? The answer can make a considerable difference to what you end up with in payment.

You should have the right to end the deal if the sponsor breaches the payment terms or otherwise doesn't fulfil their side of the bargain.

CONCLUSIONS

- Decide on the types of product you want to be associated with.

- Either target those companies that produce those products yourself, or through an agent, or decide that you'll wait until they come to you.

- Decide if you're looking for one exclusive sponsor or a series of deals for particular products.

- Decide if you want to do a worldwide or limited-country deal.

- Make sure that the services you have to provide are manageable and that you have any necessary permissions from your record and publishing companies.

- When setting the level of the fees, agree what is to be included.

- Try to get as much of the fee paid up-front as possible.

10: **TOURING**

INTRODUCTION

When you're starting out you'll probably get gigs in a very hand-to-mouth way. You or your manager will chase them up, probably starting in your home town with local pub dates. If you live in a town with a large student population, you might get on to the university/college circuit. Local bands are often very popular for 'rag' or summer balls, possibly as support to other better-known acts. Getting to know the local social secretary at the university/college can help but remember, all local bands with a bit of ambition will be doing the same thing.

If you can get the local press and radio behind you this can open up more local gigs. Don't forget college radio. If you make a fan of the station manager or a particular DJ, they'll plug not only your local dates but also those further afield. Take copies of your demo to the station and use your best selling skills to convince them they could be in at the start of a future Oasis, Radiohead or whatever.

Once you have a local following you can look to venture outside the area to bigger and (hopefully) better-paid gigs. A word of warning – don't even think of inviting A&R people to your gigs unless you're well rehearsed and 'tight' in your playing and command an enthusiastic local following. I've been to many showcases where the band makes the fatal error of treating it as just another session in front of their mates. They act far too casually and are under-rehearsed. If the local record company scout happens to be at that gig he could be put off you for life, or it could set back your campaign for a record deal by several months while the damage is repaired. The same disastrous situation could happen if there's a reporter for the local newspaper at the gig who gives you a bad write-up. Don't get me wrong. I know that every act has its off day when, for whatever reason, it just doesn't come off. Scouts and newspaper reviewers will take an off day into account. What they won't forgive is if you aren't acting in a professional way. You should treat every gig as a professional job and the potential one when you'll be discovered.

Try to find out who the local scouts are for the major record companies. It may be someone at the local college or radio station. Local bands that have been around for longer may be able to tell you, otherwise ask the reporter on music events at the local newspaper. It may even be them. Whoever the scout is, they may be looking to move into the business themselves using the discovery of a great local band as a stepping-stone.

Doing all this is very hard work and mostly unrewarding. Some bands get to play in venues in larger towns by doing a deal with the venue owner or promoter where, in return for booking the band, they guarantee there will be a minimum number of tickets sold. If you don't sell enough tickets you have to make up the shortfall. It pays to drum up 'rent-a-crowd' from among your local fans, friends and family. I know of bands that sell package tours – they hire a coach and sell tickets to the gig and a coach to get you there and back. This proves especially popular where the band manages to get a gig in a larger town or city. Then the trip to the gig is combined with the chance of a day out in the city at a reasonable price.

As I mentioned in Chapter 1, you might also consider entering one of the many competitions run around the country. These might be billed as 'Battle of the Bands' or similar. Look out for adverts in the local press or the music papers like *NME* or *Kerrang*. These contests are often viewed as slightly cheesy, not quite a credible way to break into the business. If it gets you noticed, what's the problem? If nothing happens, then you don't have to mention you were ever involved in it.

There are also some venues that have special showcase evenings for unsigned artists or writers. The ones I know about are in London, but there may well be others in a town near you – ask around. The Kashmir Club in Marylebone holds regular nights for unsigned acts. The Barfly at the Monarch pub in Camden has similar events. The PRS occasionally supports events for artists who are either completely unsigned or have only signed a record deal. The American collection societies ASCAP and BMI also hold unsigned artist events from time to time. Contact details for these venues and organisations are to be found in Useful Addresses at the end of the book.

You can try and get in on the unsigned acts part of the annual UK music conference called In The City. It's run by Tony Wilson (ex-Factory label boss) and is usually held in mid-September. As well as being a place for UK music business people to gather and have a drink or five, it's also the venue for a whole series of music events – mostly for unsigned acts. The unsigned gigs are held in local music venues and pubs and are a magnet for A&R scouts and record label honchos. This is because in the past this event has been a fruitful source of new talent, including Suede, Oasis and Kula Shaker. To be part of the unsigned section you have to submit your demo and a brief biography to the unsigned organisers, who then have the unenviable task of wading through a vast pile of material to come up with a shortlist of about 30–40 bands over the 4–5 nights of the event.

A similar event was held for the first time in 2002 in Glasgow, which also had showcases for unsigned bands. The Welsh Music Federation, backed by the Welsh Assembly, is also mandated to boost interest in Welsh artists and music companies and intends to take part in music industry events which can act as a showcase for Welsh acts.[1]

Most artists who are already signed see live concerts as an essential marketing tool. People that haven't yet bought one of your records may go to one of your gigs and love what you do so much that the next day they go and buy up your entire recording output. A good review of a live gig can give your latest release very valuable publicity. Also, the current emphasis being placed on radio-friendly artists means that if your records aren't the sort that Radio 1 or other powerful radio stations are going to play, you have little alternative than to build a fan base through live concerts (see Chapter 6).

GETTING A BOOKING AGENT

The next stage on from you or your manager doing all the legwork yourselves is to get a booking agent. This will probably happen after you sign a record deal (see Chapter 3). It may, however, happen before if you've established a reputation as a good live act and

---

[1] See www.welshmusicfoundation.com

have attracted the attention of local agents because they can see you're a safe bet for venues they regularly book acts for.

Do you need a booking agent at this stage? Possibly not. If your horizons are set at only playing local pub venues and you don't mind doing the work yourself, you probably won't need one. It's someone else that you're going to have to pay commission to, so you want to make sure it's going to be worthwhile before you get one. Also, they aren't likely to be interested in you unless you've already established a reputation for live work.

What you may find is that certain venues are closed to you, because the venue owner only books acts brought to him by selected booking agents. Having a booking agent can also give you credibility to get into more prestigious or bigger venues, and open up the possibility of supporting bigger 'name' acts. As the booking agent is on a percentage of what you get, it's in his interests to drive a hard bargain. If the agent is any good you should end up with a better deal than if you had negotiated it yourself.

You might think that your manager could do the job of a booking agent. Yes, they could and in the early days they probably will. But specialised booking agents are the experts in putting together larger events such as a UK or European tour of the medium to large venues and stadiums. They know all the promoters, they can get the best deals and have a better chance of getting the prime dates than you or your manager, who don't do this on a day-by-day basis. The agents also know about all the main venues you're likely to want to play, and one or two that you'll not have thought of. If the venue is outside the main concert circuit, they have the specialised expertise to negotiate a good deal for you. With everything else that's going on around a tour, you or your manager aren't going to have the time to do this properly. It pays to find someone who can.

HOW DO YOU FIND A BOOKING AGENT?

You can ask your mates in the music business. Which agents do they use, which ones do they rate and which have they found to be trustworthy? Word of mouth is often a very reliable method of finding a good booking agent. Be sure that the booking agent works in the same area of music as you, otherwise he won't have the contacts in the right places to be of use to you.

Booking agents are also listed in directories such as the *Music Week Directory*. You could call local ones and try to find out which sort of acts they regularly work with and what venues they book. Another good source of information on agents and who does what is the monthly magazine *Audience*. It also gives you music business news, including details of up-coming festivals and other music industry events.

If you have a record deal it's likely that your A&R man will direct you or your manager to a good booking agent. While obviously you should take on board their suggestions, you shouldn't blindly follow their advice. As with finding a manager (see Chapter 2), you should also ask around and arrange to meet more than one agent. You should get them to come and see you perform live. This should show you who seems the most enthusiastic. You should also ask around as to which booking agents are seen as having the most 'clout'. Your record company, accountant and lawyer should all have had experience of dealing with booking agents and can give you some guidance. It's also important that your agent has a reputation as being honest. You don't want a booking agent who's going to run off with the ticket takings. If the agent who is interested in you works for a big organisation, find out if you'll be dealing with him in person or if he'll be passing you on to someone else in the organisation.

Booking agents will probably approach you or your manager, either direct or via the record company, if there's a good buzz or hype about you and you're signed to a record deal. If this happens, the same tips apply. Ask who else is on their books. Ask around about their reputation, honesty and reliability. Get them to meet the band and see you perform live. Make sure the agent 'gets the picture' as to what you're trying to achieve.

One thing that you should also be aware of is that some booking agents may also be getting a financial kick-back from the record label to come on board as your agent. I know of record labels who are keen to see their artists perform live and encourage agents to get involved by paying them either a retainer or a small percentage of record sales (usually 0.5–1%). This should be at the record company's expense and not recoupable against you or deducted from your royalty or other record income. It's not necessarily a bad thing, but there could be a conflict of interest between what you want and what your record company thinks is best for you. Also, when you work out your deal with an agent who's being paid in this way, you need to bear in mind what they're also getting from the record company.

WHAT'S IN A BOOKING AGENCY CONTRACT?

Some agents don't have written contracts with the artists they represent. They prefer to work on trust. They tell the artists what commission rate they take, they leave it to the artist's tour manager to sort out things such as the riders (see page 186), security requirements and so on. The risk for an agent in not having a written contract isn't as great as for a manager, because the agent is probably only booking one tour at a time and will have sorted out in advance his commission on that tour. He has no interest in ongoing record or publishing royalties, or in merchandising or sponsorship income. That said, even though some agents don't bother with written contracts, most booking agents like to have a contract to keep things clear and to give them some certainty so that they can plan what's to happen in the future. In many ways the booking agency contract is similar to a management contract (see Chapter 2).

There are several parts of the contract that are common to all booking agency contracts.

Exclusivity

The booking agent will be looking for an exclusive arrangement. He won't want to be competing for your work with other agents. The arrangement with the booking agent sits alongside the management agreement. Indeed, the manager may be very involved in the appointment of the booking agent. The management contract will usually give the artist the right to approve the identity of any booking agent. The manager looks after all other aspects of touring other than the actual booking of the concerts. There is a danger of an overlap in the commission arrangements. The artist doesn't want to be paying a booking agent and the manager out of his gross income. The management contract will usually say that the manager takes his commission after any commission to a booking agent has been deducted. The management contract will usually give the artist approval over the terms on which the agent is appointed, particularly if he wants to charge more than the industry norm of 15–20%. The booking agent's fee should be deducted from the gross income first, and the manager's commission should be calculated on the net amount that's left after the agency commission and any other deductions agreed in the management contract have been taken off.

Territory

The contract could be a worldwide one or it could be for a specific territory, for example North America. If it's a worldwide deal then it's possible that the booking agent will want to use local sub-agents in some territories. For example, the booking agent may have his own offices in the UK and Europe, but be linked in with another company or individual in the US. The artist may want to have the right to approve the identity of any sub-agents. Any sub-agent's fees should come out of the booking agent's fee and not be payable by the artist.

If it's a worldwide deal, the artist will want to be satisfied that the booking agent has the necessary contacts himself or through established sub-agents to do a good job in all countries where the artist is likely to want to perform live. It's no good appointing a UK booking agent worldwide when he can do a great job in the UK but hasn't a clue how to deal with promoters or venues in other parts of the world.

Term

The length of the term can vary considerably. It could be for a particular tour, for example the 2003 UK Arena tour. In that case the contract will end after the last date of that tour. The artist is free to do a deal for the next tour or for the US leg of the same tour with another agent, as long as it doesn't interfere with the UK booking agent's rights.

The term could be open-ended, continuing until one party gives the other notice to end the arrangement. The usual notice period is a minimum of three months. There may also be an agreement that notice can't take effect during a tour, or that the agent gets commission on the whole of a tour they have set up, even if the arrangements with them are terminated before the tour is finished. This is only fair, because tour arrangements often have to be set up many months in advance.

Many booking agents are looking for the certainty of a fixed-term contract. This could be as short as a year, but terms of three to five years aren't unusual. Obviously, from your viewpoint, the longer you're committed to one booking agent, the more need there is for a contract that puts definite obligations on the booking agent to get work for you. The contract should also contain a get-out if it's not working out, because the booking agent can't get any work or is otherwise falling down on the job.

The booking agent's duties

As we saw with management contracts, the agency contract doesn't often set out in any great detail what the booking agent will do. The agent's duties are usually expressed in very general terms. There should at least be some kind of obligation on the agent to try to get work for you. After all, that's his job. If there's a fixed-term contract and if you're ready to do gigs and your agent can't or won't get you any work, then you should have the option to go to another agent.

On the other hand, if the agent does get you work, you should have the right to decide whether you actually want to do the work. The contract will probably give you the right to turn down offers of work if you do so on reasonable grounds. For example, if the booking agent gets you three dates in the North of England and a fourth a day later in Torquay, it might be reasonable to say that you can't reasonably get yourself and your gear from one end of the country to the other in that time. Or, if you did, it wouldn't be cost-effective once you take into account the travel costs in getting there. If, however, your booking agent has got you work which you turn down for no good reason, you can't then turn around and say that the agent hasn't done his job.

Your duties

You will usually have to agree to refer all offers for live work that come to you to your booking agent. Because of the exclusive arrangements, you mustn't act as your own booking agent. You will also usually agree to keep your booking agent aware of your plans. For example, if the plan is to release the new album in September, you'll be expecting to do live dates to help promote that release. You'll need to tell the agent at the beginning of the year so that they can begin to outline a tour in consultation with you and your manager. Many of the bigger venues are booked up months, if not a year, in advance for key dates, and the earlier the agent is told of the plans the sooner they can start to take options on the key venues and dates. These provisional bookings are confirmed when the details of the tour are firmed up. If you're tying a tour in with the release of your album, the dates won't probably be finally confirmed until the approximate delivery date for the album is known. That said, it doesn't always work to plan. If the recording overruns then the delivery date will shift and could have an impact on the tour dates. However, gigs at big venues are usually set up for a few months after the album release. This allows the public to get to know some material off the new album so that they buy up the tickets with enthusiasm. Tours also have to try and tie in with any plans to release the album overseas.

You'll usually agree to use your best efforts to do the dates that the booking agent has booked and which you have agreed to do. Obviously illnesses do occur, and sometimes tours or particular concert dates are cancelled at short notice due to this. It's usual to take out insurance against having to cancel a tour, or one or more dates, if illness or accident affects one or more band members. These insurance policies aren't cheap, but if the artist gets laryngitis halfway through a world tour or, as happened recently with Oasis, three band members were involved in a car crash causing the cancellation or postponement of some US dates, it's comforting to know that insurance will cover any losses. Insurance policies can also be taken out to cover dates that have to be cancelled because not enough tickets have been sold. These are, of course, very expensive and are probably only worth it for big stadium dates. If you've got yourself a decent manager, you shouldn't have to worry about whether the necessary insurance is in place as he, or the tour manager, will do this for you.

Insurance policies can also be taken out to cover things like bad weather on open-air gigs. The owner of the site that hosts the Glastonbury Festival described in the press how he'd been offered insurance cover against bad weather, but hadn't taken it up because the premium was too high. I wonder if he was kicking himself, because that particular year the weather was so atrocious the site turned into a giant mudbath.

You can get insurance cover for most things at a price. I remember a situation when a member of a band was spending a year living outside the UK for tax reasons. The rules at the time allowed you to return to the UK for a given number of days in that year. The band was doing a world tour, which included some dates in the UK. The last of these dates fell on the last day that he would have been entitled to be in the UK and not lose the tax advantages. The concert was due to finish at 10.30 p.m., which meant that with a helicopter standing by he should have been out of the country in time. If he wasn't he would lose significant amounts of tax savings, so an insurance policy was taken out to cover him against that happening. Everything was going very well until the band got a little too enthusiastic in the number of encores, and it was getting nearer to 11.00 p.m. when the band finally left the stage. A very swift dash to the helicopter followed and, luckily, our man was just away in time.

Your booking agent may want to have a free hand in deciding which promoter to use for particular tours. So long as you aren't being asked to agree to a worse deal as a result, you may well be happy to leave this decision to your booking agent. After all, it's also in their interests to get you a good deal.

The fee

What is the agent paid? His fee is usually a percentage of the gross income from your live appearances. It will include the appearance fee and also any benefits that you receive in kind as opposed to in cash. For example, the payment you get for a particular contract could be made up of a £10,000 appearance fee plus a car provided by the tour or venue promoter, or free travel or hotel accommodation. The agent will usually want to add the value of the car, the travel, the accommodation and so on to the gross income in working out his fee. It's here, of course, that you can see the value of a tour accountant. One of his many jobs will be to see that a proper value has been placed on these non-monetary items.

The fee is usually between 10 and 15% of the gross income. If you're paid £10,000 in appearance fees and a car worth £10,000, then your booking agent will receive 10–15% of £20,000 (i.e. £2–3,000). The agent will negotiate with the promoter or with the venue direct, and will usually agree that the promoter or venue pays them their fee direct, with the balance being paid through to you. There may be a deposit paid which the agent may well hold as security for their fee. Once it's clear that there are sufficient ticket sales to mean that date won't make a loss, the booking agent may well agree to release that deposit to you, less their agency fee. Or, the agent may negotiate guaranteed minimum payments from the venue or promoter, which aren't returnable, even if insufficient tickets are sold to make the date viable. The booking agent will usually insist on being paid for any work that has been contracted for or substantially negotiated during the term of the agency contract. For example, you may contract to a 40-date tour through a particular agent and then move on to another agent for the rest of the dates or for the next tour. While you may be free to do this, you will still have to pay the first booking agent for the work they did in putting the original 40-date tour together. Sometimes the agent will limit their commission to concert dates that you do within six months of the end of the term of their contract. This could be a little hard on the agent. If the artist is doing a world tour, it's likely that that could run well beyond six months. If the agent has done the work in setting up the tour, there are strong arguments for saying that they should be paid for that work. As it's unlikely that you will have to pay any other booking agent for that same tour, you aren't going to get a double-hit for fees. If the booking agent has done an all-right job and the contract isn't being disputed, or hasn't been brought to an end because the booking agent is in breach of contract, this position is a reasonable one to take.

Accounting

The booking agent will usually want to collect the money and deduct their commission before paying the balance through to you.

You'll want to make sure that the money is paid into a separate bank account, preferably one where the money is held in trust for you. You'll need to see detailed statements of what has been received, from where and how the commission is calculated. You'll want the balance to be paid through quickly and will need to have the right to carry out an audit of the booking agent's books and records to make sure you've received amounts properly due.

This is particularly important where some payments may be received up-front in the form of deposits from the venues, or as guaranteed sums regardless of the number of tickets sold. The deposit may be returnable in some circumstances. One of the jobs of the tour accountant is to keep a track of all these arrangements as well as keeping a close eye on any sums paid in cash on the night.

The balance due to you should be paid through at the end of each gig, but that may not be possible, in which case it should be at least weekly. Sometimes payment may come at monthly intervals if the arrangements are particularly complex or involve overseas tax issues. If you aren't going to be paid on the night and payment is to be delayed then a rough outline – called a settlement sheet – should be prepared at the end of each gig and given to the artist or the tour accountant within three days to check.

Assignment and key-man provisions

You need to establish who is going to be your agent – your key contact at the booking agency. The larger the booking agency, the more important it is to get this sorted out. There's nothing worse than signing up to an agency thinking that you're going to be dealt with by one of the hot-shots, only to discover that he has passed it to a junior with no experience or clout.

If you can, you should get a right in the contract to terminate it if that key-man isn't available to you as your agent. Obviously, a good agent is going to be working for more than one artist and is going to be in great demand. You can't therefore expect him to be there for you every minute of the day. But when it comes to putting together a big tour, whether you're the headline or support act, you need to know that the agent is there for you to lend their experience and bargaining skills to sorting out the details. The agency isn't going to be very happy about agreeing to key-man clauses in the contract. If a particularly good agent wants to go off to another agency, or wants to set up on their own account, that puts them in a very good bargaining position. You can terminate the contract if the agent leaves and then move to their new agency if you want to. The agent can use the fact that you could terminate to negotiate better terms for them if they're to stay with the agency, or better settlement terms if they still want to leave. If the agency does agree to a key-man clause then it will probably say that the right to terminate only arises when the agent is consistently not around for 30 days or more. They will also usually exclude periods when the agent is genuinely ill or on holiday.

If the agency plans to sell up or sell on the contract to another company, or it wants to buy into a bigger company, you should have the right to refuse to be tied to these arrangements unless the agency first gets your approval.

Finally, the contract should give you the right to terminate the term of the contract if the agent is insolvent or breaches his obligations, for example, if he doesn't pay the balance of the ticket money when he should and he fails to put this right within a reasonable time of you putting him on notice that they should.

PROMOTERS

A promoter is responsible for booking artists to perform live at particular venues. This could be one man promoting a single venue or a multi-million-pound multi-national corporation owning the right to promote a whole raft of large and small venues. A couple of years ago, a company owned by one of the best-known UK promoters, Harvey Goldsmith, went into receivership leaving a large gap in the marketplace. His companies were responsible for promoting many large-scale events at Wembley and Earls Court, among others. There was some concern among UK promoters at this time about the aggressive expansion by the US company SFX Entertainments into the UK media and leisure industry. SFX Entertainments owned a large number of the New York Broadway theatres and was the largest concert promoter in the US.[2] In 1999 SFX embarked on a series of acquisitions of UK promoters. In mid-1999 they bought up the Midland Concert Promotions Group and the Marquee Group. In September 1999 they bought Britain's biggest theatre operator, Apollo Leisure Group, and at the end of 1999 they bought out Barry Clayman Concerts. SFX was also said to be interested in bidding for Stoll Moss, which owns a number of London theatres including the Lyric and the Garrick, but was beaten to it by Andrew Lloyd Webber's Really Useful Group, which apparently paid £87.5 million for the theatres. In less than 3 years SFX had become the world's largest and most diversified promoter for live events. It also toyed with tie-ups with Internet companies such as World Online International, apparently with the view to setting up a pan-European live entertainment portal on the Internet. In early 2000, SFX was itself sold to a company whose stable of assets included radio stations. It has been rebranded as Clear Channel and continues as one of the most significant promoters of UK venues.

WHAT DO PROMOTERS DO?

Promoters are responsible for securing the venue and for selling the tickets. The promoter may be the venue owner himself, or they may be a separate company who have an arrangement with a particular venue. This arrangement may be exclusive or non-exclusive. The promoter may deal direct with the artist or his manager or he may negotiate through a booking agent. Promoters makes their money on their margins. If they own the venue then they want to cover their costs and make a profit. If they just deal with a venue they make their money on the difference between what they have to pay through to the venue and what they have to pay to the artist/booking agent after allowing for their own expenses. The promoter may also control the sales concessions at the venues, for example for selling food, drink or merchandise. The promoter may charge for the rental of these concessions and/or take a percentage of the takings.

2 Source: Jamie Doward's article in the *Observer* on 10 October 1999.

A promoter may promote just one venue or perhaps a festival or a series of venues. There are promoters who operate nationwide, but also those who operate only in particular parts of the UK.[3]

Once the dates are pencilled in, the promoter will want an agreement committing the artist to do these dates and laying out the terms on which they will perform.

Naturally, these sort of arrangements are only likely to affect the main artists on the bill – the top billing or headline acts. A supporting artist will have little or no say on the terms of the deal with the promoter. The promoter will usually agree a fee with the headline act and it's up to that act to agree a deal with the supporting act as to the terms on which they will appear on the bill.

WHAT'S IN A PROMOTERS CONTRACT?

Your obligations

The contract will set out what concerts you will do, when and where. The contract could spell out the length of time you are required to perform. For example, it may say that you're expected to do one 'set' (performance) of at least 40 minutes duration. For smaller venues it may say that you're expected to do two 40-minute sets with a break in between.

Promoter's obligations

The promoter will agree to provide at least the venue, ticket sales facilities and basic door, stage and backstage security arrangements. Thereafter it's down to the individual arrangements agreed in each contract. The promoter may agree to supply certain equipment and personnel, for example, a particular sound desk or sound engineer. If the dates include any overseas gigs, then any personnel they supply should be provided with all necessary permits, including work permits for overseas dates or for overseas personnel working in the UK.

The promoter will also usually be required to provide an agreed level of backstage amenities for you in the form of dressing rooms, toilets and meeting or VIP areas.

It's also usually the responsibility of the promoter to provide insurance cover against injury or death caused to members of the public. This is called public liability insurance. It's vital to ensure that this cover is in place. Obviously, this will be the manager's job once there is a manager on board, but a member of the public can get injured in the early days as well, so you should think about this. Unfortunately accidents do happen at live gigs; people do fall or get caught up in the crush at the front of the stage. If there isn't insurance in place, the person injured could look to you direct for compensation. If anyone is employed to do any construction work, for example for the stage or lighting rig, then those sub-contractors should also carry insurance or, once again, responsibility could fall back on you.

The promoter may also insure against cancellation by you, or bad weather for open-air festivals. However, they won't necessarily include you in the cover provided by the policy. They may only be concerned that their losses are covered and not be bothered

3 The Regional Promoter's Association (UK) is an informal grouping of promoters. Contact Josh Dean, Concorde2, Madeira Drive, Brighton, BN2 1EU. Tel. 01273 207241.

about whether you can recover any of the sums you've paid out to musicians, stage crew, on equipment hire, transport and so on. It's usually your or your manager's responsibility to get all necessary insurance.

Riders

Anyone who's seen the spoof film about the music business *Spinal Tap* will know about the occasionally ridiculous artist riders. These are the lists of specific requirements that the artists have for their comfort and entertainment backstage. Only black jellybeans and sandwiches cut in circles will do! I've seen some very strange riders in my time. One was twelve pages of very detailed menu requirements, including very specific types of cereal and drinks that can only be bought in the US. As this was a European tour that was pretty unreasonable and changes had to be negotiated and substitutes found. Other riders specify only a crate of good whisky and five crates of beer. Well, this *is* rock 'n' roll. Some artists take their own caterers with them or will only use a caterer that they know is familiar with their particular requirements. Some riders are there for a very good reason. For example, an artist may be a vegan or vegetarian, or allergic to particular food. I've also seen riders that insist that all hotel rooms have hypo-allergenic bedding and pillows.

It's usual to leave the negotiation of the details between the manager or the tour manager and the promoter. It's not usually cost-effective to get your lawyer involved in this. The riders do form part of the contract, so the promoter has to make sure that the requirements are reasonable, affordable and obtainable. If they don't and the omissions are sufficiently serious, this could be a breach of contract. Even if the omissions are more minor in nature, it can cause major grief with the artist, which is the last thing a promoter wants just before the artist goes out on stage.

Fees

You and your booking agent are dependent on the promoter for ticket sales and income. You'll want to be sure that you're guaranteed a certain level of income. If you're already an established artist, you may be able to get a Guaranteed Minimum included in the contract. This guarantees you will be paid this amount, regardless of whether the promoter sells enough tickets. This is where the promoter takes the risk. They have to get the level of the Guaranteed Minimum right, because they'll have to pay it even if they don't sell a single ticket.

Over and above any Guaranteed Minimum sum, you might receive a fixed percentage of the promoter's net receipts. For example, if the Guaranteed Minimum is £10,000 and, after the promoter has paid out certain agreed expenses, you are entitled to 10% of the net receipts, then if the net ticket sales are £100,000 you will only get the Guaranteed Minimum. If the net receipts are £250,000, then 10% is worth £25,000. After deducting the Guaranteed Minimum of £10,000, you are now due another £15,000. The tour accountant will have to check very carefully that the expenses that the promoter can deduct are reasonable and that the percentage you receive of the net monies represents a reasonable return. The alternative is that you receive a further fixed payment dependent on levels of ticket sales. For example, it could be agreed that you get a Guaranteed Minimum of £10,000 plus, if ticket sales exceed £250,000, you receive another £15,000. With this type of payment arrangement, you must assess how realistic it is that ticket sales will be high enough so that you have a reasonable chance of receiving further payments.

Payment and accounting

The contract should set out when any Guaranteed Minimum payment is to be made. Usually at least half of it should be paid up-front and the rest on the night of the first of the concerts.

The balance of any payments should be made on the night of each gig or possibly at the end of a particular leg of a tour or end of each week of a tour.

It's important that the tour accountant has access to the box-office tills and receipts on the night of the concert and that all ticket stubs should be kept for at least three months afterwards in case they need to be checked by the accountant. Further payments under the merchandising deal may be dependent on a given number of people being at each concert (see Chapter 8). The ticket stubs and any head count on the night will prove the number of people at a particular date, so access to this information and proof is very important. Receipts for any expense that the promoter is allowed to deduct should also be scrutinised and kept for later checking. Only those expenses allowed by the tour accountant should be deducted.

Other income

The promoter or the venue owner may have done deals with catering companies or drink suppliers. The contract should set out whether or not you should get any share of the profits from such sources. For example, the venue may have a deal with Coca-Cola that they are the official suppliers of soft drinks to the venue. An artist that commands a very loyal following of fans who will ensure that his concerts are a sell-out can only be of benefit to Coca-Cola in the considerable number of soft drinks it will sell at those concerts. If you have sufficient bargaining power, you can insist on sharing some of the money that Coca-Cola pays to the promoter or venue for the right to be the exclusive supplier.

The sale of merchandise can be an important source of income for you. The promoter/venue may make a charge for the right to set up merchandising stalls at the venue. The merchandising deal will cover whether the merchandising company is allowed to deduct some or all of this charge from the gross income before you receive your percentage.

If you have sufficient bargaining power, you could insist that you alone have the right to sell food or drink and that the promoter gets no income from these or from merchandise sales. You can then do sponsorship deals with food and drink companies as well as merchandising deals. These kind of arrangements tend only to apply to established, successful artists with a team of people able to give effect to these arrangements.

Restrictions

The contract should insist that the promoter stops anyone from recording the performances, unless of course a live recording or film of the concert is being made. Your record contract will probably say something about you not allowing anyone to make a recording of your performance. While it's very difficult to prevent a bootlegger unofficially and unlawfully recording the performance, you can show the right spirit by putting this requirement in the contract with the promoter. This will demonstrate that you don't condone this sort of activity. If you do intend to make a film of the performance, perhaps to make a video or for a live webcast or television broadcast, the contract should make sure that the promoter will allow access to the venue for the recording at no extra charge.

Each venue has its own restrictions on parking and when the stage crew can gain access to load equipment in or out. Any particular stipulations or restrictions should be set out in a rider or schedule to the contract. In residential areas, there may be severe restrictions on how late the artist can play and there may be an early curfew on when the crew can load the equipment back out. They may have to come back the next morning. If so, you need to ensure the equipment is kept securely and that it's insured against loss or damage. If it's a nationwide tour, the tour manager will need to know these restrictions well in advance. It wouldn't be funny if you had a date in Scarborough on the Friday night and your equipment was still in Torquay because the crew couldn't get in to load out the equipment after Thursday's Torquay gig until seven o'clock the next morning.

An important part of protecting your brand is to ensure that there are no sales of unauthorised merchandise inside or outside the venue. It's easier for a promoter to control illegal merchandise inside the venue, but he may say he has no control over what happens outside. In that case you should try to make sure that the venue and the promoter co-operates with Trading Standards Officers or other personnel who are trying to stop unauthorised or pirate merchandise.

GETTING FUNDING

Funding for a tour can come from a number of different places. At the lowest level, where you're just starting out and doing local gigs, you can expect to be paid little or nothing over and above some petrol money and a few free pints of beer. As you progress, you may get a small percentage of the ticket sales and may make some money from sales of T-shirts or recordings of your performances that you sell at the gigs. There probably won't be much in the way of profits after the cost of hiring a PA, paying for transport and maybe an agent or manager.

It is possible for an unsigned act to get sponsorship for live work. As mentioned in Chapter 9, companies such as Doc Marten or lager companies have sponsored live tours by unsigned acts. Pub chains like The Firkin pubs have also sponsored live music at their pubs around the country. Some artists can make a decent living from live gigs if they can keep their costs down, play decent-sized venues and have a loyal following of fans, but it's very hard work.

Once you're signed to a record deal, bigger venues may open up to you. A booking agent may come on the scene and get you slots as support bands or lower-down-the-order gigs at summer open-air festivals. Money can be made from merchandise sales or from tour sponsorship. However, it's likely that you won't make a profit on live work until you've achieved quite a degree of success and fame as a recording artist. Even then you may barely break even if you have an expensive live set with lots of special effects and a cast of thousands. If your live set is kept very simple, without loads of backing singers or a live orchestra, then you stand a better chance of making money. But it's important to balance cutting expenses back to a minimum against the risk that the show is a disappointment to the fans, which would be counter-productive.

Most artists need the support of their record company to get them out on the road. The record company will rarely agree to put this in the record contract unless you have a lot of bargaining power, or you're prepared to hold out for this support at the expense of perhaps a lower advance or royalty. Even if it's not specifically in the contract, it's usually in the record company's interests for you to be out touring and promoting your new album. If you can only do this by making a loss (the shortfall) then the record company has to come to your rescue and underwrite this shortfall. This is usually called tour support.

Tour support is usually 100% recoupable from royalties from record sales. This is, however, negotiable and could be reduced to 50% recoupable, with the remainder being treated as a non-recoupable marketing expense of the record company. Sometimes, if the tour support is for a tour in a particular part of the world, for example Japan, then you could agree that the tour support is only recouped from Japanese record sales.

In addition to making up any shortfall, the record company may pay a 'buy-on' fee. This is the fee payable to the headline artist on a tour or to his record company for the privilege of being allowed to support them. For some new artists, the association with a more established name gives them an opening to a much wider potential audience, as well as the chance to perform in bigger venues. For the headline act this is an additional source of income, reducing the amount of tour support they'll need from their record company. Buy-on fees for large venues and for concerts by big-name artists can run to tens of thousands of pounds. It's one of the reasons why you'll often see a big-name artist being supported by another smaller act who's on the same label. That way the costs are kept in the family.

HOW MUCH TOUR SUPPORT WILL YOU NEED?
Before you can go to your record company to ask for tour support, you need to have an idea how much you'll need.

First, you'll need to get someone to prepare a tour budget. This could be your manager or your regular accountant or bookkeeper. However, when doing a bigger tour, either as headline or support, consider getting a specialist tour accountant on board. The tour accountant could be someone at the regular accountancy firm, or one recommended by them, or by friends. Your A&R contact or manager can suggest people, as can your lawyer. Most importantly, the tour accountant must be honest, must understand how tour promoting works, and be brave enough to tackle unscrupulous promoters about to run off with the cash midway through the gig.

The tour accountant, or any other person doing that job, will put together an outline budget that will make guesstimates of income and expenditure. As details such as any Guaranteed Minimum, any buy-on fees, merchandise advances and so on become known they are factored in. The accountant will work very closely with you or your manager to work out what type of shows you intend to put on. The number of musicians, how elaborate the stage set or lighting effects will be, will all affect the tour budget.

Once your tour accountant has a good idea of the likely profit (or, more likely, loss) he prepares an outline draft budget which your manager then takes to your record company to negotiate the level of tour support. It's important, therefore, that he doesn't make wild guesses and is as accurate as he can be as to what you're likely to need.

The record company will usually set a maximum amount that they will pay to underwrite the shortfall. For example, the tour accountant may have estimated a tour loss of £18,000. The record company checks his figures and makes its own assessment of how valuable it will be to them in record sales if the tour goes ahead. It may decide that one or two dates should be dropped, or that some of the costs could be saved. It will set a limit on how much it will pay. In this case, after some adjustments it may say that it will pay up to £16,000 in tour support. You and your manager have to then sit down with the tour accountant, and any production manager working on the tour, to see if savings can be made. If the tour then goes ahead and it does better than expected and only loses £15,000, then the record company underwrites a £15,000 shortfall not a £16,000 one. The actual amount they will pay (up to that maximum) is determined by the actual costs supplied by the tour accountant after the end of the tour with supporting invoices. If the tour does worse than expected and makes a £17,000 loss then the record company is only obliged to pay £16,000, and may insist that you pick up the rest of the bill yourself. So it's important to get the figure for the anticipated shortfall as realistic as possible.

The record company will usually agree to pay part of the tour support up-front. This means that the essential personnel can be paid some of what is due to them and essential equipment can be hired. The tour accountant then has to juggle who gets paid along the way, and who has to wait until the final instalment comes in from the record company. Needless to say, the tour accountant is rarely the most popular man on the tour.

Even if there is something in your record contract about tour support, it's unlikely that all the details will be included and it's usual to set out these detailed arrangements in a side agreement to the main record contract. Copies of all side agreements should be kept together with the record contract. If you're reviewing the accounting statements or are considering doing an audit, you need to have details of all the arrangements you've reached about what amounts are or aren't recoupable and from what sales. Unless the side agreement is very simple, a lawyer should review it before it is signed.

This is an example of the sorts of things you'd expect to see in a tour budget for a band doing a number of overseas concerts or a tour involving overnight hotel stays and transportation.

Rough budget for overseas tour

DESCRIPTION	COMMENTS	RATE		PERIOD	TOTAL
Equipment		£/Day		Days req'd:	
Tour Rentals:	*(Add details below of all items*				
Fixed Lights	*& costs)*				
Moving Lights					
Risers					
Sound					

DESCRIPTION	COMMENTS	RATE		PERIOD	TOTAL
Security					
Band Tour Bus					
Crew Tour Bus					
Trucking					
Flight Case Rental					
Equipment Rental	*(Any extra equipment required)*				
Wages (Band & Crew Party)		Rate:		Period:	
Band members	*(Names of any band members*				
Crew members	*on wages and any crew)*		pw		
Daily Expenses	*No. of people on expenses*	Rate per day:	Days:		
Band Party	*How many in band*		pd		
Crew Party	*How many in crew*		pd		
Crew Driver	*Usually 1 per transport*		pd		
Truck Drivers	*1*		pd		
Band Driver	*1*		pd		
Accommodation	*How many needing beds*	£/Night:		No. of nights:	
Band Party					
Crew Party					
Transport	*To and from hotel/venue*				
Taxis	*Taxis & Cars*				
Travel to and from London	*Band & Crew Party*				
Flights	*Internal – to national gigs*				
Flights	*International – to overseas gigs*				
Freight	*To and from gigs for equipment*				
Local transport	*From airport/station to gig*				
Administration & Commissions/fees					
UK & Europe (or wherever tour is)					
Tour Insurance	*Cancellation of tour*				
Tour Insurance	*Equipment loss/damage*				
Insurance	*Public Liability for concertgoers*				
Tour Accounting	*Fees for tour accountants*				
Itineraries	*Printing/binding of gig details*				
Passes	*Printing/laminating of security passes*				
Tips	*Hotel/porters/taxis etc.*				
Design Fee	*Stage set design*				
Design Fee	*Lighting design*				

DESCRIPTION	COMMENTS	RATE		PERIOD	TOTAL
Commission	Booking Agent's percentage	%			
Commission	Management	%			
Miscellaneous	Any special items				
Phone & Fax	Long-distance costs				
Laundry					
Pre-production	Rehearsals				
Subsistence	Food/living expenses				
		Sub-Total:			
	(In case anything goes wrong:)	5% Contingency			
		Total:			
	(Amount you are guaranteed to receive:)	Guarantee:	US $		
	(Ticket and merchandise sales)	Income			
	Profit after costs:	Approx. UK £			

OTHER PLANNING ISSUES

There are some other things that have to be taken into account when planning a tour.

TAX PLANNING

Your accountant should advise whether there are any tax advantages to you in putting your touring services through a limited company and, if so, should that be a UK-based or offshore company (see Chapter 11).

If your accountant does advise use of a limited company, a service agreement should be put in place between you and that company. The contract with any promoter will then be with the limited company.

If some or all of the dates are in another EU country then the band (or company) may need to register for VAT in each country to be visited. This can be avoided if the promoter agrees to account for the VAT on the performance fees using what is known as the 'reverse charge' method. And no, it doesn't have anything to do with telephone calls. Essentially what it means is that the promoter takes responsibility for accounting for all the VAT in his own country and the band needn't get involved. This needs to be set out clearly in the contract with the promoter to avoid a situation where the VAT man in the country concerned demands that the band (or the company) pays VAT.

In some countries, there is an obligation to pay tax in that country on earnings from live work undertaken there. The promoter may have to deduct the tax before he hands the money over. In that case the contract with the promoter must make sure that the promoter has to hand over the sums he has withheld to the relevant tax authorities. In countries where there are reciprocal tax treaties in place, it's possible to claim exemption from some of these taxes or, if they have a tax treaty in place, you may be able to reclaim some or all of the amounts withheld. The promoter should be obliged to do all the necessary paperwork and the local tax authorities should either confirm exemption from tax on the income or provide a certificate of how much tax has been withheld so this can be offset against UK income for tax purposes.

Until recently, when a band was embarking on a long tour where a large proportion of a tax year was to be spent outside the UK, the band might have decided to take a tax year out. This meant that the band members would remain out of the country for long enough not to have to pay tax in the UK for that particular tax year. At the time it didn't mean that you had to be out for a full year and you could spend some days in the UK in that tax year. If this were carefully planned, the artist could also avoid paying any income tax at all on his earnings during that tax year. These arrangements were altered in 1998. You'll no doubt have seen the press stories about the Rolling Stones cancelling their UK dates in 1998. This was, it's said, solely on tax grounds. They and several members of the crew were apparently taking tax years out from the UK. The tightening up of the rules meant that, in order to get the maximum tax benefit, they couldn't set foot in the UK for the whole of that tax year. The UK dates were cancelled because, otherwise, the Stones and their crew would lose all of the benefit of their tax year out.

Obviously, everyone's tax circumstances are different and these are only very general comments. Nothing will substitute for proper, professional tax planning and advice. Such planning should be done as far ahead as possible.

PUBLICISING THE TOUR

This is the joint responsibility of you and the promoter. Your record company also has a vested interest and will want to co-ordinate their own marketing efforts with the tour dates. For example, if they had planned a poster campaign in particular towns in the UK, they may decide to target those towns where you're doing live dates. The tour posters may also give information on when your latest record is to be released. The promoter or the venue will publish adverts in the music and local press listing forthcoming tours. Your press officer and the internal press office at your record company will get to work placing the information in the press, getting interviews and personal appearances for you to promote the tour. You'll be expected to mention it in interviews with the press or on radio or TV.

Increasingly the Internet is being used to advertise tours. This could be on the record company's website, but more usually it will be on the artist's website, possibly with a link to the promoter's site or that of the venue. Websites are being used to offer the possibility of ordering tickets online and are offering competitions to win tickets or to meet the artist. Artist and record company websites can fulfil an important role in promoting the tour or selling tickets online.

The fan club can also be invaluable in publicising a tour. The regular newsletter sent out to fans can give details of forthcoming live events and where tickets can be bought. Sometimes the fan club does a deal with the promoter and/or a travel company to offer special travel, accommodation and ticket packages at a reduced rate to fan club members. The fan club has to be careful not to offer things that it can't deliver. For example, members of the Boyzone fan club were apparently offered special top-of-the-range seats at Boyzone concerts as part of a special package. It seems that the promoters didn't deliver the expected good seats, leading (apparently) to a demand for the return of monies. Such bad experiences can have a very negative effect on the fan base and their support for the artist.

OTHER PERSONNEL

TOUR MANAGER
Depending on the size of the tour and your degree of success, you may appoint a tour manager to work alongside your manager in organising the day-to-day details of the tour. Tour managers go out on the tour and handle all crises as they come up. They are generally paid a weekly fixed fee and receive free travel and accommodation and probably a fixed daily sum for expenses.

SOUND AND LIGHTING ENGINEERS
How your music sounds and how you look on stage is crucial to the success of your live performances. Most bands learn at an early stage the importance of having their own sound engineer and not relying on some stranger in a strange venue. As soon as they can afford it, most bands also like to bring along their own lighting engineer. Both of these will be on a daily or weekly rate with free accommodation and travel and daily expenses.

BACKING BAND AND SESSION MUSICIANS
If you're a solo artist, or only one member of your group is signed to the record label, then any backing musicians and singers have to be engaged for the tour. There are many different types of arrangements that can be reached with regular band members. They can be on an annual retainer or on a small, daily-based retainer for when they aren't needed and a higher fee when they have work to do at rehearsals, at personal appearances, interviews and during the tour. When they aren't needed they could be on a first-call basis, which means they have to drop everything to make themselves available for you. Or, they may be completely free to do other work but on the understanding that if you call for them and they aren't available you'll get someone else. You can only afford to do that if they are replaceable. If they are crucial to your 'sound' then you would be better advised to put them on a retainer on a first-call basis.

Other non-regular members of the band will generally be engaged on a daily or weekly rate plus free accommodation and travel and daily expenses. Additional fees may be payable to regular or non-regular members for other promotional work such as appearing in a video, for a live TV or radio performance or a webcast to promote the tour. The fee that they are paid could include any of these extra activities and fees. It's important that you agree a 'buy-out' of all rights on the musicians' or vocalists' performances, whether they are your regular band members or not. If they are Musicians Union or Equity members, there will be minimum rates for the work you want them to do and rules on what can be bought out in the way of rights and what will be the subject of further repeat fees (details are in Useful Addresses). If you don't buy out the rights you may get into difficulties if you then go ahead and do a TV or video deal for performances including those of the session musicians or singers. You may believe you've cleared all rights and say as much in the contract. If you haven't then the musician or vocalist or their union can come out of the woodwork at the most unhelpful moment.

All these personnel should be given written agreements specifying their fee, when it will be paid and what you expect to get by way of services and rights in return.

Personnel who aren't regular members of the team should enter into confidentiality agreements. These make it clear that they have to keep confidential anything that they find out about you from being on the road with you. They are intended to head off people selling salacious stories and pictures. If, however, they are regular band members then it could be counter-productive, because they could get upset at what they might see as you not trusting them. For more on the issue of privacy, see Chapter 12.

The importance of getting things clear in contracts with musicians is borne out by a case involving Elvis Costello.[4]

The Elvis Costello Case

Elvis Costello employed Thomas as a musician to perform on the European tour with him as part of his band. He was also going to do the US tour, but as a part of a separate contract. Costello employed Thomas through his service company, Elvis Costello Limited. The tour had breaks in it between countries in Europe when Thomas's services were not required. Thomas took a seven-day break between the UK and US tours and put in a claim for payment. When he didn't get paid, he applied to the court to wind up/liquidate Costello's company for insolvency, i.e. being unable to pay its debts when they fell due. The court declined to do that, but did order that Thomas be paid on the basis that the court did think it was part of the European tour. The lesson is to make absolutely sure that your tour agreements are clear as to when someone is working and when it is unpaid leave.

THE FUTURE

What we've talked about so far are largely traditional methods of touring and promoting yourself through live work. We're already seeing glimpses of what might happen in the near future. What I'm talking about is virtual touring – or webcasts. As the name suggests, these are broadcasts of your live performances over the Internet. Several artists, including Madonna and Robbie Williams, have done webcasts either of special concerts or as an adjunct to their normal live touring. So far the quality of the sound and visuals has been mixed, but will no doubt improve as more homes get broadband access to the Internet.

By agreeing to have your performance filmed and the sound streamed (i.e. digitally presented in a way that means it can be listened to on a computer but not downloaded), the webcast could be available on one or more sites either at the same time as the concert is taking place – called a simulcast – or at a later date.

In theory, an artist needn't go out on the road at all, but can go into a studio where his performance is streamed and filmed and then broadcast either on the artist's own website or in conjunction with another website or portal.

As I said in Chapter 8, imaginative use of your brand name and the Internet can make it possible to target marketing at potential or actual fans. For example, if you had access to a database of the people who visit your website or who listened to your last webcast, you could e-mail them all and tell them when you're going to be performing live and let

---

4 *Elvis Costello Limited* v. *Thomas*, Chancery Division June 1997.

them buy tickets to the gigs online. Or you could dispense with touring altogether and just do webcasts. There are already a couple of UK venues that are either converting themselves into specialist webcast venues or are setting themselves up from scratch as Internet venues. One of these is the East End venue, Ocean, which is also available as an ordinary concert venue.[5]

You may ask how you make money from webcasts. Well, you could have an arrangement where your fans have to pay a small fee to have access to your webcast. This would be similar to the pay-per-view system offered by some satellite and cable TV companies for special concerts or sporting events. Alternatively, you could decide to broadcast the webcast for free and get your money from other sources. For example, you could do a deal with a sponsor so that, in return for being associated with the webcast, you get a fee (see Chapter 9 for more on sponsorship). You could do a deal with one or more advertising companies who might want to put what are called 'banner adverts' on the home page of the website offering the webcast. These companies are prepared to pay for the right to advertise on that site. Or you could view it as a purely promotional activity for a tour, a record release or other activities on your website.

CONCLUSIONS

- Get yourself a good agent.

- Tie your touring in with your record company's marketing plans.

- Use the Internet to advertise forthcoming tours.

- Look at doing webcasts as an additional way to make money from touring.

---

5 For details see www.ocean.org.uk

11: **BAND ISSUES**

INTRODUCTION

The solo artists and songwriters among you may want to skip this chapter, but if you co-write or plan any kind of recording collaboration it would be worth you reading it to see some of the potential problems.

It may seem very negative to talk about problems before you've released a record or even got a deal. But that's exactly when you should be looking at the things that cause friction within bands. If you address these things at the beginning when everything is going well, it will be much easier and cause less tension. If you wait to raise these issues until you've been on the road nonstop for six months and can't stand the sight of each other then, believe me, it will seriously strain, if not destroy, the relationship.

WHO OWNS THE BAND NAME?

OWNERSHIP

As we saw in Chapter 1, choosing the right name is vital, but once you've decided on a band name and have done what you can to check that you have the right to use it, you have to decide who owns that name.

The record company won't normally expect to own the band name. There are exceptions, particularly in the field of manufactured bands or ones where the record company thinks up the name and concept and hires in people to perform. In such cases they might have a very good reason to say that they should own the name, but this then forms part of the deal. What the record company *will* expect you to do is to confirm that you have the right to use the name and that they have the exclusive right to use it in connection with the recordings you make under the record contract and a non-exclusive right after the contract ends. Music publishers will also want the exclusive right to use the name in connection with exploitation of your songs during the term of the publishing contract and a non-exclusive right after the end of the term. You don't want to give exclusive rights for all uses of the name to any one company, for example your record company, as that would mean that you couldn't then use your name to sell merchandise or do a sponsorship deal.

WHO WITHIN THE BAND OWNS THE NAME?

It is essential that you sort this out at the beginning. I also firmly believe that you should put what you've agreed in writing. But I realise that I'm probably whistling in the wind. I tell every band about to sign a deal that they should have a band agreement. They usually nod and say that they understand why they should have one, but most of them never do anything about it. It doesn't have to be a terribly formal document – although I would advise that a proper band agreement drawn up by a lawyer would be best. Even if you don't go for that it would be better than nothing to write down what you've all agreed and sign it and then keep it in a safe place. You may think that this is over the top and a bit unnecessary, but if you can't prove who owns the band name you can get the very unedifying spectacle of two or more band members arguing over who has the right to use the name.

It can happen that just one or two members of the band own the band name, for example where they form the core of the band and the others aren't permanent members. A band may be made up of a core of the vocalist and the lead guitarist who do most of the writing, and a rhythm section of bassist and drummer on a wage and not signed to the record contract. The core members may not want to share ownership of the band name with the other two unless and until they become full-time permanent band members.

It's more common to agree that all members of the band own the band name. More sophisticated band agreements could set out who gets to use the name if the band splits up. You may decide that, in that case, none of you could carry on using the name or that those who carry on performing together as a band can continue to use the band name and that the one who leaves can't. Then you get problems if two or more members leave and set up another band. There is no simple solution and it's something that you should talk over with your lawyer, as they will have some suggestions that you may want to adopt.

That said, you may not in fact get any say in what happens to the band name if the band splits up, because the record contract may well decide the issue for you. The contract might say that the record company has final say over who can continue to use the band name. This may seem unfair but, if you think about it, the record company has invested a lot of time and money in building up your name and the reputation in your name through their marketing efforts. They won't want to risk losing control of that if one or more members of the band were to leave and, as a result, no one could continue to use the name. You may get a chance to say no to this if you already have a band agreement in place or, as usual, if you have a lot of bargaining power. If the record company does decide who gets to use the band name then you have to think about whether the other band members should be paid some kind of compensation for the loss of the right to use the name. It's possible that, either under the terms of the partnership/band agreement or by the operation of the Partnership Act 1890, the band name will be treated as an asset of the partnership that forms part of its 'goodwill'. There are formulas that accountants can use to work out how much that goodwill is worth. If, for example, the partnership is dissolved because the band splits up and the vocalist continues as a solo artist, then the others could have the value of their share of the goodwill in the name calculated and paid to them as part of the settlement between the band members. It's quite a difficult and delicate question and needs to be treated carefully. This is another good reason why you should sort it out at the beginning before any tensions (or pretensions) get in the way.

BAND STRUCTURES

You can decide on the ownership of the name and other things, such as how the income is to be divided between you, but before your lawyer can put what you've agreed into a legal document you also need to decide what legal form the arrangements between you are going to take. There is no simple answer as to which is best. Each band's needs are going to be different and you have to look at each on its own merits. It's important that you involve both your lawyer and your accountant on this question, as your lawyer will be looking to protect you from a legal viewpoint and your accountant will be looking at the financial and tax implications for you of the different types of agreement. Your accountant will know your personal circumstances and will be able to advise whether one type of structure works better than another for you.

The two main types of arrangement are a limited company and a partnership.

If you decide that the band should be a partnership then the band agreement will usually take the form of a partnership deed. This is like a legal contract that sets out how the partnership is going to operate on a day-by-day basis and puts in writing what has been agreed about the band name, the split of earnings and so on. If you decide to become a limited company then you'll probably be advised to have a shareholders' agreement, which does the same thing essentially as a partnership deed but also deals with what happens to your shares in the company if the band splits up or one or more members leave. At the risk of confusing things even more, it's also possible for the band to take the form of a partnership or a limited company, and for the individual members to decide to set up their own company to provide their services to the band through the company. I'll go into this in more detail below.

LIMITED COMPANY

A few years ago, accountants regularly advised bands to set up a limited company for some or all of the band's services in the entertainment business. There were good tax reasons for doing so, especially the tax year out, which was only available to employees and not to self-employed individuals or partners in a partnership. This particular tax loophole has now been closed and so the tax advantages have been considerably reduced. The reasons now for setting up a limited company are more complex and you're going to have to take specialist advice from your accountant and lawyer.

The main advantages are:

- You can spread your income (for example, a large advance) over a number of years and therefore not have it all taxed in the year in which you get it.

- It may be a more tax-efficient way of distributing income to band members.

- Increased flexibility for pension contributions.

- Increased flexibility for capital gains tax planning.

- It might protect you from legal actions because anyone bringing such an action would have to sue the company in the first instance.

Also, if a lot of the band's income is going to be earned overseas, an offshore company can be used to avoid paying UK tax until you decide you need to have access to the money in the UK.

Among the main disadvantages are that there are more rules governing what companies can and can't do, accounts have to be published so members of the public could find out how much you earn (although there are now exemptions that allow small companies to file abbreviated accounts) and there are also higher administration charges with a limited company.

Obviously, the sooner you get advice and decide on the band structure the better. If you leave it too late and try and put the structure in place after you've already entered into contracts, things get much more complicated. If you've already done a record deal as individuals and you then decide you're going to have a limited company, the record deals would have to be 'novated' (i.e. renewed) in the name of the company. Also, if you've already received some money as an individual, this might jeopardise a scheme to take money out of the country or may result in the Inland Revenue deciding you should be taxed as individuals, regardless of the existence of the limited company.

On a more basic level, if you decide halfway through the negotiation of a record or publishing deal to change the structure, the business affairs person at the record or publishing company isn't going to find this very funny, as they'll have to redraft the contract to deal with the new structure. I was recently told an hour before a record contract was about to be signed with a major record company that the deal was to be done through a limited company. The record contract was with the individual. When I rang the record company's lawyer to let him know, he was in despair. Ten people were meeting in an hour to get this contract signed – we had no time to change it. So they had to go through a fiction that the deal was signed, drink the champagne and have the photos taken. Then we lawyers went away to turn it into a deal with the limited company so that it could actually be signed and the company paid the money.

If you do decide on a limited company, bear in mind that you'll have to pay to get the company set up, to have the name that you want (assuming that name is available) and you'll have to pay the annual running costs.

The band members will be the shareholders and you'll have to agree how many shares each member is going to have. This will probably be an equal number but need not be. Day-to-day decisions on the running of a limited company generally require a 50%-plus majority. If it's a two-member band and each has 50% of the shares then each can block a decision by the other. Major decisions of the company require a 75%-plus majority. So, if you have a four-member band with equal shareholdings, one member could block major changes but three could gang up on the fourth to push through day-to-day decisions. To get around the problems that this could bring, the band is usually advised to put a shareholders' agreement in place which will govern how day-to-day matters are to be dealt with. Major decisions could require unanimous agreement, otherwise three out of four band members could vote through a major change against the wishes of the fourth. The shareholders' agreement will also deal with what is to happen if a member wants to leave. It will usually require that they resign as an officer of the company and that they first offer their shares to the other band members. If a value for the shares can't be agreed, an accountant is usually brought in as an arbitrator to decide the matter.

PARTNERSHIP

This is the main alternative structure for bands. The band members are in partnership together for the particular venture of being a band. All partners are treated equally and profits and losses are shared by all. You'll usually be advised to put a partnership agreement in writing. That agreement will decide how the venture is going to be run on a day-to-day basis, whether all partners are equal (or whether some are more equal than others) and what is to happen to the band name if the partnership is dissolved. It will record whether anyone has put any money (or goods, such as equipment) into the partnership and, if so, whether the money is intended to be working capital of the business or a loan, and whether the equipment has been gifted to the partnership or is still owned by one member and is on loan to the band. Does each band member own the equipment he uses, for example a drum kit or a guitar? What if it was bought with band advances – does that make it joint property? What about the vocalist who has no equipment other than a microphone or two? Does he share ownership of other equipment with other band members? The partnership deed should also deal with these things.

A partnership agreement can also deal with the question of who is entitled to what shares of the songs, the publishing advances and income. This is a very tricky subject and a very emotive one, which is why I say that it should be dealt with at the beginning of the relationship before money starts to be earned from the songs (see Chapter 4).

Even if you don't have a written agreement, there can still be a partnership. The taxman will look at the reality of how you work together and how things like the band income is dealt with.

SERVICE AGREEMENTS

Regardless of the structure in place for the band, it's possible for an individual band member to have his own company, which we call a service company. This service company is exclusively entitled to some or all of the individual's services in the entertainment business. The service company can then enter into the record or publishing deal, hold shares in the band's company or an interest in the partnership. Record and publishing companies are used to these arrangements and are usually happy to incorporate them into their contractual arrangements, especially if they are told at an early stage. They will usually want the individual to sign an agreement, called an induce-ment letter, to confirm that the service company is entitled to his services and agreeing that if the service company drops out of the picture for any reason he will abide by the contract personally.

A service company is usually set up for tax reasons. In the last couple of years the Inland Revenue has announced that it will look closely at service companies, as they are often used as a device to add weight to an individual claiming that he is self-employed and not an employee. For example, if a record producer was engaged as an in-house producer/engineer at a recording studio, and he had a service company and claimed he was not an employee of the recording studio, the Inland Revenue have said that they will look behind the service company at what the real relationship is between the producer and the studio. If all the indicators are that the relationship is actually one of an employee, then he will be taxed as if he were an employee.[1]

This issue often comes up when an artist engages musicians for a particular tour or to record an album. The musicians may want to be treated as self-employed. The musicians' contracts have to be very carefully drawn up to establish the existence of a self-employed relationship.

---

1 The Inland Revenue has issued guidelines with some quite useful examples of what are the main indicators to someone being either employed or self-employed. It is called IR35 and can be obtained from your local Inland Revenue office.

JOINT VENTURES

A very recent development has been the joint venture between a record company and an artist, where they set up a company together that each party takes shares in. This type of deal was the basis of Robbie Williams's new deal with EMI and is set out in more detail in Chapter 3.

BAND INCOME

Whatever structure you put in place, you have to decide what is to happen to the income.

Record, video, touring, merchandise and sponsorship income is usually shared between all band members. As we've seen, there are exceptions where a band consists of one or two core members who are signed up to the record or publishing deal and the other members are employed to work alongside these. In such cases these 'employed' members are usually either put on a retainer or a weekly wage, or they're employed as session musicians. Session musicians are only paid when they work but, as they aren't usually signed up exclusively, they are free to work for others (see Chapter 5).

While most disputes usually arise in the area of songwriting income, this doesn't mean that arguments never arise in relation to recording income.

The Cure

> Laurence Tolhurst, the former drummer and co-founder of the band The Cure, who was asked to leave the band in 1989, sued the lead singer of the band and their record company for damages arising out of deals done in 1986.[2] Tolhurst argued that the record deal done with Fiction Records Limited in 1986 gave Robert Smith the lion's share of the recording income and left him with 'the crumbs'. He asked the court to agree that there was a partnership in place and to order Smith to account to him for 50% of all profits receivable under the 1986 agreement. He also argued that he had been forced to enter into the 1986 Agreement by undue influence exerted by the record company and its owner, Chris Parry. He said that Mr Parry and Fiction Records should account to him for all their profit under the 1986 deal after an allowance for their skill and labour.
>
> The case turned into a character attack on Tolhurst as allegations were made that his contribution to the band's success had declined as a result of his drinking problems. Part of Tolhurst's case was that he hadn't been given enough information about the 1986 deal before he signed it and that he hadn't had independent legal advice. Once again we see the familiar theme emerging – Tolhurst argued that the deal should be set aside and that the court should order an account of all record income to determine how much he was actually entitled to.
>
> The court dismissed his claim and said that the question of undue influence didn't arise because, although the record company would have been in a position to exercise undue influence, the terms offered were not obviously bad. In fact, the judge thought that Tolhurst was lucky to have been offered these arrangements at all in the circumstances, and found that he hadn't signed the 1986 agreement under undue influence. The fact that he hadn't had independent legal advice didn't affect the court's decision, because the deal was not a bad one. The judge also decided that there was no partnership in place in respect of the 1986 agreement, as Smith and Tolhurst had, in fact, come to a different arrangement on what was to happen to the income.

2 *Tolhurst v. Smith and Others* [1994] EMLR 508.

Disputes often arise in relation to songwriting income. There's no problem if all members of the band contribute equally to the songwriting process. Then the income from songwriting should be split equally. This is, however, rare. Much more common is the situation where only one or two members of the band write all the songs. This can give rise to two possible sources of resentment. Those who write the songs could come to resent sharing advances or royalties with the non-writing members of the band. Or, if the writers don't share the income, this then gives rise to resentment from the non-writers, who miss out on a potentially lucrative form of income.

Of course, leaving aside these tensions, there may also be arguments about who actually wrote what. As we saw in the Kemp case, the other members of Spandau Ballet brought a case against Gary Kemp arguing that they were entitled to a share in the publishing income as co-writers of the music on the songs they recorded. They were unsuccessful, but there will be other arguments as to how much band members actually contribute to the creative process by the way in which they interpret or perform the song. If the contribution is a genuine one then they should be credited as a co-writer, but is their contribution the same as that of the main writers? If not, what is the value of their contribution?

What do you do if not all members of the band write and a publishing advance comes in and the band is broke? Just imagine the tensions that could then occur if the main songwriter takes the publishing advance and doesn't share it with the others. Even if he agrees to share the advance equally with the others, what will happen when the advances are recouped and publishing royalties start to come through? Should the royalties then go to the main songwriters or continue to be divided equally? There isn't one answer to this, as it's so personal to the individuals concerned. You only have to look at the above cases to realise how important it is to try to sort this out.

Here are three examples of ways in which I have seen bands deal with this issue. There are many more possibilities.

One band I know had an arrangement where one member controlled all the song-writing and took all the publishing income. When this began to cause tensions, he volunteered to share percentages of his publishing income from some songs with the other band members.

I've also heard the story, which may be an urban myth, that the members of mega rock band Queen had an agreement where they got to be credited as writer of the songs on the singles in turn. If true, this is very democratic, but doesn't really deal with the problem if some of the band members are weaker songwriters and don't write such successful songs as others in the band.

A third way of dealing with it that I've come across is to share the advances and royalties equally until the advances have been recouped. After that, each band member would have his own account with the publisher and the income from each writer's contribution to the songs would then be paid into his own account.

Three very different solutions to a very ticklish issue. Whatever works for you should be written down as soon as possible. If circumstances change, review the arrangements and see if it would be fair to change them.

ACCOUNTING AND TAX

One of the main things that cause problems with a band is tax. This is often closely followed by VAT. In both cases, bands don't keep enough money back to pay the bills. The Inland Revenue and Customs & Excise (the VAT man) have very heavy powers to impose penalties on you. They are often one of the main creditors forcing a winding up of a limited company and they can and will make you bankrupt. Even if they give you time to pay, there will be financial penalties and interest to pay. Believe me, you won't get away with it.

Your accountant will advise you how much should be kept to one side for tax, and if he's doing your books for you he'll be able to tell you what to expect to have to pay the VAT man. He'll also probably advise you to keep all your receipts. You can then sort out which ones you can legitimately recharge as business expenses against tax. If you haven't kept them there is no proof. So do yourself a favour – get a big cardboard box and get into the habit of throwing all your receipts into it. If you were more organised you could have a file divided into the months of the year and put the receipts in the relevant month. This makes life a lot easier for you or your bookkeeper/accountant when it comes to doing the books.

You'll need a band account and, unless your accountant is doing all the books for you, you'll need a basic accounting system. This could be a simple computer spread-sheet. In it you'd keep a record of the income you received, where it was from and what your expenses were for doing that work. So if you did a gig in March you'd record how much you received and how much it cost you to do the gig (and don't forget to keep receipts for all your expenses).

LEAVING MEMBER PROVISIONS

These are the clauses in recording or publishing agreements with bands that deal with what happens if one or more members of a band leave or the band disbands totally before the contract is over. The record or publishing company naturally wants to try to prevent this happening. They've invested a lot of money in supporting the band, making records or videos and in promoting them around the world. The last thing they want is a band falling apart on them. But of course, no words in a contract are going to keep a band together if one or more of them have decided to call it a day. Individuals develop personally and creatively, and not necessarily in the same direction as other band members. One member of the band may get married and have children and not want to spend as much time on the road. Or they may change their artistic style, which might be more suited to a solo career than as a member of a band. Of course, there are also the possibilities that the band members will grow to hate the sight of each other after years on the road, or that the band just comes to the end of what it can do creatively. It used to be the case that when this happened the deal ended and the companies moved on to the next potential big thing. Nowadays, with so much money resting on building the reputation of an artist, when a split happens the record or publishing company wants to be able to salvage what it can of its investment. It will want to have the option to pick up the rights in any new projects that the writers or artists go into without having to compete in the open market.

The record company will also want to try to have the right to continue to use the name of the band that they've invested a lot of money in building up as a brand.

Record and publishing companies will also want to have the option to pick and choose whom they continue the deal with (sometimes called the Remaining Members) and whom they drop.

For example, if the drummer leaves the band the record company will want the right to continue with the remaining members of the band on the basis that they continue to perform and record as a band. They will also want to have a contract with any replacement drummer, who will be put on the same terms as the remaining members.

If the whole band splits up, the company will want the option to do new contracts with each individual member. A publisher might only do new contracts with those they know are writers who will probably go on to do other things. A record company may decide only to continue their deal with the lead vocalist or other main focus of the band, guessing that they will team up with other artists to form another band or will have a solo career.

There's usually a system built into the contract that gives the record or publishing company a breathing space while they try to work out what they're going to do. The record contract will usually give the company the option to call for a leaving member to deliver to them demo tapes of what he would do as a solo artist or with his new band. They will usually provide studio time for him to make these demos. The contract may also require the remaining members of the band to demo new tracks, with or without a replacement member, to see if the company think there is a future for the band or if they should drop them now. The record or publishing company may know immediately whether they want to continue with a leaving member or any or all of the remaining members and may come to a quick decision. Don't hold your breath, though – they will probably take the maximum time they have under the contract in order to look at their options.

Once demo tapes have been delivered to the record company, they usually have a month or two to decide what to do. In that time, both the leaving member and the remaining members of the band are in limbo. The term of the contract is usually suspended in the meantime.

The record company may decide to take up an option on the leaving member's new project but not that of the remaining members, or vice versa. They may also decide to take up their option on the remaining members. They may decide to abandon both to their fate.

For the leaving member or remaining members who are dropped from the contract, that is the end of their obligations to the record or publishing company. They don't have to repay to the company their share of any unrecouped balance on the account. However, their share of royalties from recordings made or songs written by them up to the time of the decision to drop them will continue to be applied to recoup the unrecouped balance. The dropped artist or songwriter won't see royalties from those recordings or songs until that advance has been fully repaid.

For example, let's assume that there was an unrecouped balance on the record account of £100,000 and that the record company continues with three remaining members and drops a fourth (leaving) member. Let's also assume that the band shared advances and royalties equally. The leaving member's share of the debt and of the royalties will be 25%. The leaving member's 25% share of royalties from recordings made while he was a member of the band will go to recoup £25,000 of the unrecouped £100,000 debt. After that's happened, 25% of any further royalties from those recordings will be paid through to the leaving member.

If the record company continues with the remaining members and pays them further advances, the leaving member's share of royalties doesn't get used to recoup those additional advances as he won't have received any share of them. His debt is fixed at the time he is dropped from the contract by the record company, or at least it should be. This is something your lawyer has to deal with when he negotiates the contract.

The situation with the remaining members whose contracts continue is slightly more complicated. Their 75% of the royalties from those old recordings goes to recoup their 75% share of the unrecouped balance (£75,000 in our example). Their share of anything else that's earned from the old recordings first goes to recoup any new advances they have received and only when both the old account and the new account is recouped will they be paid any royalties. It also works the other way around. The royalties from their new recordings go first to recoup the new advances. Any surplus goes to recoup their 75% share of the old debt. Only when both accounts are recouped will they see royalties from the new recordings.

If the contract continues with any remaining members, or if a new contract is issued to the leaving member, the record or publishing company will want to continue to have the same rights to the leaving member and/or remaining members as it had under the original recording or publishing contracts. There are, however, one or two parts of the contract that they like to try to change. The record company will often try to change the minimum recording commitment from an album to singles, the rationale being that until the record company knows how the new line-up will perform in the marketplace they don't want to risk committing to make an album. With singles being seen as largely a promotional tool for album-based artists, if your music isn't directed to the singles market you should hold out for an album commitment.

The record label will also usually want options to future albums. This could either be for the number of albums left under the original deal, or for that number plus one or two more. This should be agreed at the time the record deal is originally negotiated, when you'll have more bargaining power. There's no guarantee that the record company will want to negotiate this with you in the middle of a leaving member/band split situation.

The record royalties are usually the same as under the old agreement, but may go back to the rate that applied in the first contract period so, if you've received an increase in your royalty based either on record sales or because it's later in the contract, it will go back to the rate before the increase took effect.

The advances are usually a fraction of the advance that you would have got for that contract period. For example, if you were a four-piece band and one of you left and you would have been entitled to £100,000 for the next album, then the remaining three members will expect to be entitled to £75,000. This isn't, however, a foregone conclusion. Your lawyer will have to fight for it on your behalf.

Because an artist walks away from the unrecouped debt and has a chance to start again, many are actually crossing their fingers and hoping they'll be dropped. This is a fairly short-term response though, because it will all depend on whether they can get into a new deal. It's certainly no reason to split up a band in the hope that you'll get dropped.

There are leaving member clauses that have special arrangements. There may be different rules on recoupment, or different levels of new advances, depending on which member of the band leaves and how 'key' he is seen to be to the proceedings. They may feel that the lead vocalist/front man should command a larger advance and more preferential terms if he leaves than, say, the bassist. They may even say that they're only interested in leaving member rights for the key people.

As you can imagine, these sorts of provisions can be very disruptive and, if it's the band's first deal, such arrangements ought really to be avoided both from the record company's viewpoint and the band's. At this early stage, no one knows who is going to turn out to be the star. Who'd have thought the Genesis drummer, Phil Collins, would turn out to be an excellent lead vocalist and very successful solo artist?

Different arrangements can also occur with publishing deals. For example, one of the four writer-performers in the band may be a prolific writer for adverts or jingles in addition to his work for the band. In these circumstances, it's possible for all four members to have separate accounts and to initially receive an equal share of the advances. It only really works if each writer earns an equal share of the income, as that goes first to recoup the total band advances. After that, if this writer earns significantly more from his work as a jingles writer, his income from that source is only credited to his account. At the next accounting date he will then receive a correspondingly larger royalty cheque.

One area that will probably have to change in publishing deals is the Minimum Commitment. If one songwriter previously wrote 25% of an album and the others 75% and after a split both are expected to deliver 100% of an album each then there is going to be a problem. So in leaving member clauses in publishing deals, your lawyer will usually try to reduce the commitment to an achievable level.

WHAT HAPPENS TO A BAND'S ASSETS ON A SPLIT?

If there is a partnership or band agreement then that will say what happens to the band's assets if the band splits up or one or more members leave.

If there's no written or verbal agreement that you can prove between the band members and if they're in a partnership, then the rather antiquated Partnership Act 1890 will govern what happens. Essentially the partnership is dissolved unless all partners elect that it can continue. If agreement can't be reached on a fair way of dealing with the assets then the partnership is dissolved and the assets have to be realised (i.e. sold) and the proceeds divided equally between the partners. If agreement can't be reached on whether something such as the goodwill and reputation in the band name should be given a value and, if so, what value, the matter is usually referred to an accountant acting as an arbitrator. The way, if at all, that the record company deals with the name in the recording agreement may help determine if it has a value.

If the band were not a partnership but had shares in a limited company then the shareholders' agreement and/or the Memorandum and Articles of Association will say what is to happen. Usually, the remaining members would want to have the right to require the leaving member to resign from any office as director or company secretary and also to sell his shares. The arrangements would normally give the remaining members the right to buy those shares back at a certain price or in accordance with a fixed formula. Or it may require the shares to be valued by an independent accountant. Tax questions could arise here, so everyone should take advice from an accountant or a tax lawyer if a split occurs. In the absence of written arrangements, there is a danger that the company could become unworkable. If the leaving member is a director or a company secretary and he hasn't been guilty of any wrongdoing, then without a written agreement it won't be easy to remove him from office. If he has service contracts, employment advice should be sought before terminating those arrangements. Without an agreement you can't easily get shareholders to sell their shares and, depending on the size of their shareholding, they could block votes requiring a 75%-plus majority or, indeed, those requiring a simple 50%-plus majority if it's a two-man band or two or more members out of a four-piece band have left.

Once agreement has been reached as to what to do with the band's assets, this should be recorded in a settlement agreement, which should be drawn up by a lawyer. This is particularly important for matters such as rights to band names or copyrights.

If no agreement can be reached, the parties are headed almost inevitably towards litigation and the courts. Even though the reform of the legal system in England and Wales now places considerable emphasis on conciliation and alternative dispute resolution (ADR) we still see the largely unedifying spectacle of bands fighting it out in court.

In my view, the partnership or band agreement should be very clear as to who owns what and who has brought what into the deal. For example, if one of the band members has a transit van that he allows the band to use then that should be noted. A band member could also have put money into the band to keep it going. This is either a loan to the band, with or without interest, or, more practically, it's a gift for the use of the partnership that they may or may not be allowed to get back if they leave. It's also usual for the leaving band member to take with him any band equipment that he particularly uses. This is fair, unless one person has the use of a lot of expensive equipment, which was paid for out of band advances. In that case you would expect the equipment to be valued and for each remaining band member to either get equipment to that value, or be paid his share of its value by the leaving member who is going to take the equipment away.

If a band name is genuinely closely associated with one individual then it's fair to say that that individual should be allowed to continue to use the name after the band splits. But as it will have been all the band members that will have helped to make the name successful, the person using the name after a band splits up should compensate the others. If a figure can't be agreed it can be referred to an accountant to value it. In many cases, however, the name dies with the end of the band. Each band member should continue to be responsible for his share of the record or publishing company unrecouped balance. This will usually be covered by the record or publishing deal. Once the old accounts are recouped, the individual band members should be entitled to their agreed share of any royalties.

It's also wise to decide whether the band members have to unanimously agree before something can be done with the material that they created together, or if it's going to be a majority decision. For example, a few years after a band splits the record company wants to put out a Greatest Hits album. The record contract may give the band approval over whether the record company can do this. The band agreement should say whether all the band members have to agree or not. The democratic thing would be to say yes, they should. The practical thing would be to say that it has to be a majority decision, so that one person couldn't hold a gun to the heads of the others or their record company. The same situation arises with approvals of the use of material in adverts or films. My own view is that it should be a decision of all band members where this is practically possible but that, if the band has split up and one or more have gone out of the business and aren't easily contactable, then the decision of the remaining members who are in contact should prevail.

CONCLUSIONS

- Decide on a good name for the band and protect it as far as you can.

- Decide on a band structure and put a partnership or shareholders' agreement in place.

- Decide who is going to be allowed to use the name if you split up.

- Make sure any leaving member clauses in your contracts are fair.

- Decide these things while you're still friends.

12: **MORAL RIGHTS**

INTRODUCTION

M oral rights have their origins in well-established European principles of law aimed at protecting creatives and ensuring their works are treated with respect. These are also called *droit moral*. In this chapter I'm only going to give an overview of these rights and of where they can be used. There are many books on the subject if you want to read into this further.[1]

Moral rights are separate from copyright. In some circumstances you can keep your moral rights when you've had to assign your copyright to someone else.

In Europe it has long been felt that an artist's rights to receive economic (i.e. financial) reward for the use of his work can be adequately protected by the copyright laws. However, the integrity of the work itself deserves separate protection. Hence the development of a separate *droit moral*. The UK legal tradition makes economic rights more important than those of artistic integrity. Why doesn't the UK value the integrity of creative works, you may well ask? It's not that we don't give them a value. It's a question of emphasis and the answer lies in the cultural differences between the UK and the rest of Europe and in the different legal histories they have.

The European principles of moral rights were included in the major international legal convention on intellectual property, the Berne Convention[2] and, in particular, the 1948 Brussels Revision of the Berne Convention.[3]

The UK lagged a long way behind and, indeed, the fact that we didn't incorporate the two basic moral rights into UK law meant that for many years the UK was unable to fully comply with the Berne Convention.

As the UK became more integrated into Europe it became clear that we were out of step not only in not fully complying with the Berne Convention but also in not giving sufficient weight to these rights. The general principles of harmonisation, which govern the operation of the European Union, meant that the UK had to come in line on these moral rights. As we will see, it did so, but in a peculiarly British fashion.

The 1988 Copyright Designs & Patents Act was the first UK statute that effectively incorporated all the principal moral rights. There had been limited moral rights in the 1956 Copyright Act but the 1988 Act was the one that brought the UK in line with Europe and enabled us to comply with the provisions of the Berne Convention.[4]

The moral rights aren't linked to who owns the copyright in the work in question. They may be the same person, but not necessarily. For example, you could assign your rights to the copyright in a musical work to a music publisher, but as the author of the work in question you could retain your moral rights. In fact, in law you can't assign moral rights,

---

1 See Chapter 11 of *Copinger & Skone-James on Copyright*, (Sweet & Maxwell, 1998) for a more detailed legal description of UK moral rights.
2 It first appeared in the 1925 Rome Treaty.
3 Article 6 bis of the 1948 Brussels Revision to the Berne Convention contains two basic moral rights: the right to be identified as an author of a work and the right not to have that work distorted, mutilated or otherwise altered in a manner which would be prejudicial to the author's honour or reputation.
4 The moral rights are found in Chapter 4 of the Act in sections 77–89. The remedies are found in section 103ff.

they remain with you or your beneficiaries on your death. This is intended to protect you from unscrupulous people who may want you to assign your moral rights alongside your copyright. However, there is more than one means to an end.

If you and your fellow band members write a musical work together then you each have these moral rights independent of each other. Just because one of you has decided to abandon his moral rights doesn't mean that the rest of you have to.

In reality, the 1988 Act merely put into law what had previously been dealt with in contracts. The crucial difference was that in a contract you can only bind your contracting partner, whereas with moral rights you can enforce them against third parties who were not party to the contract. For example, you may have a clause in your contract that says you have to be credited as the composer of the music. If your publishing company forgets to do this, it's a breach of contract and you can sue them. If, however, the works are licensed for inclusion on a compilation album and the compilation company doesn't credit you, then unless you have your moral rights you can't take action because the contract is between the compilation company and your record company and not with you. If you have your moral rights, you can take action against the compilation company for breach of your moral right to be identified as the author, whether or not your publishing company wants to take any action.

WHAT ARE THESE RIGHTS?

There are four moral rights, but only three of them are likely to affect you. These three rights only exist in respect of copyright works.[5] If a work is out of copyright then you don't have moral rights in relation to it.

The right of paternity

The first moral right is the right to be properly identified as the author of the work.[6] This is also known as the paternity right.

The right is owned by the author of a copyright literary, dramatic, musical or artistic work. So, as a composer or lyricist of original songs, you would have the right to be identified as having written the words or composed of the music.

It's also possible that you'll have moral rights in the artwork used for the packaging of your records if you were the person who created that work (see Chapter 6 on artwork). You'll notice, though, that the owners of the sound recording copyright don't have moral rights in that sound recording.

The right exists in relation to a musical work and lyrics when that work is exploited in one of five ways:

1. When the work is commercially published; this includes not only sheet music but also in sound recordings or as soundtracks to films.

2. The issue to the public of copies of the work in the form of sound recordings.

3. The showing in public of a film, the soundtrack of which includes the work.

---

5 Sections 178 and 1(2) CDPA.
6 Section 77 CDPA.

4. The issue to the public of copies of a film, the soundtrack of which includes the work. Remember that the definition of 'film' will include videos.

5. If a work has been adapted and the adaptation is exploited in one of the above ways then you have the right to be identified as the author of the work that has been adapted. If the arrangement itself is capable of copyright protection then the author of the adaptation may also have a right to be identified as its author.

You'll notice that there's no moral right to be identified as the author of a musical work when that work is broadcast, performed in public or included in a cable broadcast service. Just think of all those poor DJs who'd be in danger of breaching your moral rights every time they irritatingly didn't give you a name check after playing your record on the radio. It seems it was thought to be unrealistic to put this burden on the broadcasters.

If you have moral rights in the artistic work (the artwork), that right comes into effect when that work is exploited in one of the following ways:

1. If the work is published commercially.

2. If it is exhibited in public.

3. If a visual image of it is broadcast or included in a cable broadcast service.

4. If a film including a visual image of the work is shown in public or copies of the film (which will include videos) are issued to the public.

Section 77(7) of the Act sets out details of how the author is to be identified. One example is that the author of the musical or artistic work must be identified on each copy. This is logical: you wouldn't want a record company to be able to get around the right by identifying you on the first, say, one hundred copies issued and not on any of the rest.

Assertion of the right
There is, however, one very big 'but' here. In order to be able to rely on the paternity right, you have to first have asserted that right. You may have noticed on the inside cover of books published since 1988 that there is a statement along the lines of 'the right of [author's name] to be identified as the author of this work has been asserted in accordance with sections 77 and 78 of the Copyright, Designs and Patents Act 1988'. This is the book publishing world's way of asserting the author's right of paternity. If you write a song and don't want to have the right to be identified as the author then you just don't assert your moral right of paternity and you don't insist of having a credit clause in your contracts. But why wouldn't you want to be identified?

If you do want to be identified then you can do so generally – as in the statement above – or in respect of any particular act. For example, you could assert your right to be identified as the author of the musical work in the sound recording but not if that sound recording is then included in a film. Again, you may wonder why anyone would make the distinction. You can choose to assert your rights in the document in which you assign any copyright in the work, for example in an exclusive music publishing deal where you have to assign your rights for a period of time (see Chapter 4), or you can do it by some other written means that bring your assertion to the attention of someone. They are then responsible if they breach your right. The problem with this is that it's only binding on those people to whose attention the assertion of rights is brought. For example, you could put in a written document that you asserted your right of paternity, but if that document was then put away in a drawer you wouldn't have brought it to anyone's attention and so couldn't rely on your moral right later if someone failed to identify you as the author of the work. Putting it in the assignment document is the best way of ensuring that anyone who later takes any interest in the work assigned will have notice of your paternity rights.

If the musical work has been jointly written, for example by all members of a band, then each is responsible for asserting his own right of paternity. One band member can't take it upon himself to assert it on behalf of the others.

There are a number of exceptions.[7] The most important one for you is likely to be the fact that, if the copyright is one that you created as an employee, your employer and anyone acquiring rights from him doesn't have to identify you as the author of that work. So, for example, if you wrote a jingle as part of your job as an employee of a jingle company then unless there was anything in your contract that said your employer had to give you a credit, he wouldn't have to do so and you wouldn't be able to rely on any right of paternity.

The integrity right

The second moral right is the right of an author of a work not to have that work subjected to derogatory treatment (i.e. to have someone treat your work in a way that reflects badly on the work and, indirectly, on you).[8] This is sometimes called the integrity right. The right is owned by the author of a copyright literary, dramatic, musical or artistic work and by the director of a copyright film (which includes a video). Once again, the right only applies in relation to a work that is in copyright and it doesn't apply to sound recordings.

The right has several hurdles to it. First, you have to establish that the work has been subjected to some form of treatment, i.e. that it has been added to, or parts have been deleted, or the work has been altered or adapted in some way. Something has to have been done to it. This can be as little as changing one note or one word of the lyrics. It *isn't* a treatment of a work if all you do is put it in an unchanged form in a context that reflects badly on its author. For example, if someone uses your song as part of a sound-track for a porn video, that of itself isn't a treatment of the work for the purpose of your moral rights. Nor is it a treatment if someone just changes the key or the register of the music.

In a case involving George Michael, the court was asked to consider the question of what was a treatment.[9]

Someone had put together a megamix of George Michael's tracks using 'snatches' from five songs. They had also slightly altered the lyrics. The court decided that this was definitely a treatment.

---

7 Section 79 CDPA.
8 Section 80 CDPA.
9 *Morrison Leahy Music v. Lightbond*, 1993 EMLR 144.

Once you've established that there has been some form of treatment, you then have to show that that treatment was derogatory. For these purposes that means a distortion or mutilation or something that is prejudicial to your honour or reputation.

When you've established both these points, you then have to look at whether the treatment has been subjected to a particular type of use. In the case of a literary or musical work the integrity right is infringed by:

1. Publishing it commercially.

2. Performing it in public, broadcasting it or including it in a cable broadcast service.

3. Issuing copies to the public of a film or sound recording of, or including, a derogatory treatment of the work.

In the case of an artistic work the treatment has to have been used in one of the following ways:

1. By publishing it commercially.

2. By exhibiting it publicly.

3. By broadcasting or including in a cable programme service a visual image of a derogatory treatment of the work.

4. By showing in public a film including a visual image of a derogatory treatment of a work or issuing to the public copies of such a film.

In the case of a film (which includes a video) the integrity right is infringed by a person who shows in public or includes in a cable programme service a derogatory treatment of a film or who issues to the public copies of a derogatory treatment of the film.[10]

False attribution

The third right is an extension of a right that existed under the previous Copyright Act of 1956. It is the right not to have a work falsely attributed to you. This would happen if someone says that a piece of music is written by you or that you directed a particular film and that isn't in fact the case. This false attribution needn't be in writing – it can be verbal. It also needn't be express – it can be implied. So someone could suggest on a television programme that you were the author of a particular piece of music when you weren't, or could imply that you were without coming straight out and saying so. In many ways, it is the mirror image of the right of paternity.

If there has been a false attribution then it has to be applied to a work that has been used in one of the following ways before it can be said to be an infringement of this moral right:

---

10 See section 83 CDPA for details of other persons who could be liable for infringement of this right and section 81 CDPA for exceptions.

1. If a person issues to the public copies of a literary, dramatic or artistic work or a film in which there is a false attribution. So, for example, if the credits wrongly identify you as the author of the music, this could be an infringement of your moral right.

2. If a person exhibits in public an artistic work, or a copy of an artistic work, in or on which there is a false attribution.

3. If in the case of a literary, dramatic or musical work, a person performs the work in public, broadcasts it or includes it in a cable programme service, saying wrongly that it is the work of a particular person or, in the case of a film, shows it in public, broadcasts it or includes it in a cable programme service as being directed by someone who had not in fact directed it.

4. Material issued to the public or displayed in public, which contains a false attribution in relation to any of the above acts, is also an infringement. This could catch publicity posters for films, or adverts in magazines for a book, or the false credit on the packaging for a recording of a piece of music.

There are also rights against those who indirectly infringe this right.[11]

Privacy of photographs

The final moral right is the right to privacy in any photographs that you commission.[12] This is intended to protect against unauthorised use by newspapers and suchlike of private photographs that you have commissioned. When you're starting out in the business this right may not be of immediate practical interest to you. There's always the motto that there's no such thing as bad publicity. However, later in life, when you're a megastar seeking to protect your privacy at all costs, you may remember this right and use it against unscrupulous photographers keen to sell their soul and your life to the tabloids. This right can be used alongside the privacy and confidentiality rights that are being developed by the courts implementing the Human Rights Act (see page 219).

OWNERSHIP OF RIGHTS

As we've already seen, the moral rights belong to authors – to composers of musical works and writers of lyrics intended to be spoken or sung with music. Performers on sound recordings don't have these rights unless they are also the writer or composer of the musical works. So, for example, if you have a band member performing on a record who hasn't contributed to the writing of the words or the lyrics then he can't expect to be credited as an author. The same applies to record producers. If the record producer contributed to the writing of the words or music then they may have moral rights, but they don't have them if they act purely as a record producer (see Chapter 5).

The real beauty of these rights is that they are rights of the author, who can't be

---

11 Section 84(3) CDPA.
12 Section 85 CDPA.

made to assign them. A songwriter may have been required to assign the copyright in his words and music to a publisher as part of a publishing deal (see Chapter 4), but he can't be made to assign his moral rights. If he retains his moral rights then he is in a position to take legal action against someone infringing those rights, even if the publishing company wants to take no action.

There are, of course, difficulties with the moral right of paternity, as you would have to show that you had the right, that it had been infringed and that you had asserted the right in such a way that the person infringing it had notice of the assertion. If your assertion was in an assignment document and was general in nature, you could take action against the assignee of the rights and against anyone else taking an interest in the rights subsequently. This could help you take action for infringement of your paternity right against your publisher or one of his sub-publishers, but not so easily against someone who was acting unlawfully.

The other moral rights do not have to first be asserted.

DURATION OF RIGHTS

The paternity and integrity rights last for as long as copyright exists in the work in question. The same applies to the right of privacy in commissioned photographs and films.[13] After a person's death, the right to take action for infringement passes to whomever he specifically directs. This can be more than one person. The right against false attribution lasts until twenty years after the person's death. If there is an infringement after his death then his personal representatives can take action.

THE CATCH

There is, though, one other big problem with these rights and it has been dealt with in a peculiarly British way. You'll recall that the two main moral rights were introduced into UK law in 1988 in order to enable us to fully comply with the requirements of the Berne Convention. The Convention said that the laws of signatory countries ought to contain the author's moral rights. There was, however, nothing in the Convention that prevented a country incorporating the rights into its laws but then making concessions to other economic interests. This is exactly what happened in the UK. It arose largely as a result of intensive lobbying by the powerful record and publishing interests in this country. It is also a result of the long-standing laissez-faire tradition that we spoke of earlier. In the UK we still favour economic interests over author's rights. So what happened was that, having included the rights in the 1988 Copyright Act, the law then went on to say that the author could then elect to waive his rights, to agree not to assert the right of paternity or to enforce any of the other rights. The waiver must be in writing and signed by the person giving up the right. The waiver can be for a specific work, for works within a specific description or works generally. It can apply to existing and future works, can be conditional or unconditional and can be revocable.

What was the consequence of this waiver provision? I'm sure you can guess. As soon as the industry realised these rights could be waived, all contracts were changed to include as standard a waiver of these rights in the widest possible terms. Clauses were

---

13 Section 86(1) CDPA.

included which provided for an absolute, unconditional and irrevocable waiver of any and all moral rights of whatever kind in relation to all existing or future works. They even put them in record contracts where there was little or no chance of the right existing in the first place.

CONCLUSION

So why bother discussing these rights if you're going to have to waive them anyway? Once again, it comes down to bargaining power. If creative controls are important to you then you could try and insist on not having to waive them. If you're forced to waive your moral rights then try and only waive them against uses of your works by properly authorised people. Try and retain the right to enforce your moral rights against unlawful users of your works and infringers of your rights.

If you're made to waive your rights, your lawyer will then usually use that as a lever to try and get some of the benefits of the rights through the back door. It helps us to negotiate more favourable credit clauses for you and to cover what happens if you aren't properly credited. We rely on the integrity right to get you contractual consents as to what can or can't be done with your work. For example, that your words and music can't be changed without your consent.

It's not a criminal offence to infringe your moral rights but, if proven, you have the right to seek injunctions and/or damages. Most importantly, you can exercise a degree of control over what's being done with your work.

PRIVACY OF THE INDIVIDUAL

I've been talking in this book (in Chapters 8 and 9 in particular) about how you capitalise on your fame and fortune – but there is another side to the coin. What rights does a famous person have to prevent others from cashing in on his fame and intruding into his private life? Can celebrities protect their privacy? What happens if the press gets too intrusive?

There are two opposing schools of thought at work here. On the one hand, you could argue that personalities have worked hard to create their fame; why shouldn't they be able to benefit from the results of this hard work and control what others do with that celebrity? On the other hand, some consider that the fame of a personality is created by the public – it's society at large that decides whether or not an individual is famous or not, so their name and image should belong to the public.

The courts of different countries adopt different approaches. In the US it's much easier to protect your personality and the publicity associated with it. In the UK the courts have, for over half a century, adopted the approach that if you choose to go into an arena where you get fame and maybe fortune, then your name and reputation is a matter of public interest and public property.

The cases on the laws of passing off that we discussed earlier clearly show that the courts are not keen on assisting famous personalities to clear the market of 'unofficial' merchandise (see Chapter 8). So, if there is no trademark or copyright infringement and no breach of the Trade Descriptions Act, what can you do? Well, in most western European countries you'll find that the law gives you a much broader protection, indeed a right of privacy.

The Petula Clark Case

One of the first French cases involved Petula Clark, who had authorised an agency to interview and photograph her for a particular publication. The agency concerned, however, sold the photographs to another agency that used them in a weekly publication. Petula Clark was successfully awarded damages by a French court proportional to the loss of the opportunity to earn revenue from the publication of the photographs. This line of approach has been consistently followed in France but not in the UK.

The Eddie Irvine Case

A very different case, involving the racing driver Eddie Irvine, has given some hope that the courts are starting to acknowledge that there is a commercial value in the named image of a well-known individual, which the individual is entitled to protect.[14]

Talksport produced a limited run advert with a doctored picture of Eddie Irvine showing him seeming to hold a radio, not a mobile phone, in his ear with a 'tag' line that suggested he supported a particular sport radio station.

Irvine brought an action for damages for passing off and argued that he had a substantial reputation and goodwill and that the defendant had created a false message that a not insignificant section of the public would take to mean that Irvine had endorsed the radio station. The radio station argued that there was no freestanding right to character exploitation enjoyable exclusively by a celebrity, and a passing off claim couldn't be based on an allegation of false endorsement.

The court agreed with Irvine and held that an action for passing off could be based on false product endorsement. The judge recognised the fact that it was common for famous people to exploit their names and images by way of endorsement in today's brand-conscious age, not only in their own field of expertise, but a wider field also. It was right, therefore, for valuable reputation to be protected from unauthorised use by other parties. The fact that the brochure had only had a limited distribution was not relevant. Even if the damage done may be negligible in direct money terms, the court accepted that potential long-term damage could be considerable.

The implementation of the Human Rights Act into UK law, which was effective in 2000, attracted much interest among personalities and those advising them.

The Act gives an individual the right to respect for his private and family life, home and correspondence. This must, however, according to the Act, be balanced against the importance of freedom of expression and of the press. The courts are required to perform this balancing act.

The introduction of the law saw a flood of cases, some juicy ones involving stories of sex and drugs. Others were less tabloid in nature, but both sorts centred on the very serious question of the right to privacy. Here is a selection of some of those cases:

---

14 *Irvine and Anr. v. Talksport Limited* Chancery Division 13/03/02.

The Michael Douglas case[15]

This involved a claim by actor Michael Douglas and the publishers of *OK!* magazine that *Hello!* breached his privacy by secretly photographing his wedding to Catherine Zeta-Jones and publishing the photographs ahead of the exclusive that had been given to *OK!*

Three judges reviewed the history of the developing law of *confidence*, not privacy, and the effect, if any, of the introduction of the Human Rights Act 1998. They considered the acceptance of a right to appropriate protection of one's personal privacy as an extension of the law of confidence – placing a fundamental value on personal autonomy.

The earlier CA case of *Kaye* v. *Robertson* was distinguished on the basis that the law had moved on to develop a law of privacy without the need for first establishing the relationship of confidentiality, which sometimes had to be done very artificially.

On balance, they decided Mr Douglas had a right to privacy, even though he had waived that right by agreeing a deal for publication of photographs of the event in question, his wedding.

The Venables Case[16]

This is a good example of the balancing act that the courts have to carry out. The murderers of James Bulger sought to prevent publication of their identity when they were released from prison, as it was argued that there was a serious risk to these young men's lives if their identity were revealed. The judge decided that that obligation outweighed the right of the press to freedom. While the Douglas case may have seen the judges starting to develop a distinct law of privacy, the area that most of the law is based on is that of confidence, the right to keep information confidential.

The courts have shown more of a tendency to grant injunctions in the area of privacy than, for example, libel. This fact, together with the hope of celebrities for an improvement in their right to privacy from intrusive paparazzi and tabloid reporters, has led to a whole spurt of cases in this area.

The footballer case[17]

A footballer wanted to prevent the publication of kiss-and-tell stories by getting an injunction against a newspaper. The court had to balance the interests of the individual against freedom of speech and decide whether there was a public interest to be served in allowing publication. They decided that, on balance, they wouldn't prevent publication.

This case made it clear that nearly all intrusions on privacy will be dealt with in the area of breach of confidence. This seems to be a move away from the Douglas case, which clearly wished to establish a separate law of privacy. By returning to this law of confidence, it will be necessary for celebrities to show that the information was obtained in confidential circumstances. The case also seems to show the court's sympathies tipping in favour of freedom of the press, while stressing the need for a balancing act

---

15 *Michael Douglas, Catherine Zeta-Jones, Northern & Shell Limited* v. *Hello! Ltd.* [2001] EMLR 199.
16 *Venables* v. *News Group* (April 2001).
17 *A* v. *B & C* [2002] EMLR 21.

between privacy of the individual and the public interest. By that, I don't mean that just because it's a piece of juicy news that it's in the public interest, but that public figures have to accept that their activities do, in some circumstances, make it in the public's interest that they be written about, whether they like it or not.

This approach seems to have been followed in recent cases.

The Jamie Theakston Case

Another celebrity caught, as it were, with his trousers down, was the TV presenter and actor Jamie Theakston, who visited a brothel and was photographed by one of the women there, who then threatened to sell her story to the press, apparently because he failed to pay for services rendered.[18] Theakston sought an injunction to stop her. The court applied the rules on confidence and decided that the woman owed him no duty to keep the matter secret and that the public interest was served by a story that he had visited this place. They also ruled, though, that that interest didn't go so far as photographs, and made an order preventing the publication of the photographs.

The Naomi Campbell Case

The first of the privacy cases to come to trial after the implementation of the Human Rights Act was one brought by the supermodel Naomi Campbell against the *Daily Mirror*.[19] The *Mirror* intended to publish details of Ms Campbell's drug addiction. She sought an injunction to prevent them. The court decided that, while there was a public interest in knowing of her addiction (she had, apparently, previously proclaimed an anti-drugs stance), this didn't extend to details of her therapy with Narcotics Anonymous. It granted her an injunction for breach of confidentiality, but awarded the very low sum of £3,500 in damages – a signal that the court didn't think much of her behaviour. The judge went so far as to say, 'I'm satisfied that she lied on oath.' This was a clear case where the damage caused by the publicity surrounding the case and her evidence in court outweighed that caused by the original article.

As in many other areas of English law, much can depend on the individual judge who hears your case. Lord Woolf, one of our senior judges, has been seen to try to encourage a greater role for the Press Complaints Commission, which has a code of conduct for the press. As it doesn't look as if we're going to follow the US model anytime soon, celebrities may well have to hope that the PCC does give some teeth to its code to prevent some of the more intrusive activities of the press.

CONFIDENTIALITY AGREEMENTS

What these cases also make clear is that, as they are based on the law of confidence, if a confidential relationship does exist (for example, between a celebrity and his housekeeper, driver or body guard), then it's important that they get a confidentiality agreement with those individuals. This will make the extent of the confidentiality clear and confirm that such matters will remain confidential. This will add a claim for breach of

---

18 *Theakston v. MGN Ltd* [2002 QBD] EMLR 22.
19 *Campbell v. Mirror Group Newspapers Limited* [2002].

contract to that of confidence. Prime Minister Tony Blair and his wife proved the worth of this when they got an order preventing a former nanny of theirs from publishing her 'inside story'.

The Naomi Campbell Case (No. 2)

> In another case involving Naomi Campbell, the question of her right to privacy arose again, but this time as a result of a breach by a former employee of a confidentiality agreement in her employment contract.[20] The employee sold her story to a Sunday newspaper and the court in this case found in favour of Ms Campbell.

HARASSMENT ACTIONS

Apart from seeking court orders in the civil courts for injunctions, celebrities can, and do, seek the involvement of the police to prevent the activities of paparazzi and reporters whose activities border on that of stalking. They rely on the legislation introduced in the 1990s to prevent private individuals from being hounded or stalked. If the police can be persuaded to get involved, they can be very effective in 'moving on' recalcitrant members of the press. If they won't, then private criminal actions are possible, although such cases rarely come to trial as the celebrity would have to give evidence and many are reluctant to do so. Whether it's a police or private criminal case, the court is going to want to see detailed evidence of the extent of the harassment, so private detectives are often hired to produce photographs of the paparazzi hounding the celebrity, and his private security staff are often called upon to produce detailed statements of the extent of the harassment. Many of these paparazzi are freelance and make their money from selling stories and photos to the highest bidder. 'Exclusives' can net them tens of thousands of pounds in syndication rights worldwide. No wonder they are keen, and no wonder that many celebrities are forced either into almost total isolation in the UK or to move overseas, France and the US being particular favourites, where the privacy laws are stronger.

CONCLUSIONS

- Try to retain your moral rights if you can.

- Assert your right to be identified as an author of a work as early and as widely as you can.

- If you have to waive your moral rights, use this to get improved creative controls in the contract.

- Put confidentiality agreements in place with those who work closest with you.

- Consider harassment actions if intrusion becomes too much.

- Before embarking on privacy/breach of confidence actions, consider whether the potential bad publicity of a trial could outweigh any advantages gained.

20   *Campbell v. Frisbee* 2002 EWHC328.

13: **SAMPLING AND PLAGIARISM**

INTRODUCTION

Sampling and plagiarism are two sides of the same problem. Plagiarism is the taking of someone else's ideas and passing them off as your own. Sampling is essentially the same thing. The subtle difference between them, as we will see in the cases below, is that to be guilty of plagiarism you need to show that someone had access to your material and that it was not just coincidence that it sounds very similar to your work. Sampling, of course, is always only a deliberate act. The person doing the sampling deliberately takes parts of someone's work and then, possibly after manipulating it, includes it in their own work.[1] Both sampling and plagiarism are infringements of copyright.[2] If you sample the actual sound itself by copying the digital recording, this is an infringement of the sound recording copyright.[3] If you don't actually make a copy of the sound recording copyright, you could take the piece of music that you're interested in using and get someone to replay it, to re-perform it in an identical way. This is still sampling, but it would then only be an infringement of the musical copyright in the music and the literary copyright in the words.[4]

Is sampling theft? Many people argue that all cultural evolution is based on taking bits of existing popular culture and adapting and changing them. They argue that all new musical genres 'borrow' or are influenced by earlier ones. R&B from gospel, and rock 'n' roll from R&B and so on. Those that believe this think that clamping down on sampling stifles this growth. They would be in favour of the removal of all restrictions on using parts of someone else's copyright.

This is all very well, but if you were to take this to its logical conclusion then no one would be able to protect their work, music would be devalued and people wouldn't be able to make a living from their work. Surely that's likely to lead to less creativity rather than more? I believe that it's wrong to deliberately take someone else's work without their permission, without paying them anything for it and without giving them proper credit.

HOW MUCH IS A SAMPLE?

Although sampling has been around since the 1960s, it only became more widely used when affordable digital sampling machines arrived in the 1980s. When they first came on the market they were expensive (around £20,000). Now they're available for less than £1,000.

Sampling now forms the core of the dance music scene, but there's still an awful lot of confusion about what is a sample. A lot of people think that just because they've only

---

1 For an overview on the state of sampling see also 'Plagiarism and originality in music: a precarious balance' by Reuben Stone published in *Media Law & Practice*, Vol. 14, No. 2, 1993.
2 Sections 16–21 CDPA.
3 Section 5A CDPA.
4 Sections 3 and 4 CDPA.

sampled a couple of notes or a few seconds of someone else's work they haven't sampled it at all. That simply isn't true. What the 1988 Copyright Act says is that there has to have been copying of a 'substantial part'.[5] It's a question of the quality of the part sampled and not the quantity.

There are a number of cases where the courts have considered what is a 'substantial part'.

Colonel Bogey Case

In the case of Hawkes & Son,[6] Paramount had included the sound of the 'Colonel Bogey' military march in a newsreel. They used 28 bars of music lasting about 20 seconds. The question was whether 20 seconds out of a four-minute piece was a substantial part. The music performed by the band made up the main theme of the march. The court clearly looked at the quality of what had been copied as well as the quantity and found that an infringement of copyright had taken place. Judge Slesser said, 'though it may be that it was not very prolonged in its reproduction, it is clearly, in my view, a substantial, a vital, and an essential part which is there reproduced.'

The Beloved Case[7]

So, could something shorter than 20 seconds constitute a sample?

The band The Beloved sampled eight seconds of a recording of a piece called 'O Euchari'. The sample was repeated several times in The Beloved's track, 'The Sun Rising'. The sound recording of a performance by Emily Van Evera of the work had been sampled. Hyperion owned the rights in that sound recording and sued. At a preliminary hearing, the judge gave his opinion that an eight-second sample was not too brief to constitute a substantial part. He wanted the matter to go to a full hearing. However, as happens with so many sampling cases, Hyperion settled out of court and permission to use the sound recording sample was given retrospectively.

The Macarena Case

A claim was brought by my clients Produce Records Limited, that the dance hit 'Macarena', which had been released by BMG Records, infringed the copyright in a sound recording by The Farm called 'Higher and Higher'. The sample consisted of a short sound made by the vocalist Paula David, which Produce alleged had been used or 'looped' throughout 'Macarena'.

Because so few sampling cases get to court, a lot rested on this case. If it went to a full court hearing and the court confirmed that such a short sample could constitute a substantial part, this would be a firm ruling that could be relied on in later disputes. After such a judgement it would be very difficult to rely on the widely held view that three seconds is the minimum amount necessary to constitute a substantial part. It was more important as a potential guideline for samplers than it was for BMG to win this particular case. A decision that the part sampled *didn't* constitute a substantial part would mean

---

5 Section 16(3) (a) CDPA.
6 *Hawkes & Son Ltd* v. *Paramount Film Service Limited* [1934] 1 Ch 593.
7 *Hyperion Records Limited* v. *Warner Music (UK) Limited* 1991.

success for the record company, but it wouldn't necessarily have given any guidance on what is a substantial part. Each subsequent sampling case would continue to be decided on a case-by-case basis. On the other hand, if the case had gone against BMG and such a short sample had been said to be a substantial part then BMG would have lost this particular case, but *all* record companies would also have lost the argument that such a small sample couldn't constitute an infringement of copyright. BMG settled out of court on terms that I'm not allowed to reveal. Possibly the potential downside was too great.

The question also comes up from time to time as to whether you can sample a rhythm or a drumbeat. I would argue that you can if it can be shown to be original and distinctive and if a substantial part has been copied. There are, of course, only so many rhythms in popular music and many drum and bass lines used currently are, in fact, the same as have been used in earlier works. This is particularly true in the area of reggae music. Inevitably there is going to be duplication. I tend, however, to agree with Aaron Fuchs. He's the man behind an eight-beat drumbeat used in the classic hip hop track by The Honeytrippers, 'Impeach The President'. In 1992 he brought legal actions against Sony and Def Jam alleging that this particularly drum sound is one of the more distinctive in the hip hop genre and worthy of the protection of copyright. I can find no report of that case coming to court, so I presume it was settled out of court like so many of these cases.

In a development in this area in a 2002 case, a judge ruled that certain elements such as these could be protected.[8] This may be a decision on the particular facts of this case or the start of a development to confirm protection for distinctive drumbeats or patterns.

In the United States the courts are handing down decisions that suggest they are leaning towards giving protection to a distinctive or unique 'sound'. One example of where the US courts have tended towards this view involved the actress and singer Bette Midler.[9]

The Midler Case

Ms Midler successfully stopped Ford Motor Cars using an imitation of her very distinctive voice in a television advert. There are, however, no signs that the UK courts are moving in this direction and as we saw in Chapter 12, the UK courts are much less likely to accept that someone has personality rights that should be protected.

HOW DO YOU CLEAR A SAMPLE?

If it's clear that you've sampled someone else's work then this is an infringement of their copyright – unless you get their permission to copy and reproduce their work. If you don't, they could sue you for damages for the copyright infringement and also for an injunction stopping you from continuing to use that sample. As you can imagine, record companies aren't very happy about having an artist who samples material from others and doesn't get their permission. It's very expensive for the record company if there's an injunction and they have to recall all the copies of the single or album and remove the offending sample before re-cutting, re-mastering and re-issuing the record. In fact, if it's

8 *Creagh v. Hit and Run Music Publishing Limited*, (2002) Chancery Division.
9 *Midler v. Ford Motor Company*, 9th circuit 1988 decision.

too expensive they may not bother redoing it and just kill the single or album. That isn't a very good solution for you, so it's best to get permission to use any samples. This is called 'clearing' samples.

Most record contracts, whether they're exclusive recording agreements or licences, will have a clause in them that says you are guaranteeing that all samples are cleared before the recording is delivered to them. This makes it clear that it is your responsibility. This is only fair if you're the one who put the sample in there in the first place. But bear in mind that producers and remixers also have the opportunity to introduce samples into the recording at various stages in the process. Their contract should make them responsible for clearing any samples that they introduce. Sometimes it's the record company that has the idea that including a particular sample will turn a good song into a great monster hit. If the record company is encouraging you to include a sample then they have to take responsibility for clearing it, possibly as an additional recording cost. That cost may or may not be recoupable, depending on the deal.

In a case on this point, the judge (Terence Etherton QC) had sympathy for Mr Walmsley's case.[10]

The Walmsley Case

Walmsley had recorded a track that contained two sound-recording samples. The track was licensed to Acid Jazz and the contract required Acid Jazz to pay royalties to Walmsley. Walmsley gave a warranty that the copyright in the track was free from any third-party claims. Why he signed such an agreement is unknown, but part of the explanation may be that he didn't pay much attention to it, as we will see. Acid Jazz refused to pay any royalties, even though the track was a chart success. Acid Jazz said the track had given rise to a number of disputes and that it had had to pay out monies in settlement. It said that it was relying on its warranty, which it said Walmsley had breached. Walmsley's evidence was that he'd told Acid Jazz at the time of the agreement and subsequently of the samples, and had been told by Acid Jazz that no licences were required and, if any were to be sought, Acid Jazz would do it.

The judge found that Acid Jazz owed the royalties to Walmsley and, although Walmsley was in breach of contract, Acid Jazz was not permitted under equitable principles to rely on it because it had had full knowledge of the true position from the outset.

With some types of music, particularly in the dance area, the record company is fully aware that there will be samples and will often help to clear them. This can be an advantage, as they can use their greater resources and clout to pull favours and get things cleared quickly. This clout can have its downsides. If you're a small, struggling dance label that asks to clear a sample, the person whose work is sampled is less likely to ask for large amounts of money than if you were EMI or a Sony, for example.

WHEN SHOULD YOU SEEK PERMISSION?

Ideally, you should try and get clearance before you've recorded the sample. Then if you don't get permission you haven't wasted recording costs and time. In reality, this won't usually be possible. It can take time to track down the owners of the work sampled to

10 *Richard Walmsley v. Acid Jazz Records Limited,* Chancery Division 2000.

find out who you have to ask for permission. Even once you find them they may take their time in getting back to you. You may then have to negotiate terms for the clearance. In the meantime you can't get on with finishing the recording of that track. This could hold up delivery of the record and its eventual release. Also, you're going to need a recording of what the sampled work is going to sound like in your version of it, even if it's only a demo. In practice therefore, the clearance process takes place after the recording has been made or during the recording process. Sometimes it's left until the record has been delivered. I think this is too late to start the clearance process. Some feelers should have been put out beforehand, at least to find out who owns it and to get an idea of whether they're likely to give you a problem.

Most record contracts and licences will say that delivery of a recording hasn't taken place until evidence has been produced (usually in the form of clearance letters or agreements) that all samples have been cleared. If you haven't used any samples they will want you to give a warranty (a sort of guarantee) to that effect. Until delivery has taken place, it's unlikely that you'll get any advances due to be paid on delivery (see Chapter 3). Nor will time start to run for your record to be released and the marketing plan won't be put into action. Therefore, the sooner samples are cleared the better.

Some people say that they're willing to take a risk that the use of a sample won't be spotted. They think that if it's sufficiently obscure or hidden in the track, the sample won't be discovered. Well, it's just possible that you could get away with it if it was a limited edition low-key release. For example, if you were only going to press up 5,000–10,000 copies of the record for release on your own small dance label then you might be lucky. Even if it were spotted, the copyright owner of the sample may not bother to take any legal action because the amounts involved and the legal costs and hassle of suing you wouldn't warrant it. But what happens if a bigger record company licenses your track in and gives it a big marketing push? Or if you make it a big success in your own right and find you're licensing it to loads of different compilations? If you haven't cleared it and you're found out you'll end up with a big problem on your hands, because now the copyright owner of the sampled work has an incentive for taking you to court. The bigger record company that has licensed the track from you may get sued by the sample owner. The record company will in turn usually have an indemnity from you. This means that, if they are sued, they can make you responsible for the damages and costs involved because you've breached your warranty that there were no uncleared samples in the recording. By lying to them you may also have irretrievably damaged your relationship with that label for the future. Is it worth the risk? That is for you to judge.

TO WHOM DO YOU GO TO CLEAR SAMPLES?

If you decide to clear samples, who do you go to for clearance? If you've sampled the actual sound recording, you need to seek permission from the owner of the original sound, although they may have passed it on to someone else by licence or assignment of rights (see Chapter 3). You can start by looking at the recording that you sampled it from. It should have a copyright notice on it that will say who was the copyright owner at that time, for example '© Sony Music 1999'. So your first point of call would be Sony. They should be able to tell you if they still own the rights. If you don't want to show your hand too soon, you might want to do this through your lawyer on a 'no names' basis.

You must allow yourself plenty of time. The first thing you should be trying to achieve is an agreement from them in principle to the use of the sample. Some artists won't allow their works to be sampled under any circumstances, so it's best to know this as early as possible. Once you've got the agreement in principle then you can negotiate the terms. This can also take time, but you should know fairly early on whether they are going to ask for a ludicrous amount for the clearance, which will make it uneconomical for the sample to be used.

Remember that, as well as clearing the use of the sound recording sample, you have to clear the use of the underlying music and, if appropriate, words. In 1991 a US court granted a preliminary injunction against a rap artist called Biz Markie to stop him from exploiting a sample of three words and the accompanying music from Gilbert O' Sullivan's hit song 'Alone Again, Naturally'.[11]

The owner of the copyright in the words and music may be the writer credited on the sampled recording.[12] It's quite possible, though, that the writer may have assigned or licensed his rights to a music publisher (see Chapter 4). So you'll have to look at whether a publisher is credited and go to them to see if they still own or control the rights. They may only do so for part of the world or they may have passed the rights on or back to the original writer. The MCPS/PRS database should contain details of who claims to own or control the publishing rights (see Chapter 15). They would be a good starting point if you're a member of either MCPS or PRS. If the title or the writer's name is a common one, for example John Smith, then the database is going to throw up a lot of names. Try and narrow down the search by giving them as much detail as you can.

In another recent case on sampling, the importance of clearing samples with the correct party is emphasised.[13]

The Ludlow Case

Ludlow published the song 'I'm The Way'. Robbie Williams and Guy Chambers co-wrote 'Jesus In A Camper Van', which was published by EMI and BMG.

Because two lines of 'Jesus' resembled 'I'm The Way', Mr Williams approached Ludlow to acknowledge the resemblance and to agree that Ludlow would be a co-publisher. Ludlow wanted 50% – Williams and Chambers offered 10%. Ludlow refused and, just as the album containing the track was to be released, repeated their demand. EMI registered Ludlow as having a 50% share in the lyrics i.e. 25% of the whole song. Ludlow then brought a claim for 100% of the copyright and of the income and sought an injunction.

The judge found there had been an infringement of copyright, but thought it was borderline. He gave his opinion that what the defendants had offered was generous, but left it to another court to determine the amount of damages. He also decided that, on balance, Ludlow's conduct had been oppressive, governed by money and that they had gone along with things and had seemed to have been agreeing to things up to the last minute before release. He refused an injunction at summary judgement. An injunction was granted at the final hearing, so future copies of that Williams album will have to be minus this track.

This is another example of how one party's conduct can prejudice their case when relying on another's bad conduct.

---

11 *Grand Upright Music Limited* v. *Warner Brothers Records Inc.*, No 91 Civ. 9648 1991.
12 See section 9 (1) CDPA and Chapter 4 for a description of who is the first owner of copyright in a musical or literary work.
13 *Ludlow Music Inc.* v. (1) *Robert P. Williams*; (2) *Guy Chambers*; (3) *EMI Music Publishing Limited*; (4) *BMG Music Publishing Limited*, Chancery Division (2000).

What sometimes happens is that it's possible to clear the underlying words and music but not the sound recording. If you're adamant that you have to use that sample then you can try and get it reproduced almost identically by having it replayed or recreated. Then you haven't sampled the sound recording, so you only have to clear the underlying music/words. Of course, if you do a very good job of it and it sounds identical to the original, they may not believe you've replayed it and still sue you. Then you may need independent evidence from, for example, the studio engineer, that you didn't use the sample sound recording.

My firm was also involved in a case where this happened. The client sampled part of a sound recording, asked for permission, which was denied, so set about replaying the sample to recreate the sound. He even went to the trouble of getting a specialist report from a musicologist to confirm that he hadn't used the original sound recording but had replayed it. Nevertheless, the owner of the original sound recording wasn't convinced and threatened to sue my client's record company, who had released the track. Using a right they had under their record contract with my client, they 'froze' the royalties that would otherwise have been payable to my client on the track in question until there was an outcome to the dispute. The money has now been 'frozen' for over a year and, as it's a substantial amount, my client is understandably very frustrated. Ah, but I hear you say, it serves him right for copying someone else's work. Well, before you get all high and mighty, just make sure that no one can ever accuse you of sampling or plagiarism.

HOW MUCH DOES IT COST?

This is always a question of negotiation. It will depend on how important the track is that you've sampled and how crucial it is to you that you use it.

Record companies will usually clear sound recording copyrights for an up-front sum, with a further sum when you sell a certain number of records. For example, £1,500 up-front and another £1,500 when you've sold 10,000 copies of the record that includes the sample. This usually comes out of the artist's royalty, but may be shared with the record company if it really wants you to keep the sample in.

Publishers of sampled works may clear rights for a one-off fee or a fee and a further sum based on numbers of records sold. More likely, however, is that it will want a percentage of the publishing income on the track. In effect, the publisher of the sampled work is saying that their writer should be treated as a co-writer on the work and receive a co-writer's share of the income. That share could be as much as 100% if a substantial use has been made of their work. For example, in a track by All Seeing I called 'The Beat Goes On', substantial use was made of a Sonny and Cher song of the same name, although the band had altered the track and given it a more up-to-date sound. Warner Chappell, who publish the Sonny and Cher song, insisted that the All Seeing I version be treated as a cover version and they retained 100% of the publishing. If the use is less substantial then a lower percentage may be agreed.

As we saw with the Ludlow case above, claims for 50% or more of a song may be claimed even if a relatively small percentage is sampled – it's a copyright infringement that the owner of the sampled works is entitled to be compensated for. If it's a blatant offence, the court will be asked to award additional damages.

If you're going to do a lot of sampling in your work and are going to end up having to give away some or all of your publishing on certain tracks, do bear in mind that this may make it very difficult for you to fulfil your Minimum Commitment to your publisher – make sure you take this into account when setting the original level of that commitment.

WHAT HAPPENS IF YOU DON'T CLEAR SOMETHING?

If a sample isn't cleared and a dispute arises, your record company may suspend payment to you until the dispute is resolved. There may be a limit on how long it can suspend payment, but this could be a year or more. MCPS also has the right to suspend any payments of publishing income and has a disputes procedure that has to be followed. MCPS won't directly intervene to resolve a dispute, but can sometimes be used as an arbitrator.

The Shut Up And Dance Case

> In 1992 the MCPS brought an action against dance label Shut Up and Dance (SUAD) on behalf of ten of their publisher members, claiming 12 separate infringements of copyright of works by writers such as Prince and Suzanne Vega. Legal action was taken after the owners of SUAD, PJ and Smiley, told the music press that their policy was never to clear samples. At the time a very macho culture prevailed over the use of samples, with some one-upmanship going on over who could get away with the most in terms of uncleared samples. It's thought their comment reflected this cultural approach to sampling. SUAD didn't defend the case and damages were awarded against the label.

Failure to clear samples in good time could result in an injunction preventing distribution of copies of your record, or an order that they be brought back from the distributors and destroyed. You could also be sued for damages for the copyright infringement.[14]

However, it's not all bad. Not all copyright owners sue or want payment when their work is sampled. The track 'Ride On Time' by Black Box may have attracted a fair amount of litigation in its time, but there was no claim from Don Hartman, whose work 'Love Sensation' was sampled. Apparently Mr Hartman loved the new work so much he wanted neither payment nor a writer credit.

PLAGIARISM

For the purposes of this chapter, when I'm talking about plagiarism as opposed to sampling I'm talking about a situation where someone takes another's work and copies it, passing it off as his own work. There are, of course, overlaps with the situation where you replay a sound sampled from another's work. But what I'm describing here are cases where a writer has claimed that another writer has stolen or copied his work; where the similarities between two pieces of work are so striking that you would have to believe the one was copied from the other. As we will see from the cases below, once you've established similarities between two pieces of work the crucial test is whether the person being accused of plagiarising the work has had access to the other work. It's possible to unconsciously copy something or indeed to arrive at a very similar-sounding piece of work purely by chance.

---

14 As to remedies for infringement of copyright see sections 96–100 CDPA for civil remedies and sections 107–110 CDPA for criminal sanctions.

The John Brett Case

The composer Lord Andrew Lloyd Webber is no stranger to claims of plagiarism. In the late 1980s a songwriter, John Brett, accused him of copying two songs written by him in Lloyd Webber's musical *Phantom Of The Opera*. Although there were similarities between the pieces, Lloyd Webber was able to show that he had written the song first. He produced evidence that it had been performed in mid-1985, whereas Mr Brett's evidence suggested that he had not sent demo recordings of his songs to his solicitor until a month later.

The Ray Repp Case

In another case involving Lord Lloyd Webber, a songwriter called Ray Repp brought a legal action in New York accusing Lloyd Webber of plagiarism. Mr Repp claimed that Lloyd Webber had stolen a passage from his song 'Till You' and had used it, again, in *Phantom Of The Opera*. Once again Lloyd Webber was cleared, and afterwards made a passionate statement condemning the increase in cases alleging plagiarism. He blamed the lawyers (oh dear, us again) and people with an eye to the main chance. He said there were too many people around who thought it was worth a chance, because record companies would rather settle than fight potentially damaging court cases. I understand that he returns unopened all unsolicited demo tapes sent to him or to his office. The same policy is, I believe, adopted by other well-known songwriters who wish to avoid any such claims.

The Francis Day & Hunter Case

An early case in this area that set out a number of guidelines for what constitutes plagiarism is the case of Francis Day & Hunter.[15]

In this case it was argued that eight bars of the chorus of a song entitled 'In A Little Spanish Town' had been copied in the song 'Why'. The judge found a number of similarities between the two works but decided that copying (i.e. plagiarism) had not been proved. It went to the Court of Appeal. That court also agreed that copying had not been proved, but took the opportunity to consider the subject of copying generally. The Appeal Court judges said that you had to establish that there was a definite connection between the two works, or at the very least to show that the writer accused of copying had had access to the work of the other.

The Chariots of Fire Case[16]

The film *Chariots Of Fire* and the music written for it has also been the subject of a number of court cases.

The writer Logarides had written a piece for television called 'City Of Violets'. He claimed that the writer Vangelis had copied four crucial notes from 'City Of Violets' when writing his theme tune for the film *Chariots Of Fire*. Logarides said that, consciously or unconsciously, Vangelis had infringed his copyright. The court decided that there was

---

15 *Francis Day & Hunter v. Bron* [1963] Ch 587.
16 [1993] EMLR 306.

insufficient similarity between the works for there to have been an infringement. This ruled out the argument that Vangelis had unconsciously copied it, because it wasn't similar enough. The evidence that was produced to show that Vangelis had had access to the work was also not very strong, although the court thought that it was possible that Vangelis had heard the song 'City Of Angels'. Logarides was not able to prove that Vangelis had actually had access to his work.

Other cases involving plagiarism include a claim by an Italian writer Al Bano, who has been described as a middle-of-the road crooner, that Michael Jackson plagiarised his song 'I Cigni di Balaka' in his song 'Will You Be There' on Jackson's *Dangerous* album. That wrangle ran on in the Italian courts for over two years.

Tyneside group Lindisfarne took on pop star Whigfield in 1996, claiming that her hit 'Saturday Night' sounded like a copy of their 1969 hit record 'Fog On The Tyne', and Polygram Music Publishing sued Oasis, alleging that their song 'Shakermaker' sounded too much like 'I'd Like To Teach The World To Sing' written by Roger Cook and Roger Greenaway. More recently we've had the Mike Batt 'Sound Of Silence' dispute. There seems to be no end to these claims. This is further proof, if it were needed, that where there's a hit there's a writ.

MORAL RIGHTS

These are dealt with in detail in Chapter 12. If, however, you sample or copy the work of another and you don't credit the original author, or if you do something to the work you've copied or sampled that distorts it, you may well also be infringing the author's moral rights of paternity and integrity of their work.

SOUND-ALIKES

This is where someone deliberately sets out to imitate a successful piece of music. It's often used by advertising agencies when they don't want to pay the price for the right to use the original of a piece of work. Instead they commission songwriters to write a piece that is a close imitation of the original. This is an artform in itself.

The Chariots of Fire Case (No. 2)[17]

In another *Chariots of Fire* case, Clarks Shoes deliberately set out to gain a financial advantage from using a piece of music that had a very close similarity with the *Chariots Of Fire* theme. This was found to be blatant plagiarism, but because it was so obvious the case didn't really set any guidelines.

The Williamson Music Case

Another case, involving the advertising company Pearson, used a parody of the song 'There Is Nothing Like A Dame' in an advert for a coach service.[18] The lyrics were changed but the layout of the verse and chorus was similar. The manager of the licensing

---

17 *Warner Brothers Music Limited and Others v. De Wilde* [1987].
18 *Williamson Music Limited v. The Pearson Partnership and Another* [1987] FSR 97.

division of the MCPS heard the advert and thought it sounded very like the original song 'There Is Nothing Like A Dame'. He told the publishers of the song, Chappell Music Library. Williamson Music Limited were the exclusive licensees of the song in the UK. They and the other plaintiffs complained of infringement of copyright. Williamson Music Limited retained the right of approval to all requests for a synchronisation licence in relation to that song. No such consent had been given. The judge applied the test of whether an ordinary, reasonably experienced listener would think on hearing the track that it had been copied from the other work. He granted an interim injunction on the basis that the plaintiffs had established that there was a case to answer, but it seems he was of the opinion that there had been infringement of the music but not of the words.

It seems that the test for whether something is a parody that is allowable and one that infringes copyright is that, in the case of the former, the parody has to only conjure up the idea of the original – it becomes an infringement if it uses a substantial part of the original.

CONCLUSIONS

- If you sample someone's work, you'll have to get permission to use both the sound recording copyright and the copyright in the underlying music and/or lyrics.

- Put the process of clearing samples in hand as early as possible.

- If there is any chance of an uncleared sample being found and legal action taken, don't take the risk, clear it or remove it.

- If you can't clear the sound recording copyright then see if you can replay the sounds to sound like the original and clear the rights in the underlying music/lyrics instead.

- If you copy another's work and pass it off as your own then you're guilty of plagiarism, unless you can show that the similarity was completely coincidental and that there was no way that you could have heard the work you're accused of copying.

- There is a very fine line to be drawn between sound-alikes, parody and plagiarism.

14: **PIRACY**

INTRODUCTION

Piracy is a huge, worldwide problem. The worst offenders are Eastern European and Far Eastern countries with weak copyright laws and little or no means of enforcement. In Eastern Europe, pirate recordings account for over 50% of the marketplace. In Ukraine, domestic piracy is around 80%. Of course, countries in which piracy is rife also export these illegal records into the UK. Even though the UK has strong copyright laws and a vigorous enforcement policy, pirate records account for about 3% of the total retail market for records.[1] Levels of commercial piracy in the UK rose by 30% during 2001.[2] This is before you even begin to think about what's happening on the Internet. Even the most cursory search of the Internet will show up thousands of sites offering MP3 or similar music files for free download. Some of these are put up there legitimately by artists or record companies who want to promote their music. There are companies such as Peoplesound.com, whose purpose it is to make music by unsigned artists available as downloads as a means of getting the artists noticed. However, for every site with legitimate MP3 files, there are many more that feature illegal pirated works (see Chapter 7).

Another area where growth has tripled in the last twelve months is that of CD-R piracy. This is particularly prevalent in developed countries like North America and Western Europe. Its spread is facilitated by the widespread availability of cheap CD burners.[3] An even more worrying potential problem is that of DVD piracy.

WHAT IS PIRACY?

Piracy is theft. It is the reproduction of someone's copyright without their approval and generally on a commercial scale.

There are three different types of pirate records.

COUNTERFEIT RECORDINGS

These are copies of CDs, cassettes or vinyl records that also copy the packaging, artwork and graphics. For example, someone gets hold of a master recording; they use it to make copies of it, which they then pass off as the original. They don't usually care what the sound quality is like, or even if the tape or CD will play at all. They just want to make them look as much like the original as possible so that they take your money and you don't find out until you get home that it's a pirated copy. The trademarks and logos of the original copyright owners are also copied to make them look as much as possible like the originals. This is an infringement of the trademark, which could give rise to a legal

---

1 IFPI Music Piracy Report June 2002.
2 BPI Market Information Report June 2002.
3 This worrying development is considered in some detail in the IFPI report referred to above.

action in its own right (see Chapter 8). Of course, if you're buying these CDs or tapes from a market stall at half the usual retail price, you've only yourself to blame if they turn out to be dodgy copies.

PIRATE RECORDINGS

This is the unauthorised duplication of an original sound recording. The pirate takes a master recording and copies it without the permission of the original copyright owner. The sound quality is usually as good as the original. This has been made much simpler with the introduction of digital recording processes. Pirate recordings are usually put out on a different label from the original and in different packaging. The trademarks and logos of the original copyright owners aren't usually on the record or packaging. The aim is to undermine your market for the original by putting out a pirate copy first, or in a different form from the way you were going to present it. For example, you release so-called 'white label' copies of your next single release to the press and to DJs for review in advance of its commercial release. They are called white labels because, in their vinyl form, they have a white label, which says they aren't for commercial use. Unscrupulous characters then copy that recording and put it on their own compilation record without getting permission and without paying anything for it. Confusingly, the music industry has now taken to calling these releases 'bootlegs'. They aren't, as we'll see below, but this is a term that's being used more and more to mean all illegal copying of records.

Pirate recordings are generally made in countries with little or no copyright protection and then exported to other countries. The practice is, however, spreading to other countries where the agencies in charge of anti-piracy are less effective. Sometimes publishing rights have been cleared and authorisation obtained from a collective body like the MCPS, but no permission has been obtained to reproduce the master sound recording. For example, if you were putting a pirate copy of a master recording on your own dance compilation, you might apply for a mechanical licence from someone like MCPS to get the right to reproduce the song on that master. This lends an air of respectability to the release and means you have one less collective body to worry about. You don't bother to get permission from the owner of the sound recording. You hope that he either doesn't get to hear about the release, or hasn't the money or the inclination to sue you for copyright infringement.

You could, in some cases, take advantage of different laws on copyright. For example, you might get permission to use the song, and the original sound recording might now be out of copyright in your country. You make copies of it without going back to the original copyright owner and you can import it into other countries where the recording is still in copyright, undercutting the legitimate market in that country. This was more of a problem when the sound recording copyright in the EU was different in different countries. For example, the sound recording copyright in Denmark was 20 years after the end of the year in which it was first released, while in the UK it was 50 years. This meant that after 20 years Danish companies could legitimately say that the sound recording was out of copyright, so no permission was required to reproduce it in Denmark. They then used the principles of freedom of movement of goods within the EU to export these recordings into other EU countries. This began to be a real issue when early Beatles and Stones albums started to come out of copyright in Denmark. It has become less of a problem since the Directive on the Harmonisation of Copyright and

Related Rights made the duration of the sound recording copyright 50 years throughout the EU.[4]

Sometimes pirates argue that they have a valid licence to release a sound recording because of a chain of contracts going back many years. Often, in the 1960s and 70s, ownership of copyright was not properly recorded and there have been many changes of ownership down the years.[5] In those days it wasn't unusual for deals to be single-page, sketchy outlines, that didn't make it completely clear who owned what and who could do what with the recordings. This confusion has been successfully exploited by later record companies claiming to have the right to put out recordings under some dodgy deal struck 20 years earlier. It's sometimes very difficult to prove them wrong.

BOOTLEGS

A bootleg is a recording of a live performance, whether it's at an actual gig or off a television, satellite, radio or Internet broadcast, which is made without permission of the performers.

You used to see shifty-looking people at gigs with tape recorders under their macs making terribly bad recordings of the performance. With the improvements in technology and the miniaturisation of the devices, it's now easier than ever to make reasonable digital recordings.

The Phil Collins Case

In the early 1990s, Phil Collins, ex-Genesis drummer turned successful solo artist, brought an action against Imrat, a record distributor, in respect of royalties for sales in Germany of a CD recording of one of his US concerts, which was made without his consent. Under German law, German nationals are entitled to stop distribution of performances made without their consent, regardless of where the performance takes place. Foreign nationals couldn't rely on this law where the performance had taken place outside Germany.[6]

The court decided that all European Union countries should provide nationals of other European Union countries with the same degree of protection as they would have had in their own country. This has been a key decision in the tightening up of performers' rights across the EU.

HOW DO YOU SPOT A COUNTERFEIT, PIRATE OR BOOTLEG RECORD?[7]

COUNTERFEITS

These are often on sale in markets, at car-boot sales and are often obtainable from street traders selling goods out of suitcases on street corners. The prices are usually 50% or less than a full-price record in the shops.

The packaging will often be of poor quality, possibly blurred print, especially when it gets to the small print. Sometimes there is a white border on the edges of the inlay card

---

4 This was implemented into UK law as section 13A CDPA. The term is 50 years from the end of the year in which the sound recording was first made or, if it is released in that time, 50 years from the end of the year in which it was first released.
5 See *Springsteen* v. *Flute* as discussed on pages 109–10.
6 *Collins* v. *Imrat Handelsgesellschaft mbH* [1994] W.M.L.R 108.
7 Source: 'Protecting the Value of British Music' published by the BPI Anti-Piracy Unit (see below).

for the cassette or CDs where it's been copied. These inlay cards may look genuine on the outside; it's only when you open it that you see it's a poor representation on the inside. The trademarks may be removed, smudged or partly obscured as the pirates try to get around an allegation of infringement of trademark. The name and logo of the original record company may also be missing, blurred or obscured. There may not be a Source Identification Code. This was something introduced a few years ago to show the place of manufacture. The sound quality will often be very poor, particularly on cassettes. Copy protection devices will definitely be absent.

BOOTLEGS

These are often found on sale at music festivals, second-hand or 'underground' record stores and collectors' fairs. They are aiming at the die-hard fans who want to own every available recording by their favourite artist. The price is often the same or higher than the legitimate product to reflect how desirable they are to collectors and fans.

The packaging may leave off company information; there could be no catalogue numbers or proper credits. Bootleg CDs can be very good sound quality, particularly when compared to the very bad quality of bootleg cassettes. The inlay cards will often be simple colour photocopies.

HOW CAN YOU STOP PIRACY?

Most people in the music industry now accept that it's not possible to prevent illegal uses of music on the Internet, and that rights owners should accept this and concentrate on putting systems in place to make sure the copyright owners and creators are paid whenever their music is used. There is certainly the view that not much can be done to prevent pirate recordings of sound recordings that are already in the marketplace. What the music industry is putting its efforts into is putting security systems in place in the digital computer files of the music (see Chapter 7).

When it comes to physical copies of records like cassettes and CDs, the problem is a different one – how to control the illegal manufacturing plants and seize illegal copies.

In both cases the underlying rights being infringed are the same.

COPYRIGHT

Pirate recordings may infringe the sound recording copyright and the rights in the music and lyrics as well as the artwork. It's an infringement of copyright to reproduce, issue copies to the public, perform in public or include it in a cable programme (including online). These are what we call direct infringements of copyright.

Indirect infringements of copyright include importing, possessing in the course of trade, selling or exhibiting infringing copies in public and/or distributing them in the course of business.[8] These are obviously aimed at the distributor or retailer. They have to know or have reason to believe that they are dealing with an infringing copy.

MORAL RIGHTS

If the writer or composer of the lyrics and music isn't identified, or the work has been

---

8 Sections 22–26 CDPA.

subjected to derogatory treatment, this may well be an infringement of moral rights if these have not been waived (see Chapter 12).

TRADEMARKS

If the artist's or record company's trademark name or logo is reproduced without permission of the trademark owner, this is an infringement of the Trade Marks Act 1994.

TRADE DESCRIPTIONS

If the record has been misdescribed or represented as something that it is not, this may be a breach of the Trade Descriptions Act.

ENFORCEMENT

First, decide who you're going to go after. Who have you got evidence against? You could try to take action against the pirate manufacturer, but this may be difficult if they're based overseas. You could decide to try to stop distributors from starting or continuing to distribute pirate records. You'll have to move fast. If nothing has been distributed you could try to get an injunction to stop distribution taking place. If it's already been distributed you may need court orders against the person retailing the product.

So, when you've decided whom you want to target, what can you do?

CIVIL ACTION

You can apply for an injunction, although you have to move quickly. You can ask the court to make an order preventing infringement of your rights. The court can make orders preventing further sale, distribution and/or import of pirated products. You'll probably also make a claim for financial damages and reimbursement of your legal costs.

CRIMINAL ACTION

You have to show that the defendant had reason to believe he was dealing with an infringing copy of a copyright work. The penalties are imprisonment and/or a fine. For this kind of action you need to involve the police, who will need to have explained to them how copyright exists in the product and how it is being breached. You also have to convince them that it's sufficiently serious for them to put resources into the case.

PRIVATE CRIMINAL PROSECUTIONS

The CDPA gives you the right to bring a private criminal prosecution.[9] This was first used successfully in a case run by my firm in 1994 to prosecute someone who was using computer bulletin boards to copy computer games illegally.

The CDPA also makes it possible for an officer of a company to be liable to prosecution for an offence committed by the company.[10] This is to avoid companies slipping through the net.

If someone is found guilty of infringement, the court can order that all the offending articles are handed over[11] and can order their destruction. I'm sure you'll all have seen

---

9 Section 107 CDPA.
10 Section 110 CDPA.
11 Section 108 CDPA.

pictures of companies like Rolex using a steamroller to crush fake copies of their watches.

TRADING STANDARDS OFFICERS
These are local government officials and they can be very helpful if you get them on side. A good friend of mine is an ex-Trading Standards Officer and he tells me they like nothing better than a good raid on a pirate. They usually act to enforce breaches of trademark using powers given to them under the Trade Descriptions Act among others. They can enter premises and seize goods. They can prosecute for offences such as fraudulently applying a trademark[12] and the application of a false description to goods.[13]

ANTI-PIRACY UNIT (APU)
The APU was set up by the BPI and also receives financial support from the Musicians Union and the British Association of Record Dealers (BARD).

The APU investigates complaints about piracy. They take information from record companies, musicians and members of the public. They also monitor new technology and how that might affect the record industry. The APU runs training courses and seminars for the police and Trading Standards Officers.

The APU can assist in both civil and criminal actions and work with a number of other industry bodies. In 2001 they attended or gave evidence in more than 500 criminal cases. They closed down some 400 websites trafficking unauthorised MP3 files and others who threatened to deal illegally with unreleased tracks. They also closed down 2,315 auction websites offering illegal MP3 compilations and bootleg recordings.[14]

THE INTERNATIONAL FEDERATION OF THE PHONOGRAPHIC INDUSTRY (IFPI)
This represents the international recording industry. If you're a member of the BPI you automatically become a member of the IFPI. It has about 100 members in over 70 countries. It is involved in the international fight against piracy. It lobbies governments for appropriate copyright protection and helps to ensure the laws are enforced. Its contact details are in Useful Addresses.

OTHER BODIES
Other bodies involved in the fight against piracy include the Federation Against Software Theft (FAST), which was set up in 1984 to represent the software industry (both publishers and end users);[15] the Federation Against Copyright Theft (FACT), which represents film and video producers, manufacturers and distributors as well as TV and the satellite industries,[16] and the European Leisure Software Publishers' Association (ELSPA), which represents publishers of interactive software such as computer games and has an anti-piracy hotline.

12 Section 300 CDPA.
13 Section 1 Trade Descriptions Act.
14 Source: BPI Market Information June 2002.
15 For more details of their activities see www.fast.org.uk.
16 For more details of their activities see www.fact-uk.org.uk.

FACT, FAST and the Music Publishers Association (MPA), which looks after the interests of music publishers, also set up a hotline in the autumn of 1999 for people to report suspected cases of film, music or software piracy. You can also get legal advice on copyright and trademark issues and they will tell you about their education and training initiatives.[17]

17 The hotline number is 0845 603 4567.

15: **COLLECTION SOCIETIES**

INTRODUCTION

As you know by now, copyright is the right of an individual and, in most cases, that right should be exercised as the individual decides and on his own behalf.

However, there comes a time when it makes more sense for these rights to be exercised collectively by an organisation set up to represent the interests of its members. To make doing business as easy as possible requires a one-stop service. For example, it wouldn't be commercially viable for the owners of a radio station to have to go to the copyright owners of the sound recording copyright and of the rights in the songs on each of the records that the station bosses want to play on their programmes. It would be far too time-consuming and costly. The practical difficulties of this became obvious when it came to setting up online radio stations. What the radio station bosses want to be able to do is go to one body representing the copyright owners of the songs and to another body representing the broadcast rights in the sound recordings and get a one-off permission to use all the songs and all the records that these bodies control.

The problem was that these didn't exist for online rights, although over time a number of collective bodies had been set up for terrestrial/non-Internet uses. The first ones were set up to collectively license and administer public performance rights and others have come along as technological advances have brought new means of using music. The difficulties that the lack of online one-stop licensing were causing meant that it was even more important to have efficient and effective collecting societies offering one-stop global solutions. In 2002 the music publishers got together to authorise the MCPS/PRS to collectively license their music for certain online uses. It is therefore now possible to legitimately apply for a one-stop clearance for sound recordings.

WHAT ARE COLLECTION SOCIETIES?[1]

They are, in effect, organisations set up by the various categories of rights owners to administer their rights collectively as their sole, or one of their main, purposes.[2]

On the whole, collection societies are private as opposed to state-owned bodies, but they are subject to some form of government or state supervision. In the UK, that supervision is provided for partly by the 1988 Copyright Act, which established a form of compulsory arbitration in the shape of the Copyright Tribunal,[3] and in part by the Monopolies and Mergers Commission.

The purpose of most collection societies is to provide a practical and economical service to enable its members to enforce and administer certain of their copyrights.

---

1 For a more detailed description of collection societies and their history, see Chapter 29 of *Copinger and Skone-James on Copyright*.
2 Section 116(2) CDPA defines a licensing body as 'a society or other organisation which has as its main object, or one of its main objects, the negotiation or granting, either as owner or prospective owner of copyright or as agent for him, of copyright licences, and whose objects include the granting of licences covering works of more than one author'.
3 Sections 116–123 CDPA.

These bodies make it easier for others to get licences to use copyright works. There is also certainty in that the payment for these uses will usually be at a fixed rate or one individually negotiated within certain guidelines. The idea is also that, by acting collectively, administration costs are reduced.

There are, of course, possible dangers inherent in that these collection societies are, by their nature, monopolies. It's the job of the Monopolies and Mergers Commission to police whether that monopoly position is being abused.[4]

BLANKET LICENCES

One of the features of collection societies is that they grant so-called blanket licences for the right to use certain rights in all the works controlled by the society for a particular purpose, for a particular period of time and at a particular rate. Anyone wishing to take advantage of these blanket licences has to take a licence for the whole catalogue. For example, the Performing Right Society Limited (PRS) can negotiate a blanket licence with radio broadcasters for the right to broadcast to the public all the works controlled by PRS. The licence would be for a given period of time, say a year, and would then be subject to review. PRS would negotiate with individual radio stations or, more likely, with their representative bodies, the rate that would be applied to these licences. It could be a flat fee per annum or it could be linked to the revenue that the radio station earns, for example, a percentage of the advertising revenue earned by commercial radio stations, or it could be a combination of both.

ADMINISTRATION

A main role for the collection societies is the administration of the rights, making sure that a member's interests have been properly registered, that people using the rights have the necessary licences and have paid the negotiated rate. They have to collect in the monies, allocate and distribute them. Most societies charge their members a fee of some kind for the administration of the rights, usually a percentage of the gross income they collect.

There is usually one society for each category of rights. A major exception is the US, where three societies doing identical things compete for the right to administer publishing rights, namely ASCAP, BMI and SACEM.

Sometimes a society will administer more than one right. For example, in Europe a number of the collection societies administer not only the performing rights but also the right to copy or reproduce works. In fact, in the UK, the PRS and the Mechanical Copyright Protection Society Limited (MCPS) have now combined many of their managerial and administration functions while continuing to maintain separate identities.

RIGHTS GRANTED

The societies either take an assignment of certain rights from their members or they have a licence from their members or act as agents for them. The terms of membership

---

4 In the last ten years there have been two major reviews of individual collection societies. The first, published in 1988 (HMSO Cm. 530), dealt specifically with Public Performance Limited. The second, published in 1996 (HMSO Cm. 3147), dealt with the Performing Right Society Limited. That report contained several criticisms of the Society, which has since altered its rules to try to deal with these concerns.

of a collection society will usually dictate what form the rights granted will take. The idea is to establish through these membership rules a clear mandate to grant licences to use certain rights. As we will see in the section on new issues below, there has been less certainty than is desirable in the mandate of some of the collection societies to deal with new technologies.

The collection societies usually have reciprocal arrangements with other societies so that they can protect their members worldwide. This system is still developing in the area of online licensing. These reciprocal arrangements mean that the UK societies can represent the interests of their UK members and of foreign artists, writers and composers within the UK, with both categories of writers receiving the same treatment. However, in the online world, the extent of the reciprocity is still largely untested and, as the law and practice in different countries isn't the same, complete harmonisation of the arrangements isn't easily achieved.

One of the main advantages of collective licensing is, of course, the greater bargaining power that you can get by being part of a big collective effort. The rates and rewards for uses of your works that the collection societies can get for you should be better than what you could get on a one-to-one basis.

Collection societies have been around for over 150 years. The French Performing Right Society, SACEM, was the first to be set up back in 1852. MCPS and PRS were established in 1911 and 1914 respectively. Some are of more recent origin such as Public Performance Limited (PPL), which was established in 1934. A more detailed description of what each of these societies does is set out below.

OTHER COLLECTIVE BODIES

There are a number of other music business bodies that represent the interests of various parts of the business. These could be collective bargaining or interest groupings such as the Music Managers Forum (MMF) and AIM (The Association of Independent Music). They also include unions like the Musicians Union (MU) and Equity. More recent additions have been the two societies set up in the last couple of years to administer the income from exercise of the rights of performers, P@MRA and AURA.

What all these groupings have in common is that they act as a forum for debate and, to a greater or lesser extent, as a means of using collective bargaining power to get things for their members that as individuals they could find it very hard to achieve. A brief description of the aims of each is set out in the section on useful addresses at the end of the book.

THE FUTURE AND CHALLENGES FACING THE COLLECTION SOCIETIES

The main challenges to the collection societies come from the development of new technologies. The Collection Societies are slowly getting to grips with agreeing rates for the licensing of new formats like Digital Versatile Disc (DVD) and CD-ROMs. As we saw earlier in this chapter, not all of the members of UK societies give their mandate to negotiate and grant licences for these formats on their behalf. Getting the mandate required, in many cases, a change of the membership rules and it took time for members to sign up to the new deals. These rates are often negotiated on a case-by-case basis, but a precedent of previous licences is building up.

At least these formats are just new forms of providing physical copies of recordings of music. The collection societies are used to dealing with these sort of things. More recently, they have been getting to grips with the challenges of online licensing and the commercial pressures that they are under to grant blanket licences for online uses. Many societies still don't have the mandate from all their members to grant rights for online uses, although that is changing, particularly on the music publishing side of the business. Rates and possible pricing models for the new uses are being developed as we've seen, but progress is slow. Indeed, as this work goes to press I hear that the record companies are unhappy with the blanket rate the publishers have set for online uses and may take the issue to the Copyright Tribunal.

An example of the difficulties the societies face is the rate for digital download of music off the Internet, which the MCPS announced on behalf of its members in 1999. It recommended a 10 pence per download rate for up to 5 minutes of music and 2 pence per minute over that. The announcement was met with howls of protest from Internet Service Providers and content providers, who felt that it was too high and would stifle business. But the MCPS was under considerable pressure to do something. In fact, the rate was not accepted and the MCPS/PRS went back to the drawing board to come up with a new blanket licence that is, in respect of rights, controlled by both MCPS and PRS and is based on a sliding-scale percentage of turnover. But, as we've seen above, it too is meeting with resistance.

The other big issue that remains unresolved and where in many cases the question has been fudged is whether the societies can grant worldwide rights. Reciprocal arrangements are in place for a UK society to be able to grant worldwide rights for terrestrial uses of a song or a recording. With the Internet, it's so easy to make your music available globally that it's essential for the collection societies worldwide to put in place reciprocal arrangements for online uses, so that these are afforded the same degree of protection. In January 2000, the major collection societies in the US, the UK and Europe announced that they were in accord (the so-called 'Santiago Agreement') over the need for a global solution and were working on a common solution. Sources are slowly signing up to it, but one of the major American societies is, I understand, still wavering. In the meantime, online uses are going ahead globally and in many cases probably without the permission of the rights owners or the collection societies of which they are members. This isn't such a problem when the use being made of the music or the recording is primarily promotional, but it will become a pressing problem when it takes off commercially, as the rights owners will be losing out on valuable sources of income.

Even though global solutions are necessary to the problems of online licensing, there is still a need to deal with the fact that each country applies a different means of rewarding rights owners for different sorts of uses of the songs. For example, the mechanical royalty rate in Europe is, on average, slightly higher than in the UK, but does vary between countries. If the rights owners are to be properly rewarded for these uses then there need to be systems in place that can identify where the use took place and calculate the rate of reward applicable in that country. These rights management systems are being developed but there is still a long way to go.

Another aspect of these rights management issues is the whole question of piracy.

This is dealt with in more detail in Chapters 7 and 14. It is, however, a huge problem for all rights owners and for all the organisations set up to deal with these problems both on a domestic and international level.

All these issues are ones that will require flexibility from the various rights bodies so as not to stifle trade, but at the same time to protect the rights of their members.

THE SOCIETIES

In the following section I'm going to briefly describe the structure and function of some of the main bodies that exist in the UK at the moment. I'll tell you what they are, where they are and how you can contact them. I'll describe their basic aims and what are their basic criteria for membership. More details can be obtained from the individual societies, most of whom publish brochures describing what they do for their members.

THE BRITISH PHONOGRAPHIC INSTITUTE (BPI)

Strictly speaking, this isn't a collection society as such, but an organisation that represents the interests of UK record companies. It's a non-profit-making trade association that was set up in 1973.

The BPI is based in Central London (see Useful Addresses) and its members are UK record companies. There are currently about 318 members. There is a fee to become a member and these fees mainly fund its activities. The subscriptions for full members are calculated on a percentage of the member's turnover in the preceding calendar year. Turnover is defined as 'net sales of owned and licensed finished recorded music product to retailers and wholesalers in the UK'. There is a minimum fee. Any established record company able to afford the membership fee can join, provided they agree to be bound by the membership rules and the Code of Conduct that the BPI maintains. If you're a member of the BPI you automatically also become a member of the IFPI.

The Code of Conduct deals with how the music charts are drawn up and involves the BPI investigating alleged irregularities, for example if there is an attempt to buy up unusually large numbers of copies of a particular record in order to artificially gain a higher chart position. If the BPI finds that a member has been guilty of infringing the Code it can employ sanctions against that member, including expelling them as a member and/or imposing a fine.

Because it's a trade association rather than a rights body, it doesn't take any rights from its members nor does it grant licences or otherwise administer or collect money from exploitation of rights.

The BPI provides a forum for discussion and acts for its members generally on matters in which they have a common interest. It has a lobbying function at Westminster and in Brussels, and also negotiates agreements with other groups such as music publishers, the Musicians Union or Equity.

Its Rights Committee monitors developments in the law and advises its members on implications for their businesses.

It's responsible for the collection of data on UK record sales and for matters relating to the profile of the record business through its Public Relations Committee.

A very important part of its job is to co-ordinate anti-piracy efforts through its Anti-Piracy Unit, which is active in trying to reduce the amount of piracy in the UK. Its role includes taking high-profile litigation cases against pirates and giving publicity to successful seizures of pirate goods.

PHONOGRAPHIC PERFORMANCE LIMITED (PPL)

This is the record industry's licensing body. It licences records for broadcasting and public performance.

It represents a large number of record companies (about 3,000), some of which, but not all, are members of the BPI.

The PPL is based in London and was incorporated as a company limited by guarantee in 1934. (See Useful Addresses for contact details.)

The PPL negotiates collective agreements with broadcasters. It also protects the rights of its members and takes legal action to protect those rights. It doesn't, however, have its own anti-piracy unit or staff, but relies on its members to bring infringements to its attention.

PPL has a number of different tariffs that apply to the various uses of the music in its repertoire. These are usually payable annually. There are minimum charges and how much is paid out to the members depends on the use. It does take assignments or exclusive agency rights of various rights from its members. These include broadcasting, public performance, dubbing of background music (a role it took over in 1985), multi-media uses and digital diffusion rights.[5]

The membership agreement allows the member to elect to assign all the rights or to keep some rights back. Most record companies assign broadcasting, public perform-ance and dubbing rights to PPL. Many keep back the multi-media and digital diffusion rights. The fact that PPL doesn't have the mandate from all its members to grant digital rights is hampering its ability to negotiate licences for online uses of the repertoire. As at September 2002 the PPL still doesn't have the right from all its members to grant blanket licences for online uses where any element of interactivity or consumer choice is involved. This is holding back the development of online commercial uses of sound recordings. The major record companies obviously prefer to license such uses direct. In November 2002, EMI announced it had struck new licensing deals with nine online music distribution firms allowing permanent, portable and burnable downloads of music, including rarely available US radio singles. This is seen as a positive step forward.

PPL is also now charged with distributing a proportion of performing income to performers.[6]

VIDEO PERFORMANCE LIMITED (VPL)

This is a company associated with PPL. It is the record industry's licensing body for music videos.

Its members are the owners of public performance rights in music videos being publicly broadcast or included in a cable broadcast service.

It's a company limited by guarantee and has about 800 members. It's based at the same office as PPL.

Like PPL, VPL licenses music videos for broadcasting, public performance and

---

5 Dubbing is the right to 'copy, produce, reproduce or make records embodying a sound recording'. An example would be a television sports programme that has music in the background. The sound recording of that music is dubbed into the television programme.
6 See Chapter 4 for performers' rights and the description of P@MRA and AURA in Useful Addresses.

inclusion in a cable broadcast service. It applies a number of different tariffs to the different uses of the music videos.

Again like PPL, VPL takes an assignment of its members' public performance and dubbing rights in music videos and a non-exclusive licence of the broadcasting rights.

VPL collects performing income from use of music videograms but, unlike PPL, it's not obliged by law to share this income with performers, only with its record company members.

ASSOCIATION OF INDEPENDENT MUSIC LIMITED (AIM)

This is a relatively new association, set up in 1999. Its members are drawn from the independent sector of the music business, mostly the record company side but including publishers, production companies and manufacturers

It is a trade association acting as a forum for debate and also has a lobbying function. Its function as a trade association means that it also has a collective bargaining role.

AIM is based in London, and provides a legal advisory service to its members with a number of checklists of points to look out for in negotiating various types of deals. It has been forward-looking in the licensing deals it has struck with online distributors on behalf of its largely independent membership. Its website is very informative.[7]

THE PERFORMING RIGHT SOCIETY LIMITED (PRS)

As we saw in Chapter 4, PRS is the UK collection society for composers, songwriters and music publishers and is charged with administering the public performance and broadcasting rights in music and lyrics. It also administers the film synchronisation right.

Both music publishers and songwriters are members. It was set up in 1914 as a company limited by guarantee. It also represents almost a million foreign music copyright owners through its affiliations with overseas collecting societies.

PRS is based in central London. When you become a member of PRS you have to assign your performing right and the film synchronisation right to PRS. Although members assign rights, they can reserve some categories of rights or types of use of rights in all their works, and the rules do allow members to request that PRS doesn't license the performing right in a particular work, for example, if it is unlawfully sampled.

There are three categories of membership: provisional, associate and full. To be eligible for membership a composer has to have had one piece of work already or about to be exploited. The admission fee is approximately £50 for a composer or lyricist.

PRS grants both individual licences and enters into collective licence schemes with various categories of users.

In 1994 PRS was accused of being anti-competitive and in restraint of trade. The band U2 served a writ on PRS, requiring, among other things, that PRS change its membership rules and re-assign to the band their live performance rights. The band objected to the requirement of PRS that rights are exclusively assigned. They thought that members should have the freedom to choose whether to allow PRS alone to administer all or part of the performing right or to administer it themselves. PRS rules don't allow for members to 'opt out'. The equivalent societies in the US do allow their members to license individual music uses direct.

U2 were dissatisfied with the administration by the PRS of live performances. The

7 www.musicindie.org/intro.

system that PRS operated meant that getting income from live performances could take over a year to come through, and there were deductions for administration fees. U2 said they would rather administer the live performance right themselves. The trouble is that if big earners like U2 pulled out of the collective system this would greatly weaken the collective bargaining power. It would also represent a huge drop in income for PRS. This could have had a negative effect on the rights of less successful members who rely on their quarterly PRS cheques.

The case settled on the basis that PRS would allow U2 to administer the live performing right and U2 then agreed that it would license the right to PRS in return for a reduced administration fee.

THE MECHANICAL COPYRIGHT PROTECTION SOCIETY LIMITED (MCPS)

This company was set up in 1911 in order to collectively licence mechanical reproduction of music, i.e. the copying of music and the synchronisation of music with visual images (see Chapter 4).

MCPS has both publishers and songwriters as members. Its main area of activity is the negotiating and administering of collective licence schemes with record companies. It has reciprocal arrangements with similar societies worldwide.

MCPS is a subsidiary of the Music Publishers' Association Limited, a company limited by guarantee. MCPS has offices in Streatham, south London, although many of its day-to-day activities are now carried out at the same offices as PRS.

MCPS doesn't take assignments of rights, but its membership agreement provides that the member appoints MCPS as his agent to manage and administer the mechanical copyright in the UK. It has the mandate to grant licences and collect royalties. It's also obliged to use its best efforts to prevent infringement of its members' rights. It can take legal action in their name and often does so.

There are three types of licence agreements with record companies. The AP1 agreement is given to those record companies who have a trading record and can satisfy the financial and accounting criteria set by MCPS. Under the AP1 agreement, a record company can record any work in the MCPS repertoire provided MCPS is notified at least seven working days before its release. Royalties are calculated on the basis of actual sales and are payable quarterly in arrears. The AP2A agreement is the next best thing and is for record companies with a trading history but which can't satisfy the accounting and financial criteria. Record companies with this type of agreement have to notify the MCPS before manufacture. They are obliged to account for royalties on records manufactured even if they aren't ever actually sold. There's a 60-day credit period up to an agreed limit. The third type of agreement is the AP2 agreement. It's basically the same as the AP2A agreement, but it's used for companies with a limited release schedule and there is no credit period.

MCPS has also negotiated blanket licence schemes with UK television and radio stations and many other types of specialist music providers.

MCPS charges its members a commission for administering the rights and collecting the royalties. This is between 9.5% and 12.5%. Its website contains details of its rates[8] and of the production music rate card.

---

8 www.mcps.co.uk.

APPENDIX

WORKING IN THE MUSIC BUSINESS

ere is a brief overview of some of the information available on the music business. It's not meant to be a complete list; it is information I've come across when researching this book. All the contact details are in the next section, Useful Addresses

If you're interested in more formal training in the music business then there are a number of courses now available. If you have access to the Internet this is an excellent resource for finding out about courses. The University and College Clearing site at www.ucas.co.uk is a good start point. Or do a general search, using any good search engine, for education/music. For short or evening courses, check *Floodlight* and Local Authority publications for courses outside London.

My own researches have turned up the following universities and colleges who run courses either in the media or the music business. Qualifications vary from NVQs, through HNDs, to degrees. Some don't offer a nationally recognised qualification but more of an overview with a certificate when you complete the course. Check the course details to make sure they meet your requirements. The list isn't a complete one by any means, and neither is it a recommendation of any particular course.

HIGHER EDUCATION

LEGAL AND BUSINESS COURSES

Bath Spa University College is running a full-time Commercial Music course presently leading to an HND/Foundation degree. They are applying to be able to provide the option of a 3rd-year BA (Hons) course. The course involves a good core grounding.

The University of Westminster offers a BA (Hons) degree in Commercial Music involving music production and music business practice at its Harrow campus.

Buckinghamshire Chilterns University College offers HND and BA (Hons) full-time courses in Music Industry Management and Music, as well as Live Production, Studio Production and Marketing.

The Continuing Education Department of City University, London runs a number of part-time introductory courses such as 'Making Music Work: An Introduction to the Music Industry'. They also offer distance learning and weekend courses in Cultural Industries and the Law and An Introduction to the Music Industry as well as Marketing and Event Management.

Greenwich Community College, south London, also offers part-time courses in The Music Business and Musicianship, which covers Copyright Law and Marketing.

Dartington College of Arts in Devon runs a BA (Hons) degree course in Music, which can be performance- or composition-based with Arts Management. Although this isn't a law course, it may suit those looking at arts management.

De Montfort University, Leicester, offers BSc (Hons) courses in Music and Media Studies, Technology and Innovation as well as BA (Hons) in Arts Management and Media Studies.

Kingston University offers a full-time or part-time course leading to a Higher Diploma in Recording, Music Technology and Music Business studies.

Oxford Brookes University offers a number of combined modules involving music, including Law/Music and Business Administration and Management leading to a BA, BSc or LLB (Hons) degree. They may suit those more interested in a general as opposed to a specific legal course.

The University of Paisley also runs a BA course in Commercial Music and it stresses the involvement of industry professionals.

Roehampton Institute, London Southlands College, has a module in Business Studies and Music within its Business Studies Combined Honours courses. These are either full- or part-time courses leading to either a BA (Hons) or BMus (Hons).

The University of Sunderland offers a number of combined BAs, including Business and Music and Business Law and Music. Intriguingly, it also offers a course entitled Gender Studies and Music.

TECHNICAL COURSES

For those looking for a more technical emphasis, there is a highly regarded Tonmeister course at my old university, the University of Surrey. This is a BMus (Tonmeister) degree course in Music and Sound Recording. It's a four-year sandwich course with time spent out in work placements. The intention is to prepare you for a career in the professional audio industry.

Canterbury Christ Church University College runs a full- or part-time HND course in Popular Music and Technology at its Thanet campus.

Thames Valley also offers various two- and three-year full-time courses covering Music Recording and aspects of the music business, for example Advertising with Sound and Music Recording.

Salford also offers a BA (Hons) course in Popular Music and Recording. The emphasis is on popular music and music technology, but it also aims to prepare you for a career in the music business or in the recording industry. They say you'll be directed towards modules as a Studio Performer or Producer depending on your aptitude and interests shown in entrance tests, interviews and by your profile. The course is accredited by the Association of Professional Recording Services.

The Nottingham Foundation for Music and Media is offering further and higher education courses, as well as commercial training courses for the music and multi-media industries. Their courses are validated by New College, Nottingham. They offer BND and HND Certificates in Music Technology as well as Music Industry.

MASTERS DEGREES

Westminster and Bournemouth Universities are both offering Masters degrees in aspects of the music business. In the case of Westminster, it's in Music Management. The University of Bournemouth is offering an LLM/MA in Media Law and Finance.

COMMERCIAL COURSES

There are also courses run by commercial organisations that aim to give practical overviews of aspects of the music business. One of the more established organisations is the Global Entertainment Group. They are offering evening courses over eight weeks as a Music Industry Overview. This can be taken together with their Skills Link programme, which provides more specialised subjects such as Music Marketing, PR and Promotion or Successful Artist Management. All courses are delivered in central London.

The Music Managers Forum (MMF) offers short courses called Master Classes to its members and AIM members on aspects of music management and the industry. These are either short evening courses or week-long intensive ones.

The British Phonographic Institute (BPI) occasionally offers one-day training workshops.

The Academy of Contemporary Music, based in Guildford, has link-ups with many industry bodies. Part of each course is a module in Business Studies.

BECOMING A SOLICITOR

If you want to become a solicitor, the Law Society can give you information. If you already have a first degree in law, you need to complete a one-year Legal Practice Course and a two-year training contract. A fast track to qualifying may be available for those who already have relevant business experience.

The Law Society now includes Media Studies or Intellectual Property as optional courses as part of the Legal Practice Course. The Law Society also requires practising lawyers to keep up to date on the law by undertaking further training during their working life.

If your first degree isn't in law, you'll need to do an additional one-year conversion course called the Common Professional Examination.

IN-HOUSE OR PRIVATE PRACTICE?

Once you've qualified as a solicitor, you can choose whether to work in a private law firm or in-house as a lawyer in a record or music publishing company. Managers don't usually employ an in-house lawyer, nor do small labels or publishing companies. They usually use lawyers in private law firms.

The competition between specialist music business lawyers is intense. It takes considerable effort, both in and out of normal working hours, to build up a 'practice' – a body of clients who use you regularly for legal advice. Without a practice you are unlikely to be promoted to Associate, salaried or full partner sharing in the profits (or losses) of the business. The financial rewards and job satisfaction can, however, be considerable.

Those of you who think you would find it difficult to build up a practice, or who aren't interested in becoming a full profit-sharing partner or owning their own business, may decide to work in-house instead. That isn't to say that this is an easy option. The work in-house can be very intense. There's no job security and you have to follow company policy, the 'corporate line'. The up-side is that the working atmosphere can be more relaxed, you don't have the stresses of building a practice or running your own business and it can be a very good way to move into management positions.

It is possible to move between the two. A partner in Harbottle & Lewis left to go in-house at one of the big music publishing companies and ended up running the whole of their European operation. Another went into artist management; both are now back in private practice as legal consultants.

BECOMING A BARRISTER

Instead of being a solicitor you could choose to do a law degree, a follow-up course at a recognised Bar School and a minimum of one year's training to become a barrister. Barristers can't be partners in law firms without re-qualifying as a solicitor, but they can, and often do, work as in-house lawyers. For further information on becoming a barrister, contact the Bar Council.

BECOMING A LEGAL EXECUTIVE

You can also get a qualification as a legal executive. For information on legal executive qualifications, contact the Institute of Legal Executives. It doesn't entitle you to become a partner in a law firm but it does give you a legal qualification. It can be done in evening and day-release classes while you're working and it can be a stepping-stone to becoming a fully qualified solicitor although this would take many years. You find legal executives in important support roles in media law firms. In the smaller firms, their role isn't that different from that of fully qualified solicitors. Legal executives also work in-house and, to all intents and purposes, they do the same work as qualified solicitors. However, there is often the view in music companies that, unless you're a fully qualified lawyer or have an additional business qualification such as an MBA (a masters degree in business administration), you're unlikely to get promoted to a management role. On the other hand, you may not have any desire to go into management and may be happy with a non-management role.

NON-LEGAL JOBS

For a general overview of types of careers available in the music business, a good place to start would be Sian Pattenden's book on the music business (see Further Reading).

You could also refer to your Careers Advisory Service and government-backed enterprise and job advisory centres. The government's Jobseekers scheme now extends to specialist advisers dealing with the music business and the particular needs of musicians.[1]

It's less easy to learn about jobs in other areas of the music business on formal courses. Those wishing to become A&R contacts will generally start as hopeful 'scouts', running around the country, often for little more than out-of-pocket expenses, chasing down likely new bands. Another way in is if you've already had some kind of success as an artist and then cross over into the business side. A common quality is a passionate love of music.

---

1 Fair Deal For Musicians, launched in Autumn 1999. For details, ask at your local Job Centre.

USEFUL ADDRESSES

ACADEMY OF CONTEMPORARY MUSIC
Rodboro Buildings, Bridge Street, Guildford GU1 4SB
Tel: 01483 500800
Fax: 01483 500801
Website: www.acm.ac.uk

AIM – Association of Independent Musicmakers
Lamb House, Church Street, London W4 2PD
Tel: 020 8994 5599
Email: info@musicindie.com

AMIA – Association of Music Industry Accountants
Becket House, 1 Lambeth Palace Road, London SE1 7EU
Tel: 020 7931 3184
Fax: 020 7401 2136

ASCAP – American Society of Composers and Performers
8 Cork Street, London W1X 1PB
Tel: 020 7439 0909
Fax: 020 7434 0073
Email: info@ascap.com
Website: www.ascap.com

AURA – Association of United Recording Artists
7 Russell Gardens, London W14 BEZ
Tel: 020 7751 1894
Email: website@ukmmf.net
Website: www.ukmmf.net

AURA was set up to administer and collect the performers' share of income from broadcasters and cable service programme providers. It's based at the same offices as the MMF and is closely allied with them.

BAND REGISTER
Tel: 020 8940 7518
Website: www.bandreg.com

BAR COUNCIL, THE
1 Deans Yard, London SW1P 3NP
Tel: 020 7222 2525

BATH SPA UNIVERSITY COLLEGE
Newton Park Campus, Newton St Loe, Bath BA2 9BN
Tel: 01225 875875
Email: enquiries@bathspa.ac.uk
Website: www.bathspa.ac.uk

BMI – Broadcast Media Inc.
84 Harley House, Marylebone Road, London NW1 5HN
Tel: 020 7486 2036
Website: www.bmi.com

BOURNEMOUTH UNIVERSITY
Studland House, 12 Christchurch Road, Bournemouth, Dorset BH1 3NA
Tel: 01202 524111
Email: postmaster@bournemouth.ac.uk
Website: www.bournemouth.ac.uk

BPI – British Phonographic Institute
The Riverside Building, County Hall, Westminster Bridge, London SE1 7JA
Tel: 020 7803 1300
Email: general@bpi.co.uk
Website: http://www.bpi.co.uk

BUCKINGHAMSHIRE CHILTERNS UNIVERSITY COLLEGE
Queen Alexandra Road, High Wycombe, Bucks HP11 2JZ
Tel: 01494 522141
Website: www.buckscol.ac.uk/bchome.html

CANTERBURY CHRIST CHURCH UNIVERSITY COLLEGE
North Holmes Road, Canterbury, Kent CT1 1QU
Tel: 01227 767700
Email: admissions@cant.ac.uk
Website: www.cant.ac.uk

CHAMBERS & PARTNERS PUBLISHING
Saville House, 23 Long Lane, London EC1A 9HL
Tel: 020 7606 8844
Website: www.chambersandpartners.com

CITY UNIVERSITY
Northampton Square, London EC1V 0HB
Tel: 020 7477 8028
Email: r.s.broom@city.ac.uk
Website: www.city.ac.uk

CONCERT PROMOTERS' ASSOCIATION
54 Keyes House, Dolphin Square, London SW1V 3NA
Tel: 020 7834 0515
Fax: 020 7821 0261

DARTINGTON COLLEGE OF ARTS
Totnes, Devon TQ9 6EJ
Tel: 01803 8622246
Email: registry@dartington.ac.uk
Website: www.dartington.ac.uk

DATA PROTECTION REGISTRAR
Wycliffe House, Water Lane, Wilmslow, Cheshire SK9 5AF
Tel: 01625 545745
Fax: 01625 524510
Email: data@notification.demon.co.uk
Website: www.dpr.gov.uk

DE MONTFORT UNIVERSITY
The Gateway, Leicester LE1 9BH
Tel: 0116 255 1551
Email: enquiry@dmu.ac.uk
Website: www.dmu.ac.uk

EQUITY (British Actors' Equity Association)
Guild House, Upper St Martin's Lane, London WC2H 9EG
Tel: 020 7379 6000
Fax: 020 7379 7001
E-mail: info@equity.org.uk
Website: www.equity.org.uk

Equity is an independent trade union representing not only actors but also other performers including singers and dancers. Equity negotiates industry agreements with TV and radio broadcasters, theatres and record companies (through the BPI).

GAVIN
140 Second Street, San Francisco, CA 94105
Tel: +(415) 495 1990
Fax: +(415) 495 2580
Email: gstaff@gavin.com

GLOBAL ENTERTAINMENT GROUP, THE
Music Training Division, HMS President (1918), Victoria Embankment, London EC4Y 0HJ
Tel: 020 7583 0236
Fax: 020 7583 7221
Website: www.globalmusicbiz.co.uk

IAEL – International Association of Entertainment Lawyers
Tara Donovan – General Secretary
Denton Wilde Sapte, 5 Chancery Lane, London EC4A 1BU
Tel: 020 7242 1212
Email: tgd@dentonwildesapte.com
Website: www.iael.org

IFPI – International Federation Phonographic Ltd
54 Regent Street, London W1B 5RE
Tel: 020 7878 7900
Email: info@ifpi.org
Website: www.ifpi.org

ILEX – Institute of Legal Executives
Kempston Manor, Kempston, Bedford MK42 7AB.
Tel: 01234 845718
Website: www.ilex.org.uk

KINGSTON UNIVERSITY
River House, 53–57 High Street, Kingston-upon-Thames, Surrey KT1 1LQ
Tel: 020 8547 2000
Email: d.milner-walker@kingston.ac.uk
Website: www.kingston.ac.uk

LAW SOCIETY, THE
113 Chancery Lane, London WC2A 1PL
Tel: 020 7242 1222
Fax: 020 7831 0344
Website: www.lawsociety.org.uk

LONDON SOCIETY OF CHARTERED ACCOUNTANTS, THE
53 Tabernacle Street, London EC4 4NB
Tel: 020 7490 4390

MCPS – Mechanical Copyright Protection Society Limited
29–33 Berners Street, London W1T 3AB
Tel: 0800 684828
Email: musiclicence@prs.co.uk
Website: www.mcps-prs-alliance.co.uk

MIRACLE PUBLISHING LIMITED
1 York Street, London W1H 1PZ
Tel: 020 7486 7007
Fax: 020 7486 2002
Email: info@audience.uk.com

MMF – Music Managers Forum
7 Russell Gardens, London W14 BEZ
Tel: 020 7751 1894
Email: website@ukmmf.net
Website: www.ukmmf.net

MMF – Training
Ground Floor, Fourways House, 57 Hilton Street, Manchester M1 2EJ
Tel: 0161 228 3993
Email: dramsay@mmf-training.com

This is the UK trade association for artist managers. It was set up approximately eight years ago as the International Managers Forum to act as a representative body for managers, as a forum for debate on matters of interest to its members and as a lobbying body.

MUSIC WEEK
United Business Media, 8th Floor, Ludgate House, 245 Blackfriars Road, London SE1 9UR
Tel: 020 7579 4150
Website: www.dotmusic.co.uk

MUSICIAN'S ATLAS, THE
33 Porter Place, Montclair, NJ 07042-2036
Tel: +(973) 509 9898
Fax: +(973) 655 1238
Email: MRGroup3@aol.com

MUSICIANS UNION
60–62 Clapham Road, London SW9 OJJ
Tel: 020 7582 5566
Fax: 020 7582 9805
Website: www.musiciansunion.org.uk

The MU is the only UK trade union solely representing musicians. It was formed in 1893. It has about 40,000 members and about 100 local branches. It acts as a collective body by seeking to improve the status of musicians and the money they earn. The MU makes national agreements with various organisations, including with the BPI (for recording sessions and promotional videos) and with television companies (for broadcasts).

NET SEARCHERS
Nick Wood
Tel: 020 7565 4090
Fax: 020 7565 4099

NEW MUSICAL EXPRESS

IPC Music Magazines, Kings Reach Tower, Stamford Street, London SE1 9LS
Tel: 020 7261 5813
Fax: 020 7261 5185
Website: www.nme.com

NOTTINGHAM FOUNDATION FOR MUSIC AND MEDIA

The Square Centre, Alfred Street North, Nottingham NG3 1AA
Tel: 0115 947 0044
Fax: 0115 941 8866
Website: www.the-foundation.org

OXFORD BROOKES UNIVERSITY

Gypsy Lane Campus, Headington, Oxford, Oxon OX3 0BP
Tel: 01865 741111
Website: www.brookes.ac.uk

P@MRA

29–33 Berners Street, London W1T 3AB
Tel: 020 7580 5544
Fax: 020 7306 4340
Website: www.pamra.org.uk

P@MRA was set up in late 1995 for the purposes of collecting, distributing and administering on behalf of performers income arising from the granting of the right to performers to receive equitable remuneration when a performance is played in public, is broadcast or is included in a cable programme service. It is a non-profit-making company limited by guarantee and is appointed as an agent to collect and administer the performing right income and also to enter into reciprocal arrangements with producers and performers' organisations overseas.

PINNACLE ENTERTAINMENT

Electron House, St Mary Cray, Orpington, Kent BR5 3RJ
Tel: 01689 870622
Fax: 01689 873144
Website: www.pinnacle-entertainment.co.uk

PPL – Public Performance Limited

1 Upper James Street, London W1F 9DE
Tel: 020 7534 1000
Fax: 020 7534 1111
Email: member.info@ppluk.com
Website: www.ppluk.com

PRS – Performing Right Society Limited
29–33 Berners Street, London W1T 3AB
Tel: 020 7580 5544
Fax: 020 7306 4455
Email: info@prs.co.uk
Website: www.prs.co.uk

REGIONAL PROMOTERS' ASSOCIATION
Riverside Promotions, 7–15 Pink Lane, Newcastle upon Tyne NE1 5DW
Tel: 0191 232 9729
Fax: 0191 261 4129
Email: andyhockey@yahoo.com

ROEHAMPTON INSTITUTE LONDON
Roehampton Lane, London SW15 5PU
Tel: 020 8392 3000
Email: admissions@roehampton.ac.uk
Website: http://www.roehampton.ac.uk

THAMES VALLEY UNIVERSITY
911 University House, Ealing Green, London W5 5EA
Tel: 020 8579 5000
Email: christine.marchant@tvu.ac.uk
Website: http://www.tvu.ac.uk

UCAS – University Clearing Advisory Service
Rosehill, New Barn Lane, Cheltenham, Gloucestershire GL52 3LZ
Tel: 01242 227788
Email: chq@ucas.ac.uk

UNIVERSITY COLLEGE NORTHAMPTON
Park Campus, Boughton Green Road, Northampton NN2 7AL
Tel: 01604 735500
Email: admissions@nene.ac.uk
Website: www.nene.ac.uk

UNIVERSITY OF GREENWICH
Maritime Greenwich Campus, Old Royal Naval College, Park Row, Greenwich SE10 0LS
Tel: 020 8331 8000
Email: courseinfo@greenwich.ac.uk
Website: www.gre.ac.uk

UNIVERSITY OF NEWCASTLE UPON TYNE
Newcastle NE1 7RU
Tel: 0191 222 6000
Website: www.newcastle.ac.uk

UNIVERSITY OF PAISLEY
Paisley PA1 2BE, Scotland
Tel: 0141 843 3000
Website: www.paisley.ac.uk

UNIVERSITY OF SALFORD
Salford, Greater Manchester M5 4WT
Tel: 0161 295 5000
Email: r.humphreys@salford.ac.uk
Website: www.salford.ac.uk

UNIVERSITY OF SUNDERLAND
Langham Tower, Ryhope Road, Sunderland SR7 7EE
Tel: 0191 515 2000
Email: student-helpline@sunderland.ac.uk
Website: www.sunderland.ac.uk

UNIVERSITY OF SURREY
The Registry, Guildford, Surrey GU2 7XH
Tel: 01483 300800
Email: SPA@surrey.ac.uk
Website: www.surrey.ac.uk

UNIVERSITY OF WESTMINSTER
309 Regent Street, London W1B 2UW
Tel: 020 7911 5000
Website: www.wmin.ac.uk

VITAL
Unit 6, Barton Hill Trading Estate, Herapath Street, Bristol, Avon BS5 9RD
Tel: 0117 988 3300
Fax: 0117 988 0600

GLOSSARY

T he term **artist** is used throughout the book as shorthand for performing artist. This could either be a solo artist or a group of artists. I have chosen to use 'band' rather than 'group' but that is just personal taste.

An **A&R** person is the person in a record or music publishing company whose job it is to find and develop new talent. They may find it themselves or someone else may bring it to them. They develop the artists creatively, helping to find the right manager, record producer, musicians or co-writers. They are the artist's link with the company. The name stands for Artistes and Repertoire, but no one uses the full title these days.

A **demo** is a recording of an artist's performances or a songwriter's songs. It's the showcase (or demonstration) of their talents. It could be recorded in a professional recording studio or in your back bedroom on begged or borrowed equipment. The quality isn't expected to be good enough to release as a record. But it must be good enough to clearly hear the quality of the material (if you're a songwriter) or the performance (if you're a recording artist). The demo used to always be on a cassette tape, but it's now just as likely to be on a recordable compact disc (CDR), minidisc or digital audiotape (DAT).

A **gig** is a live concert. This need not be a big, lavish affair. It could be an artist playing to two men and a dog in a back room of a pub.

A **scout** is a person whose job it is to go around the country hunting out new talent. They are at the bottom of the pecking order but they can be crucial to the whole process of finding and developing talent. They may not be full-time employees. They are likely to be passionate music fans trying to get into the music business. They may work for nothing or for expenses only. If they are good at finding new talent, they may be offered a job as an A&R person and get on to the first rung of the ladder.

FURTHER READING

As well as the books referred to in the footnotes, you may find the following of interest:

Ashurst, Will, *Stuff the Music Business: The DIY Guide to Making It,* Sanctuary Publishing, 2002.

Beale, Hugh (Ed.), *Chitty on Contracts,* Sweet & Maxwell, 1999.

Burgess, Richard James, *The Art of Record Production,* Omnibus Press, 1997.

Chambers, Michael (Ed.), *Chambers Guide to the Legal Profession,* Chambers & Partners, 2001.

Cornish, William R., *Intellectual Property,* Sweet & Maxwell, 1999.

Dann, Allan and Underwood, John, *How to Succeed in the Music Business,* Omnibus Press, 1997.

Flint, Michael, Fitzpatrick, Nicholas and Thorne, Clive, *Flint: A User's Guide to Copyright,* Butterworth's, 2000.

Frascogna, Xavier M. Jr. and Hetherington, H. Lee, *The Business of Artist Management,* Billboard Books, 1998.

Garnett, Kevin, Rayner James, Jonathan and Davies, Gillian (Eds.), *Copinger and Skone-James on Copyright,* Sweet & Maxwell, 1998.

Gibson, David and Petersen, George (Eds.), *The Art of Mixing,* Hal Leonard Publishing Corporation, 1997.

Golvan, Colin, *Introduction to Intellectual Property Law,* Blackstone Press, 1992.

Kanaar, Nicholas (Ed.), *Bagehot on Music Business Agreements,* Sweet & Maxwell, 1998.

Krasilovski, M. William and Shemel, Sidney, *This Business of Music,* Billboard, 2000.

Laddie, Mr Justice, Prescott, Peter, Vitoria, Mary and Lane, Lindsay, *The Modern Law of Copyright and Designs,* Butterworth's, 2000.

Lathrop, Tad and Pettigrew, Jim Jr., *This Business of Music Marketing and Promotion,* Billboard, 1999.

Legal 500 UK Edition, Legalese (published annually).

Passman, Donald S., *All You Need to Know about the Music Business,* Penguin, 2001.

Pattenden, Sian, *How To Make It in the Music Business,* Virgin Books, 1998.

Purce, Teresa, *Copyright, Designs & Patents Act 1988,* The Stationery Office.

Stone, Reuben, 'Plagiarism and Originality in Music: a precarious balance', in *Media Law & Practice*, vol. 14, no. 2, 1993.

Strong, William S., *The Copyright Book: A Practical Guide*, MIT Press, 1999.

Underhill, Rod, *Complete Idiot's Guide to Music on the Internet with MP3*, Que, 1999.

Wall, Raymond A., *Copyright Made Easier*, ASLIB, 1998.

INDEX